WOLVERINE
THE DAUGHTER OF WOLVERINE

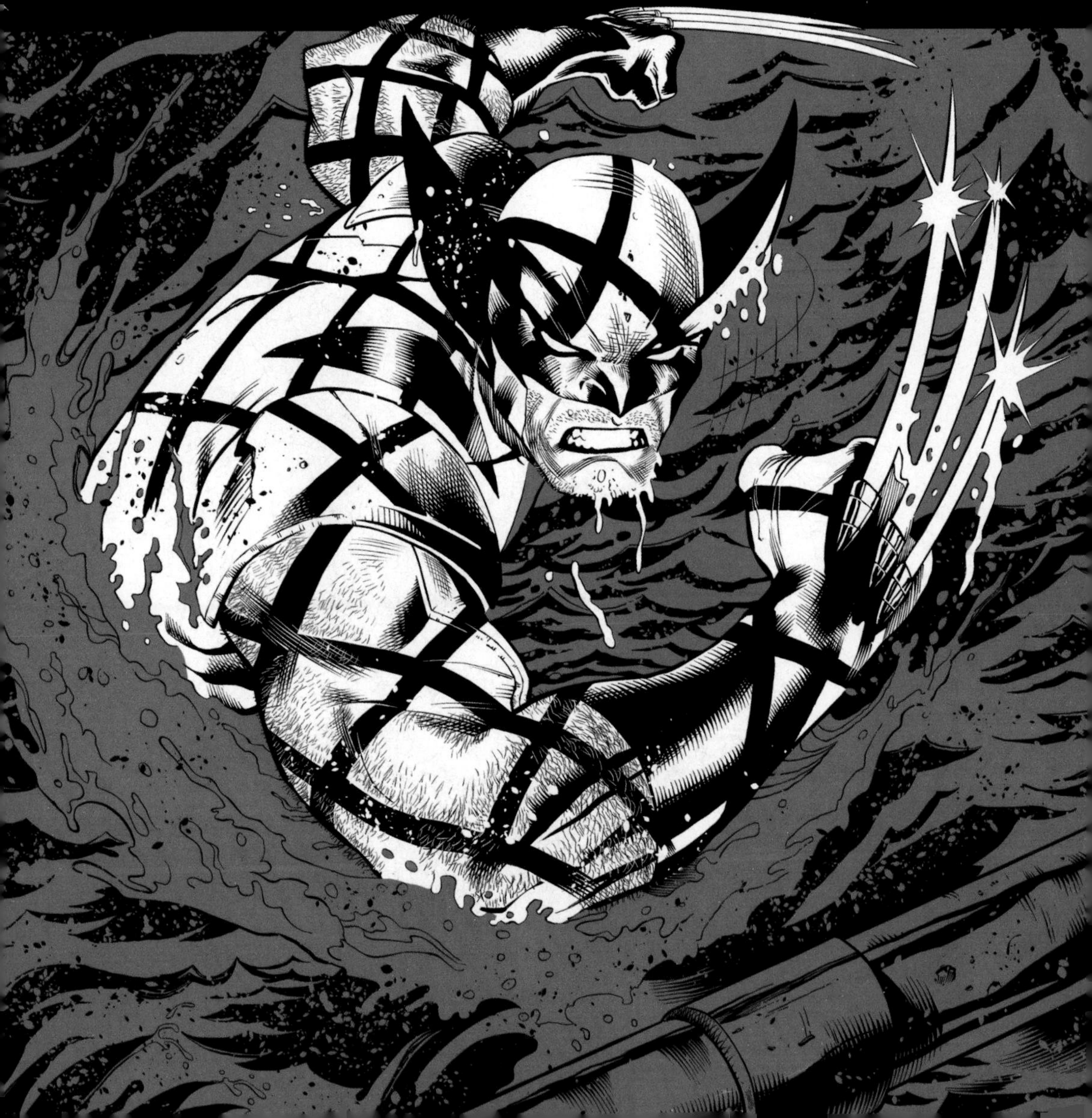

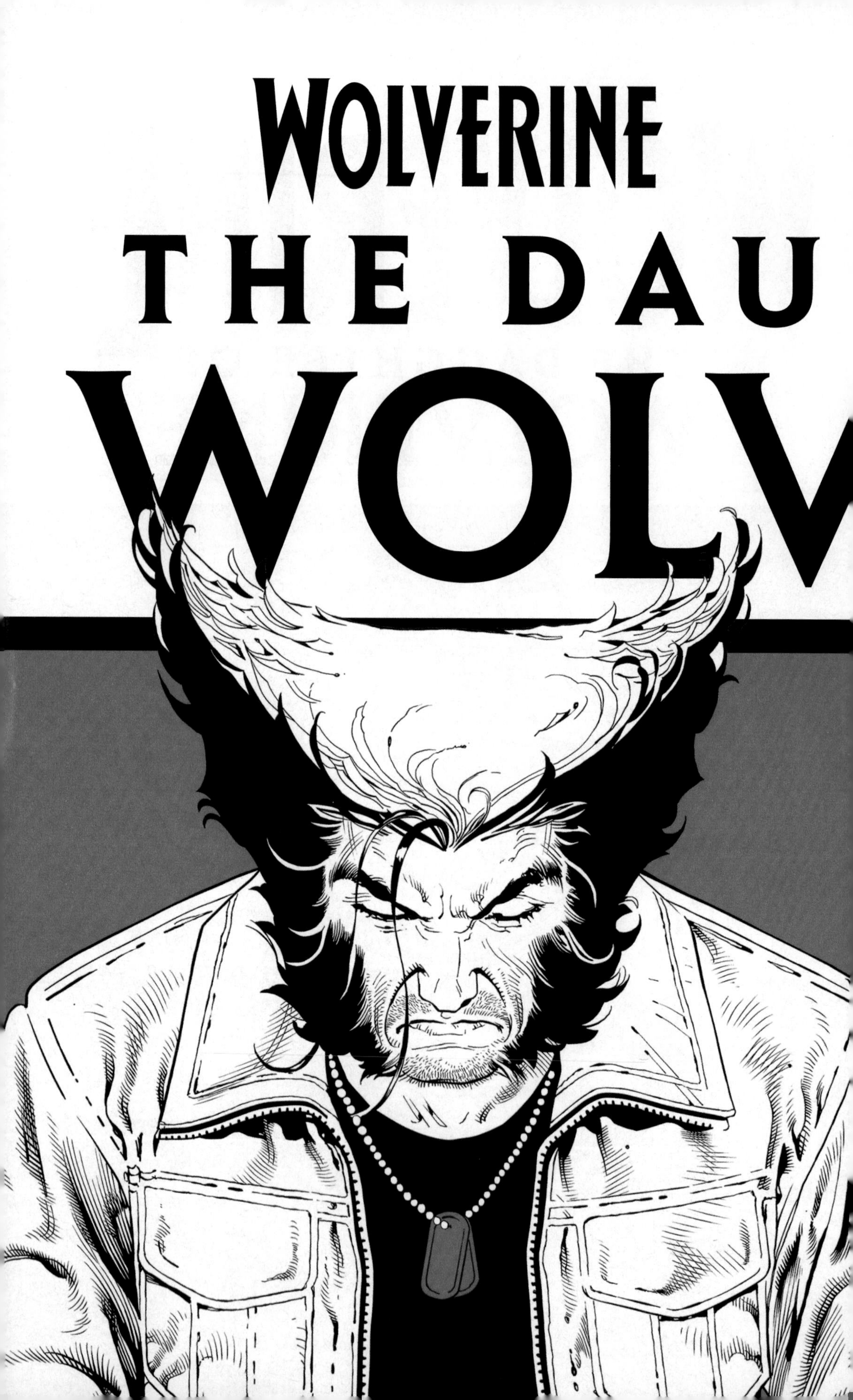
WOLVERINE
THE DAU
WOLV

HTER OF

ERINE

CHARLES SOULE
WRITER

PAULO SIQUEIRA
(#1-4, #6-7, #9) &
DIO NEVES (#5, #8-9)
PENCILERS

OREN JUNIOR
INKER

FRANK D'ARMATA
COLOR ARTIST

VC's JOE CARAMAGNA
LETTERER

**ARTHUR ADAMS &
FEDERICO BLEE** (#1-8);
DAVID YARDIN (#9)
COVER ART

CHRIS ROBINSON
ASSISTANT EDITOR

JORDAN D. WHITE
EDITOR

JENNIFER GRÜNWALD
COLLECTION EDITOR

MAIA LOY
ASSISTANT MANAGING EDITOR

CAITLIN O'CONNELL
ASSISTANT EDITOR

MARK D. BEAZLEY
EDITOR, SPECIAL PROJECTS

JEFF YOUNGQUIST
VP PRODUCTION & SPECIAL PROJECTS

JAY BOWEN
BOOK DESIGNER

DAVID GABRIEL
SVP PRINT, SALES & MARKETING

C.B. CEBULSKI
EDITOR IN CHIEF

WOLVERINE: THE DAUGHTER OF WOLVERINE. Contains material originally published in magazine form as MARVEL COMICS PRESENTS (2019) #1-9. First printing 2020. ISBN 978-1-302-91836-1. Published by MARVEL WORLDWIDE, INC., a subsidiary of MARVEL ENTERTAINMENT, LLC. OFFICE OF PUBLICATION: 1290 Avenue of the Americas, New York, NY 10104. © 2020 MARVEL No similarity between any of the names, characters, persons, and/or institutions in this magazine with those of any living or dead person or institution is intended, and any such similarity which may exist is purely coincidental. **Printed in Canada.** KEVIN FEIGE, Chief Creative Officer; DAN BUCKLEY, President, Marvel Entertainment; JOHN NEE, Publisher; JOE QUESADA, EVP & Creative Director; TOM BREVOORT, SVP of Publishing; DAVID BOGART, Associate Publisher & SVP of Talent Affairs; Publishing & Partnership; DAVID GABRIEL, VP of Print & Digital Publishing; JEFF YOUNGQUIST, VP of Production & Special Projects; DAN CARR, Executive Director of Publishing Technology; ALEX MORALES, Director of Publishing Operations; DAN EDINGTON, Managing Editor; SUSAN CRESPI, Production Manager; STAN LEE, Chairman Emeritus. For information regarding advertising in Marvel Comics or on Marvel.com, please contact Vit DeBellis, Custom Solutions & Integrated Advertising Manager, at vdebellis@marvel.com. For Marvel subscription inquiries, please call 888-511-5480. **Manufactured between 1/3/2020 and 2/4/2020 by SOLISCO PRINTERS, SCOTT, QC, CANADA.**

10 9 8 7 6 5 4 3 2 1

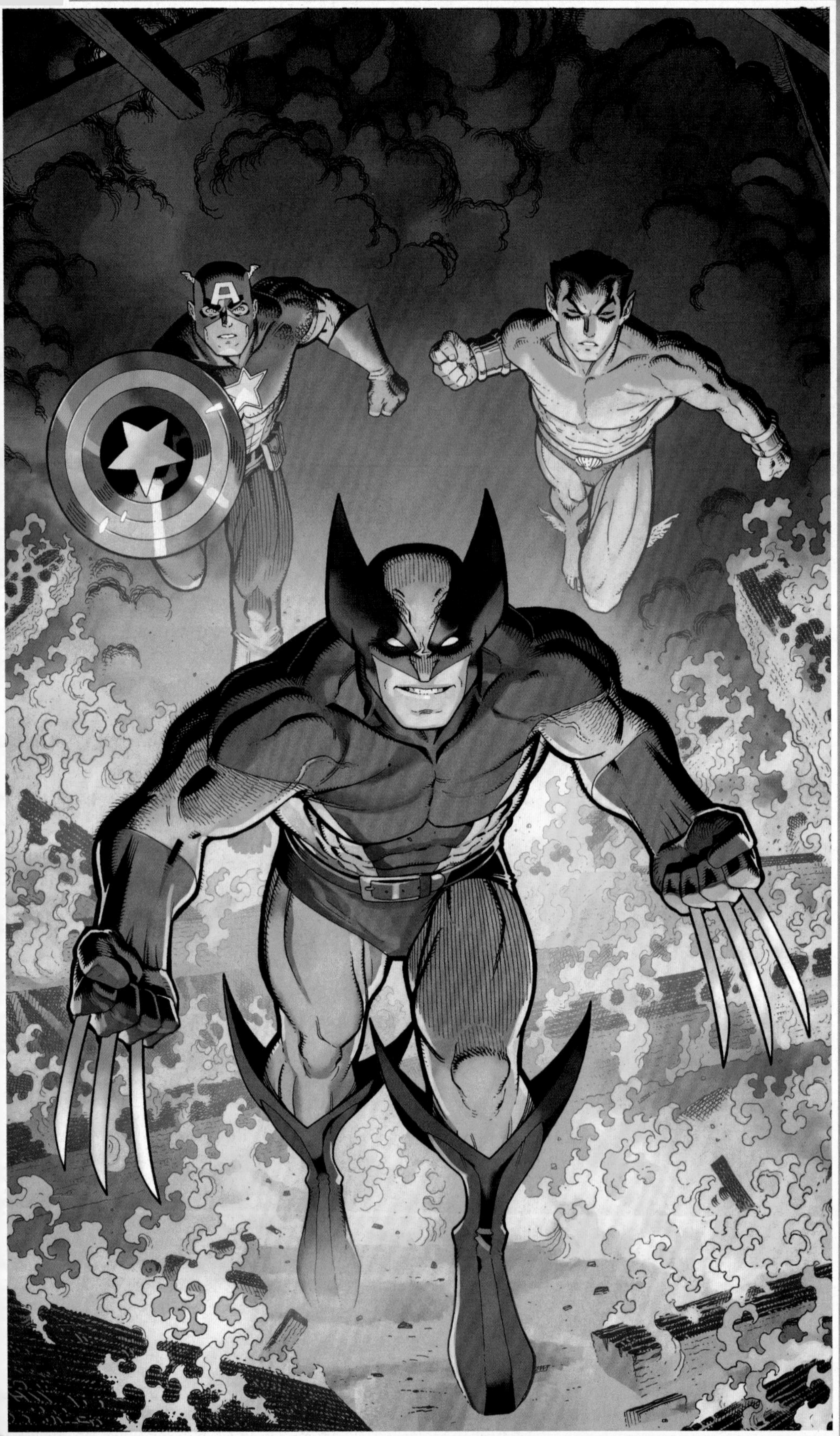

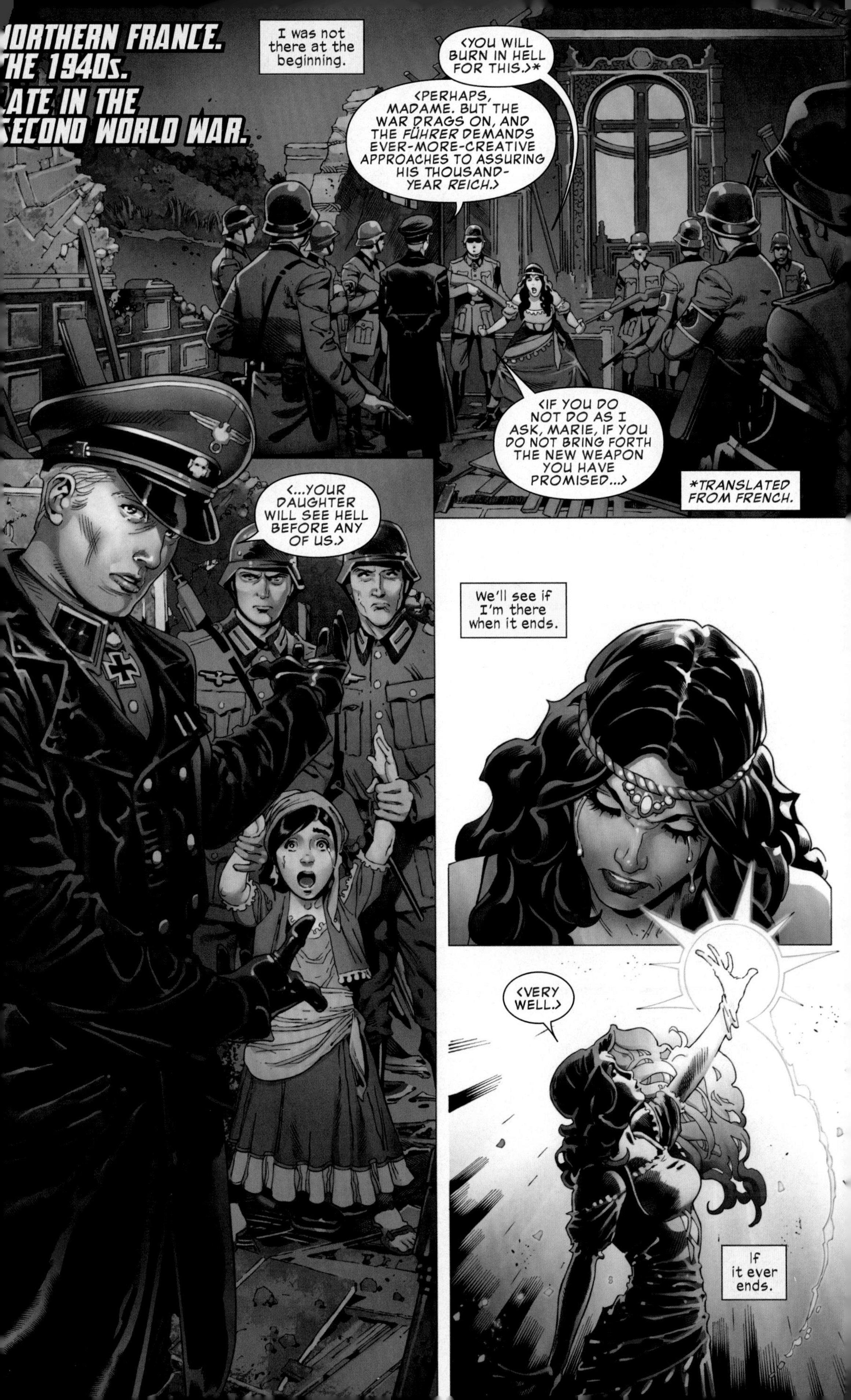
ORTHERN FRANCE. HE 1940s. ATE IN THE ECOND WORLD WAR.
I was not there at the beginning.
<YOU WILL BURN IN HELL FOR THIS.>*
<PERHAPS, MADAME. BUT THE WAR DRAGS ON, AND THE *FÜHRER* DEMANDS EVER-MORE-CREATIVE APPROACHES TO ASSURING HIS THOUSAND-YEAR *REICH.*>
<IF YOU DO NOT DO AS I ASK, MARIE, IF YOU DO NOT BRING FORTH THE NEW WEAPON YOU HAVE PROMISED...>
*TRANSLATED FROM FRENCH.
<...YOUR DAUGHTER WILL SEE HELL BEFORE ANY OF US.>
We'll see if I'm there when it ends.
<VERY WELL.>
If it ever ends.

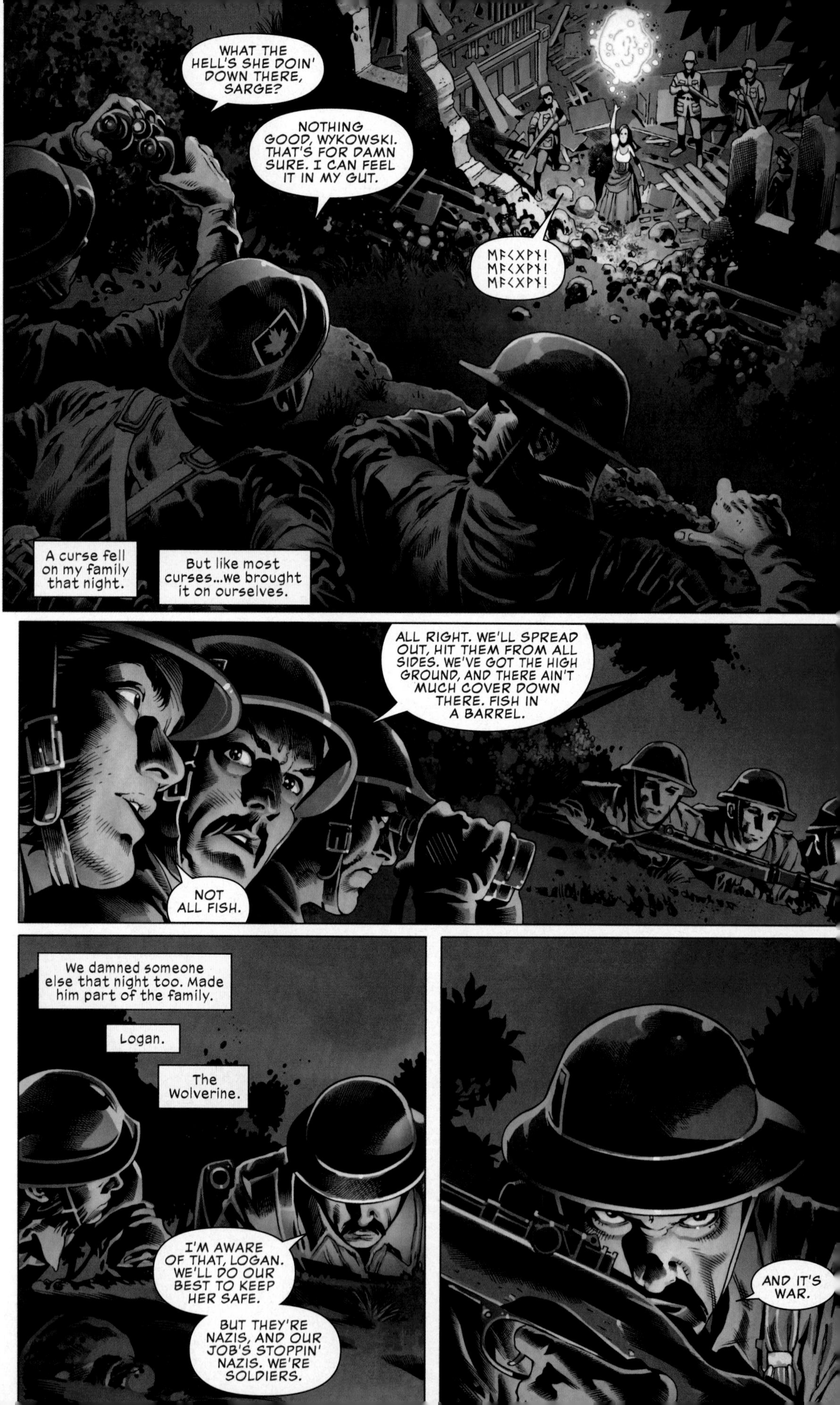
WHAT THE HELL'S SHE DOIN' DOWN THERE, SARGE?
NOTHING GOOD, WYKOWSKI. THAT'S FOR DAMN SURE. I CAN FEEL IT IN MY GUT.
ᛗᚨᚲᚷᚹᚺ! ᛗᚨᚲᚷᚹᚺ! ᛗᚨᚲᚷᚹᚺ!
A curse fell on my family that night.
But like most curses...we brought it on ourselves.
ALL RIGHT. WE'LL SPREAD OUT, HIT THEM FROM ALL SIDES. WE'VE GOT THE HIGH GROUND, AND THERE AIN'T MUCH COVER DOWN THERE. FISH IN A BARREL.
NOT ALL FISH.
We damned someone else that night too. Made him part of the family.
Logan.
The Wolverine.
I'M AWARE OF THAT, LOGAN. WE'LL DO OUR BEST TO KEEP HER SAFE.
BUT THEY'RE NAZIS, AND OUR JOB'S STOPPIN' NAZIS. WE'RE SOLDIERS.
AND IT'S WAR.

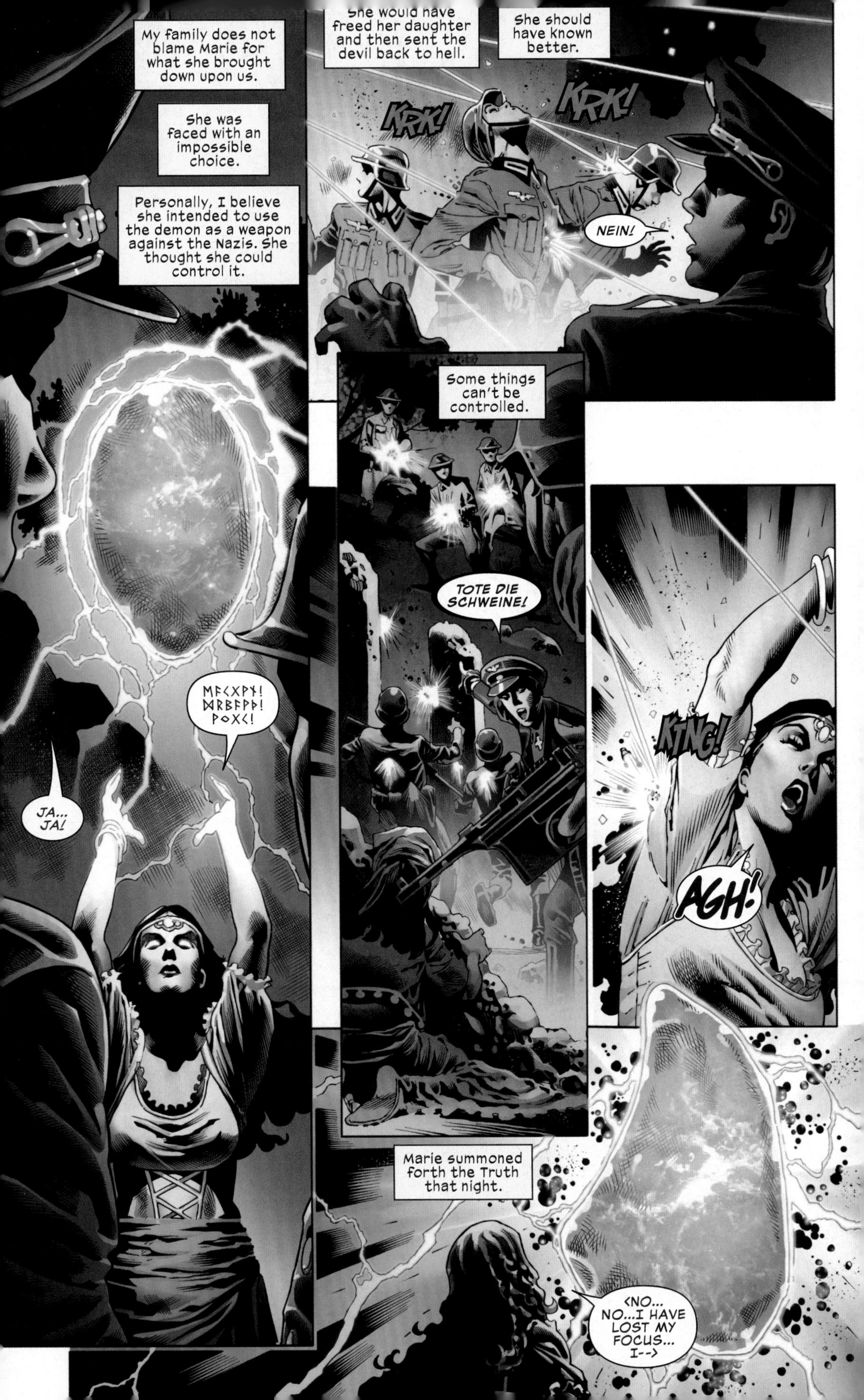
My family does not blame Marie for what she brought down upon us.
She was faced with an impossible choice.
Personally, I believe she intended to use the demon as a weapon against the Nazis. She thought she could control it.
MFCXPY! DRBFPP! POXC!
JA... JA!
She would have freed her daughter and then sent the devil back to hell.
She should have known better.
KRK!
KRK!
NEIN!
Some things can't be controlled.
TOTE DIE SCHWEINE!
KING!
AGH!
Marie summoned forth the Truth that night.
<NO... NO...I HAVE LOST MY FOCUS... I-->

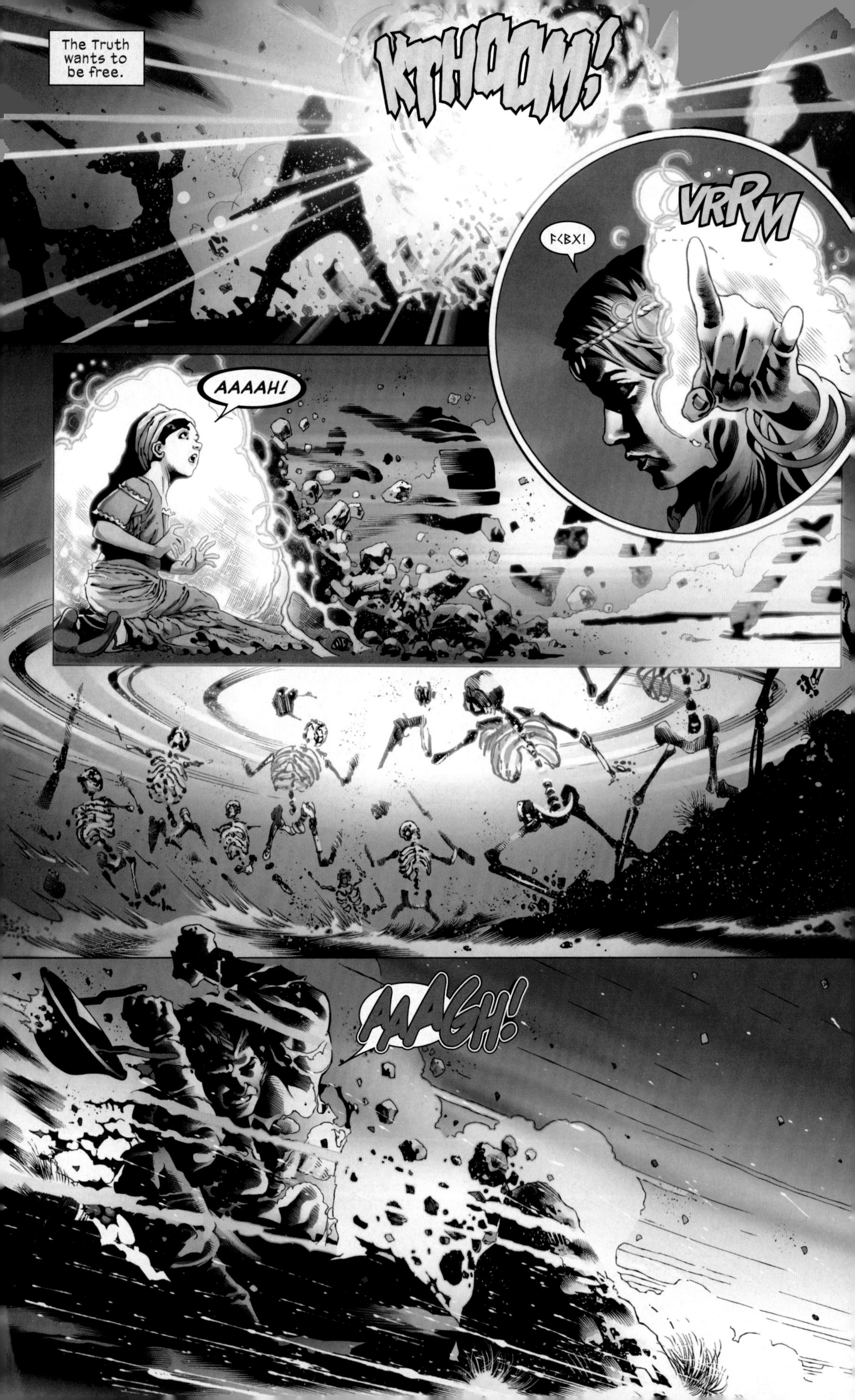
The Truth wants to be free.
KTHOOM!
VRRM
F<BX!
AAAAH!
AAAGH!

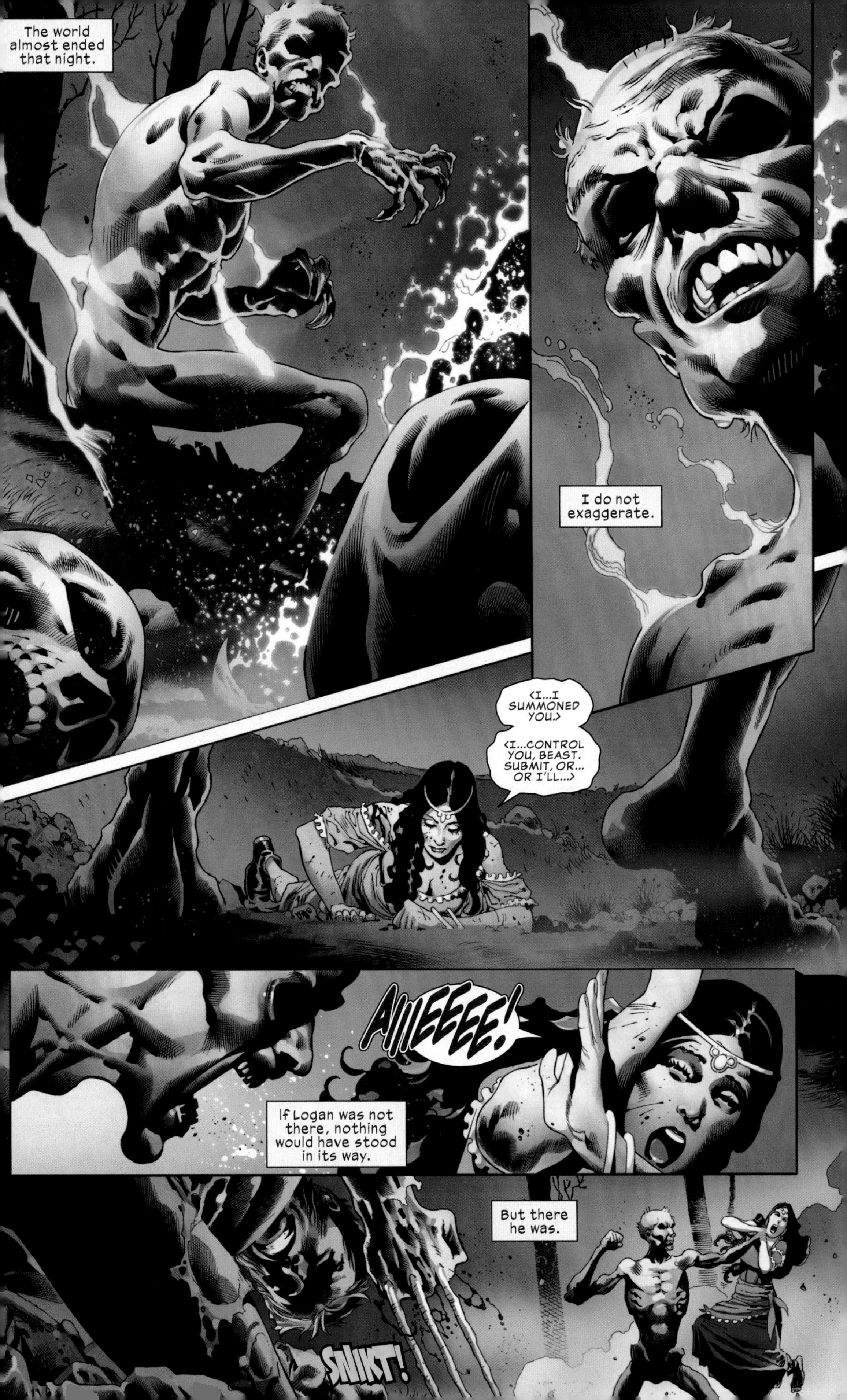
The world almost ended that night.
I do not exaggerate.
<I...I SUMMONED YOU.>
<I...CONTROL YOU, BEAST. SUBMIT, OR... OR I'LL...>
AIIEEEE!
If Logan was not there, nothing would have stood in its way.
But there he was.
SNIKT!

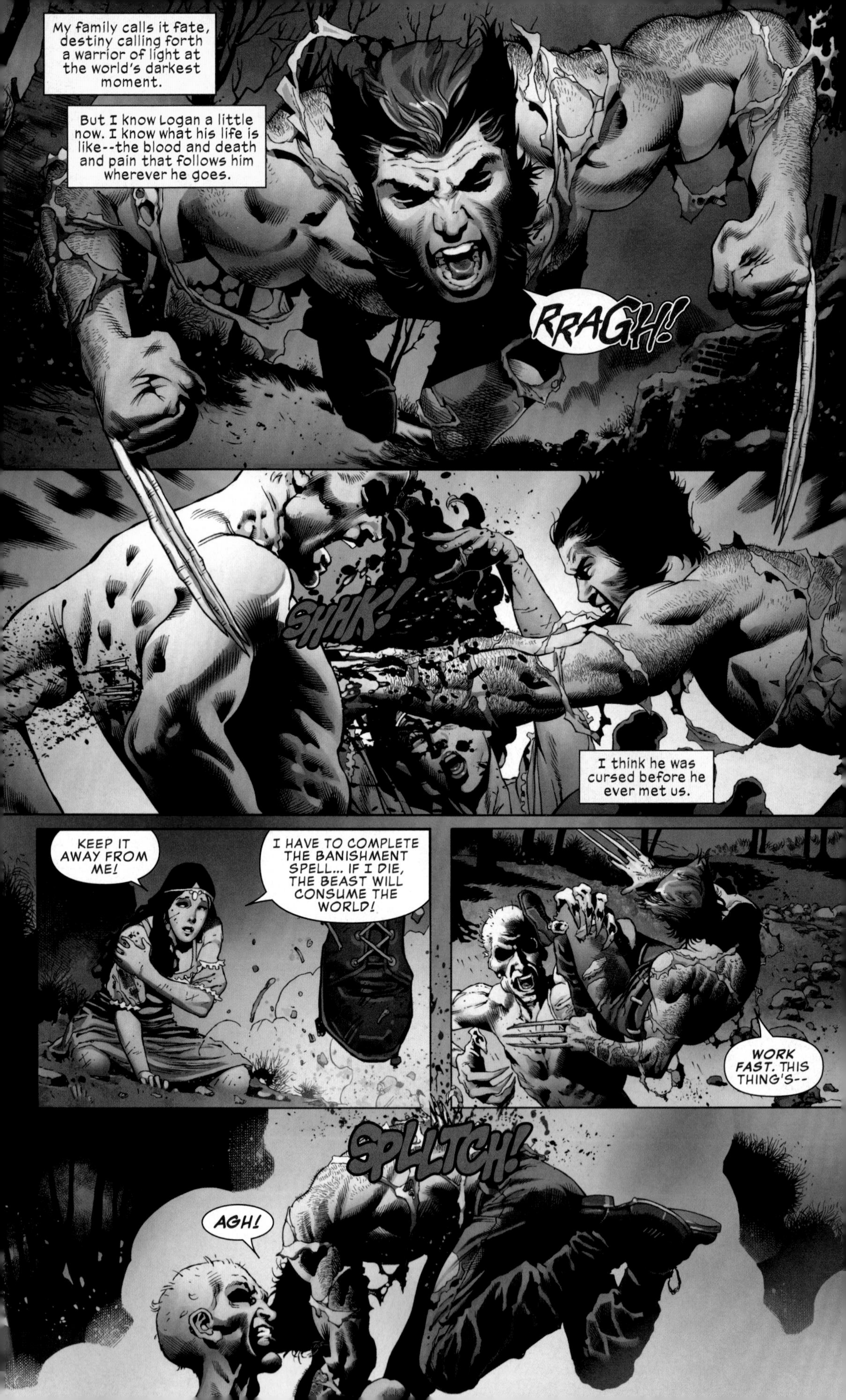
My family calls it fate, destiny calling forth a warrior of light at the world's darkest moment.
But I know Logan a little now. I know what his life is like--the blood and death and pain that follows him wherever he goes.
RRAGH!
SHHK!
I think he was cursed before he ever met us.
KEEP IT AWAY FROM ME!
I HAVE TO COMPLETE THE BANISHMENT SPELL... IF I DIE, THE BEAST WILL CONSUME THE WORLD!
WORK FAST. THIS THING'S--
SPLLTCH!
AGH!

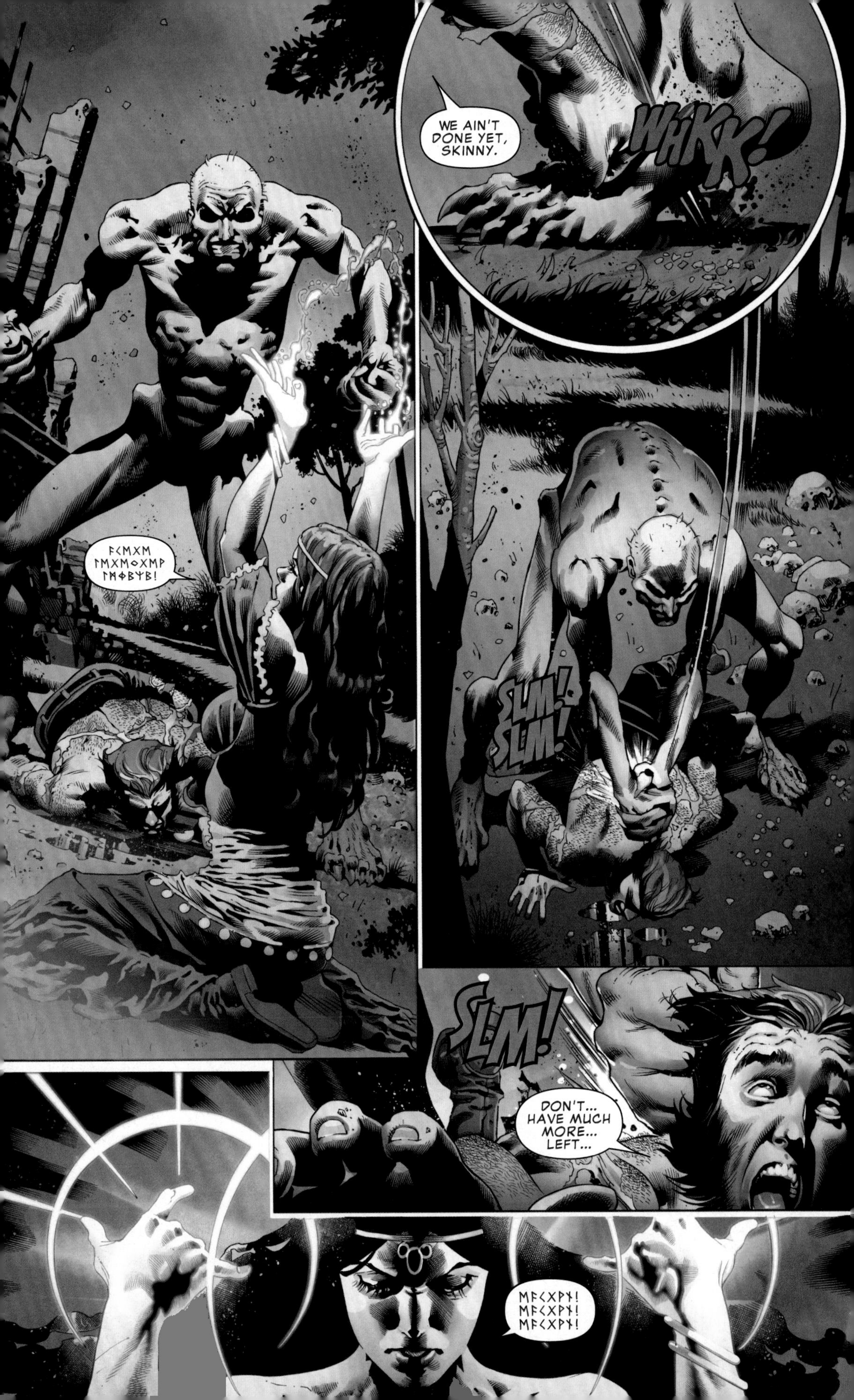
WE AIN'T DONE YET, SKINNY.
WHKK!
SLM! SLM!
SLM!
DON'T... HAVE MUCH MORE... LEFT...

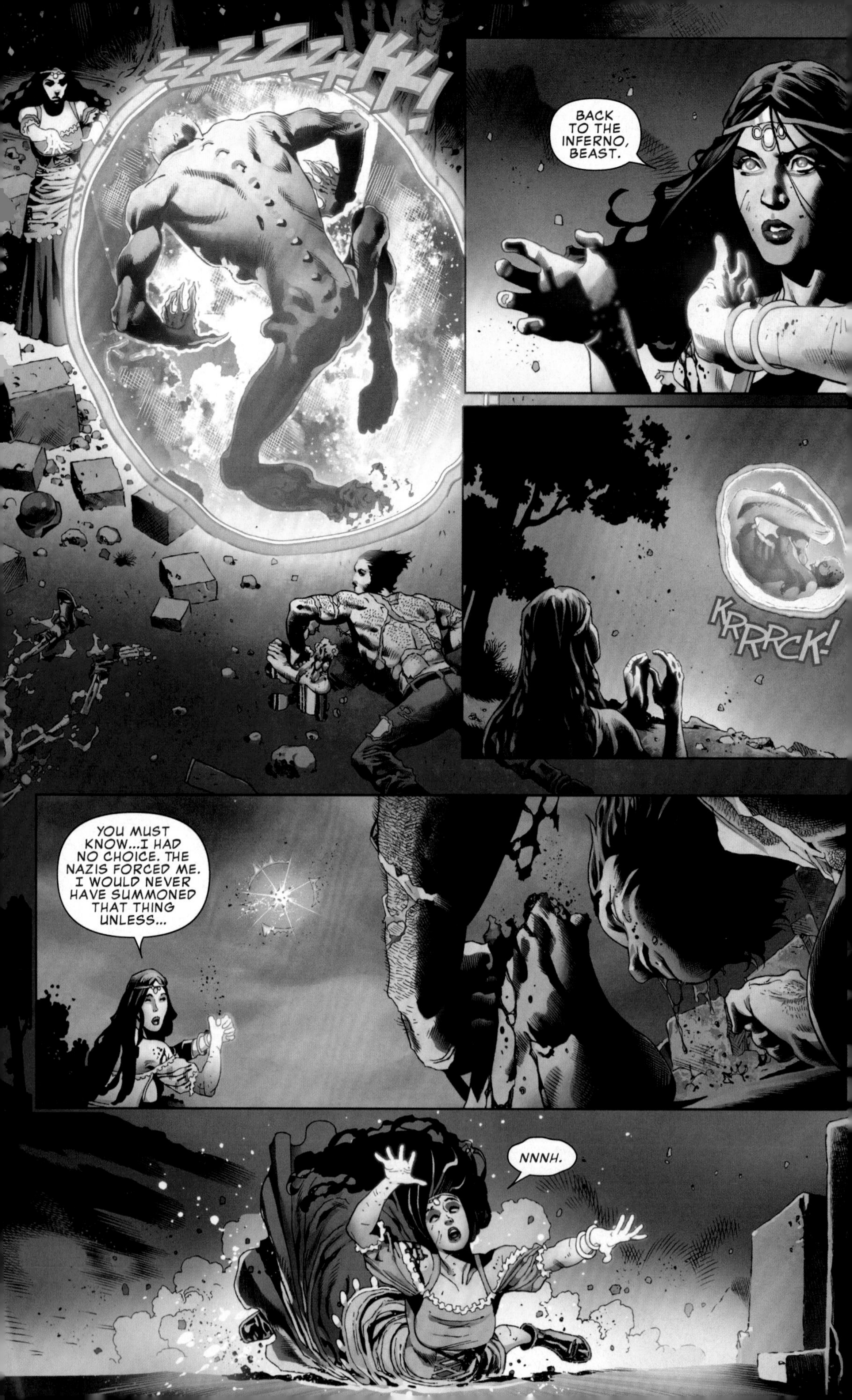
ZZZZZZKKK!
BACK TO THE INFERNO, BEAST.
KRRRCK!
YOU MUST KNOW...I HAD NO CHOICE. THE NAZIS FORCED ME. I WOULD NEVER HAVE SUMMONED THAT THING UNLESS...
NNNH.

TRY TO REST. THERE WAS A MEDIC IN SQUAD. SHOULD HAVE SOME SUPPLIES. I'M NO DOCTOR, BUT MAYBE--

NO. THERE IS NO HELPING ME. LISTEN, WHILE I AM STILL ABLE TO SPEAK.

THE BEAST, THE DEMON-- ITS NAME IS TRUTH.

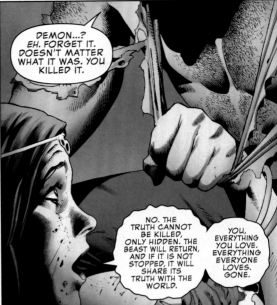

DEMON...? EH. FORGET IT. DOESN'T MATTER WHAT IT WAS. YOU KILLED IT.

NO. THE TRUTH CANNOT BE KILLED, ONLY HIDDEN. THE BEAST WILL RETURN, AND IF IT IS NOT STOPPED, IT WILL SHARE ITS TRUTH WITH THE WORLD.

YOU, EVERYTHING YOU LOVE, EVERYTHING EVERYONE LOVES, GONE.

WHEN?

TEN YEARS, PERHAPS. ONE NIGHT, THE DEMON WILL RETURN, AT THE VERY WORST PLACE IN THE WORLD. LOOK THERE.

AND THEN WHAT? CAST A DAMN SPELL? I'M NOT--

NOT YOU. YOU WILL BE THE GUARDIAN. YOU SURVIVED THE TRUTH. EVEN NOW, THE WOUNDS IT GAVE YOU ARE HEALING.

YOU WILL PROTECT HER FROM THE TRUTH, WHILE SHE DOES THE WORK.

IF SHE IS KILLED, IF SHE CANNOT COMPLETE THE SPELL... THE DEMON WILL BE SET FREE, AND ALL WILL BE DEATH.

YOU MUST PROTECT HER. ONLY SHE CAN DO IT.

SHE HAS THE BLOOD, AND I TAUGHT... HER...

Marie's death bound Logan to us. Made him part of the family. It was another curse.

His...but also ours.

WAIT... SHE...?

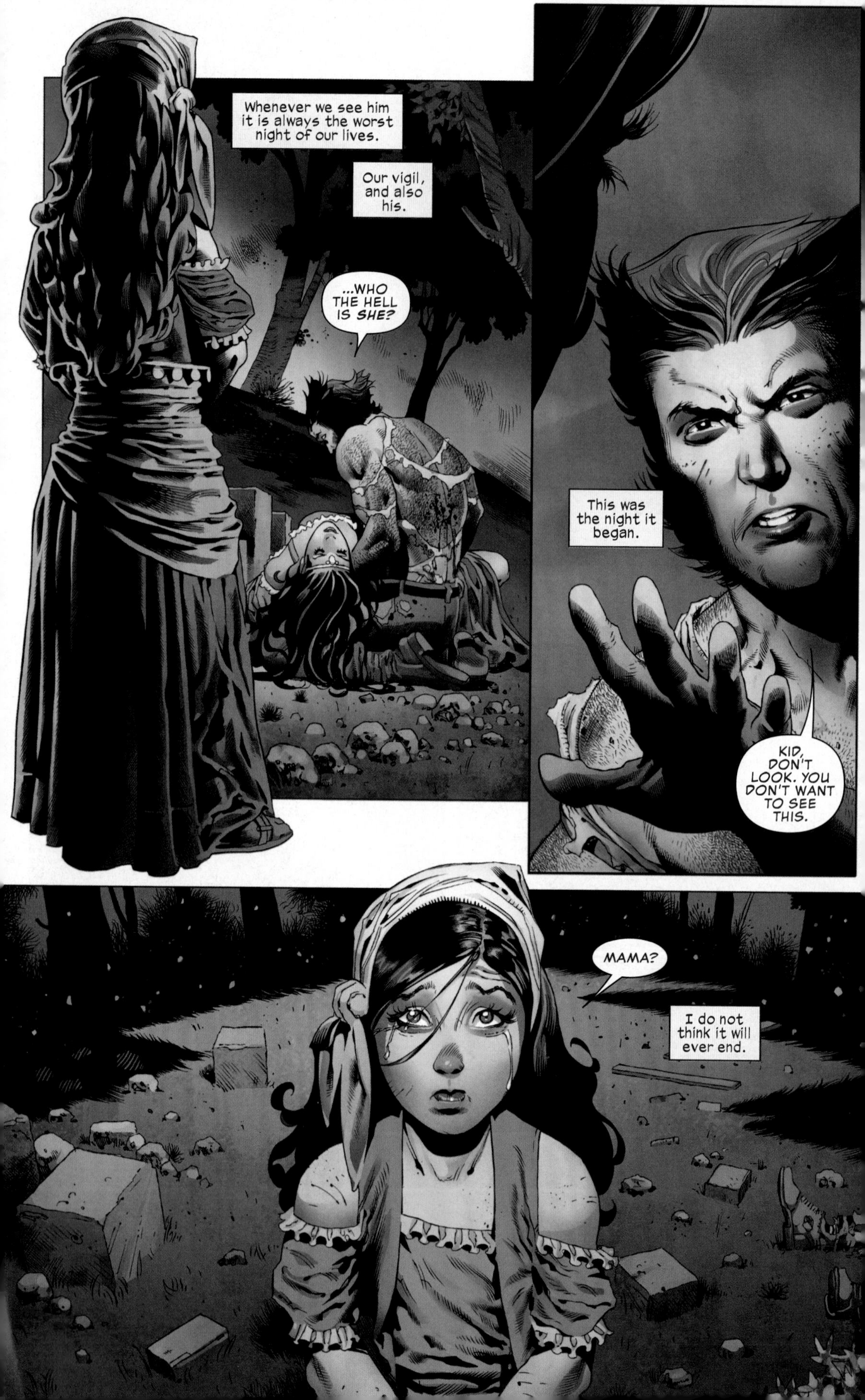
Whenever we see him it is always the worst night of our lives.
Our vigil, and also his.
...WHO THE HELL IS SHE?
This was the night it began.
KID, DON'T LOOK. YOU DON'T WANT TO SEE THIS.
MAMA?
I do not think it will ever end.

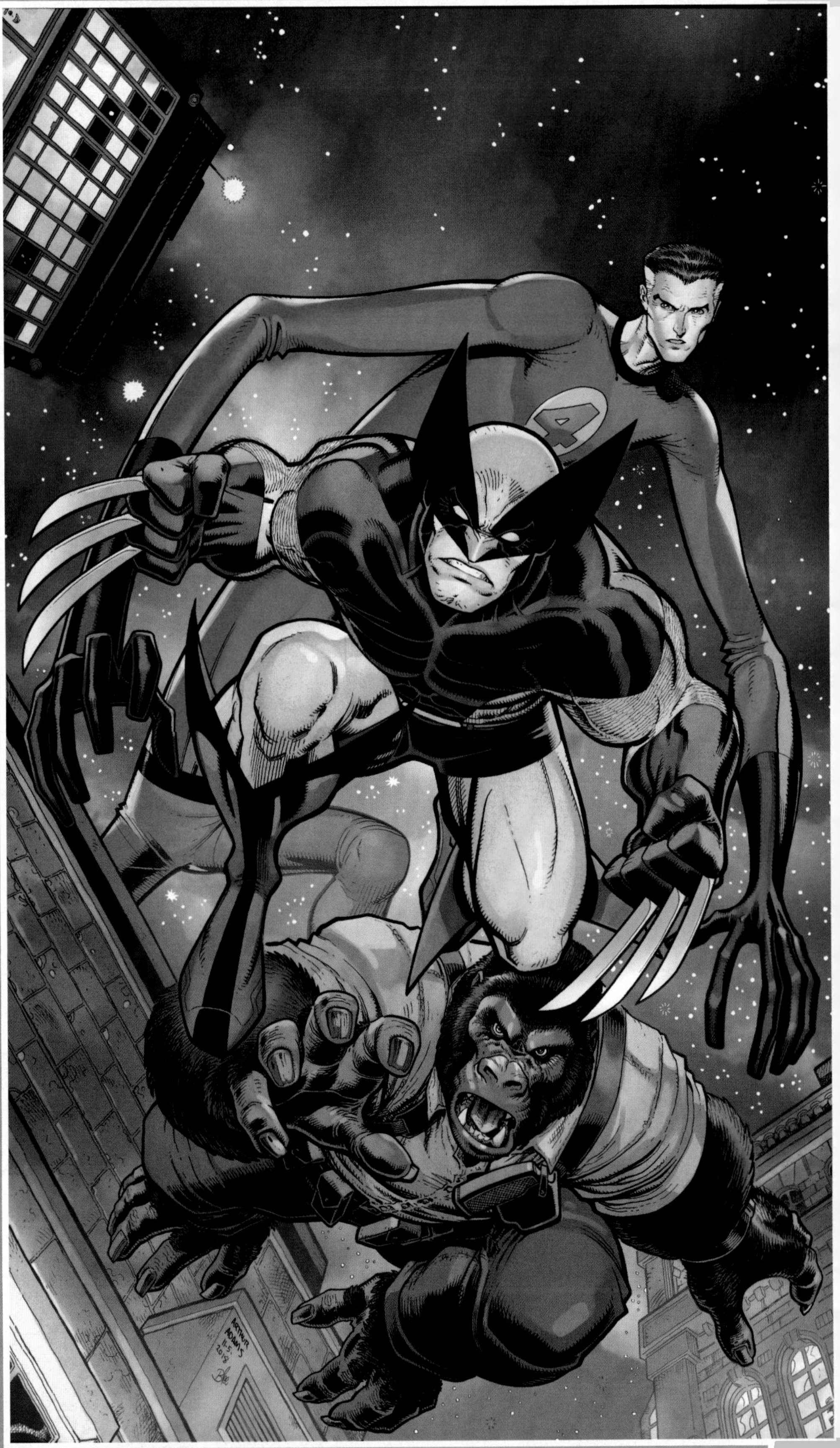

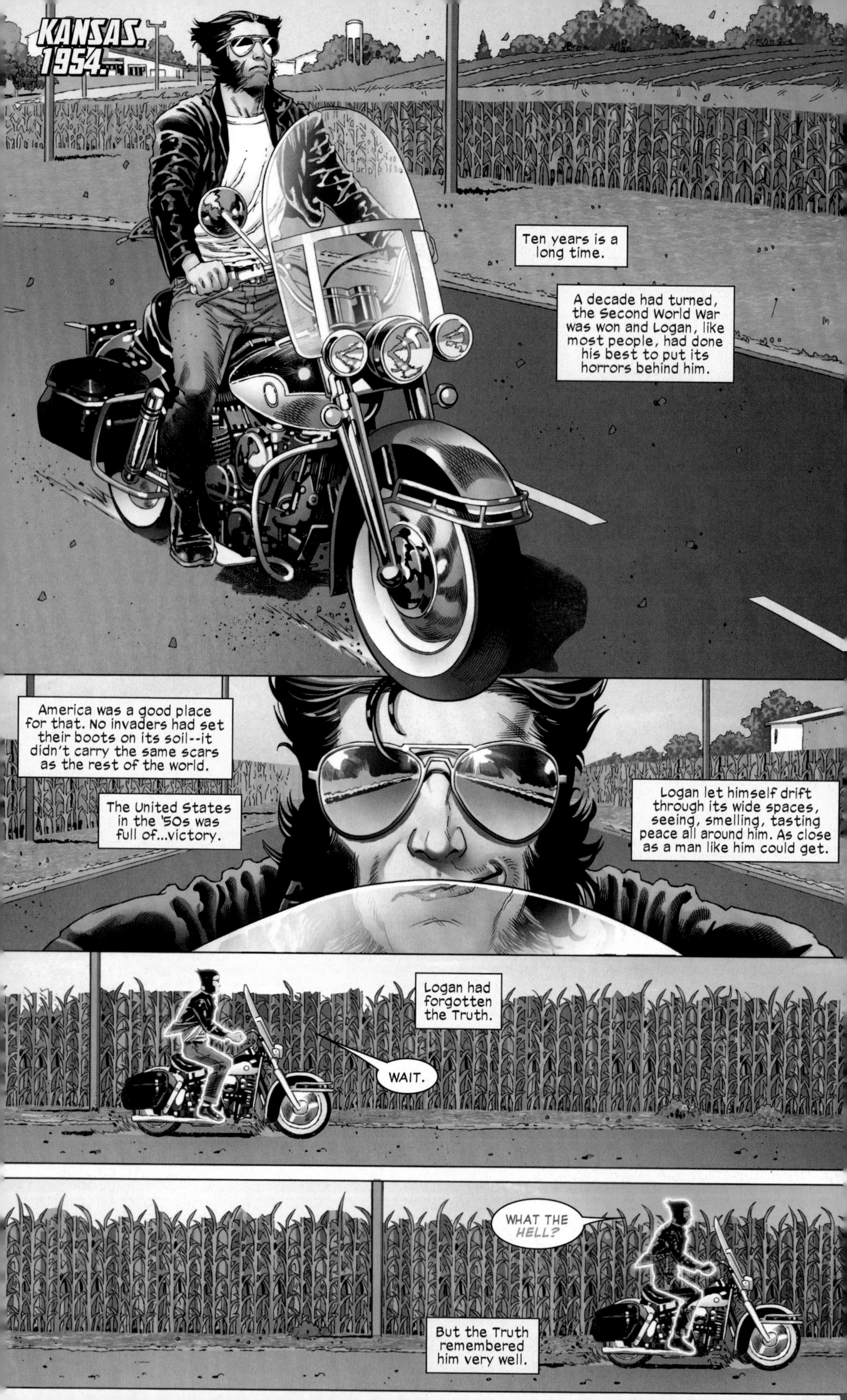
KANSAS. 1954.
Ten years is a long time.
A decade had turned, the Second World War was won and Logan, like most people, had done his best to put its horrors behind him.
America was a good place for that. No invaders had set their boots on its soil--it didn't carry the same scars as the rest of the world.
The United States in the '50s was full of...victory.
Logan let himself drift through its wide spaces, seeing, smelling, tasting peace all around him. As close as a man like him could get.
Logan had forgotten the Truth.
WAIT.
WHAT THE HELL?
But the Truth remembered him very well.

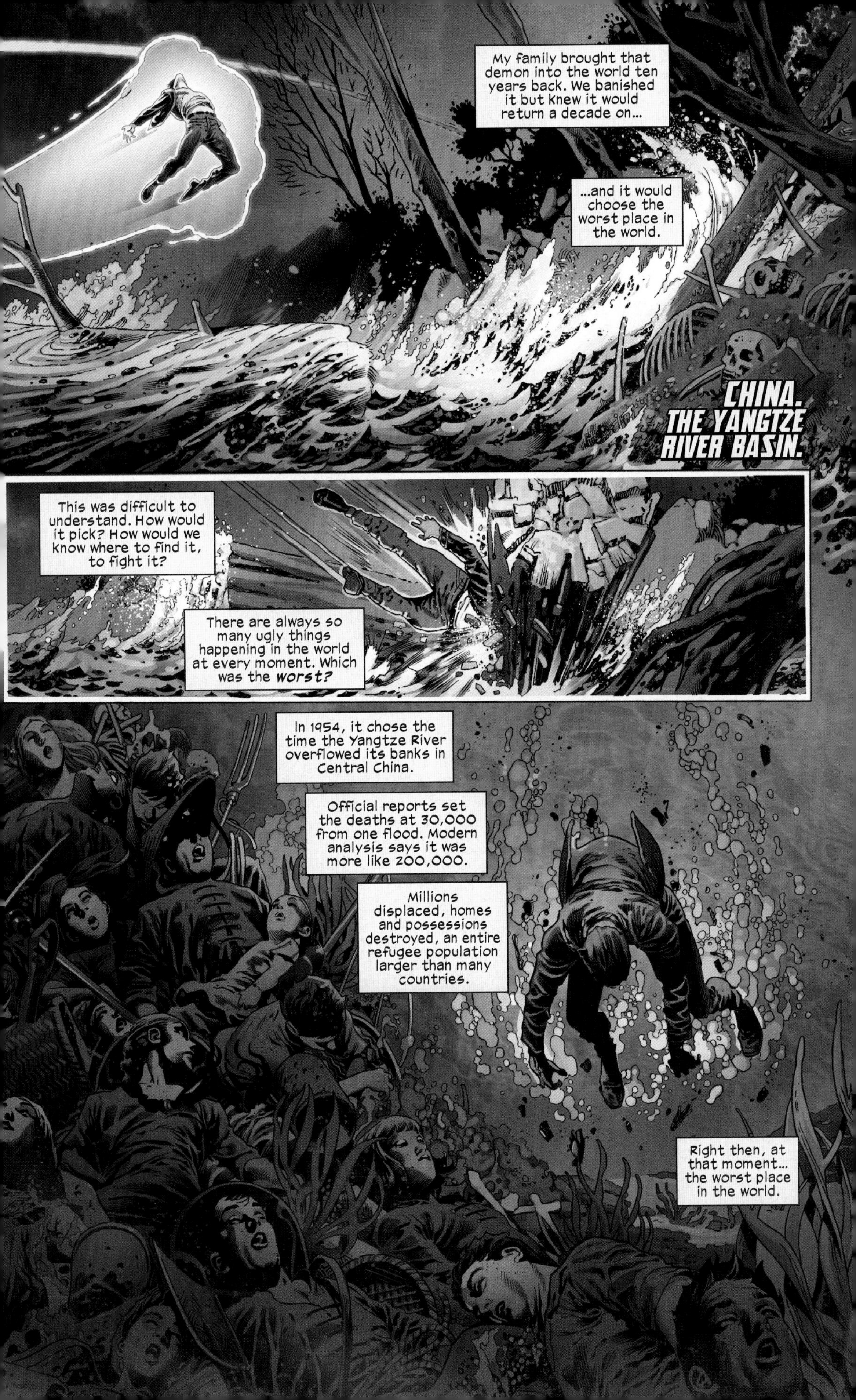
My family brought that demon into the world ten years back. We banished it but knew it would return a decade on...
...and it would choose the worst place in the world.
CHINA. THE YANGTZE RIVER BASIN.
This was difficult to understand. How would it pick? How would we know where to find it, to fight it?
There are always so many ugly things happening in the world at every moment. Which was the *worst?*
In 1954, it chose the time the Yangtze River overflowed its banks in Central China.
Official reports set the deaths at 30,000 from one flood. Modern analysis says it was more like 200,000.
Millions displaced, homes and possessions destroyed, an entire refugee population larger than many countries.
Right then, at that moment... the worst place in the world.

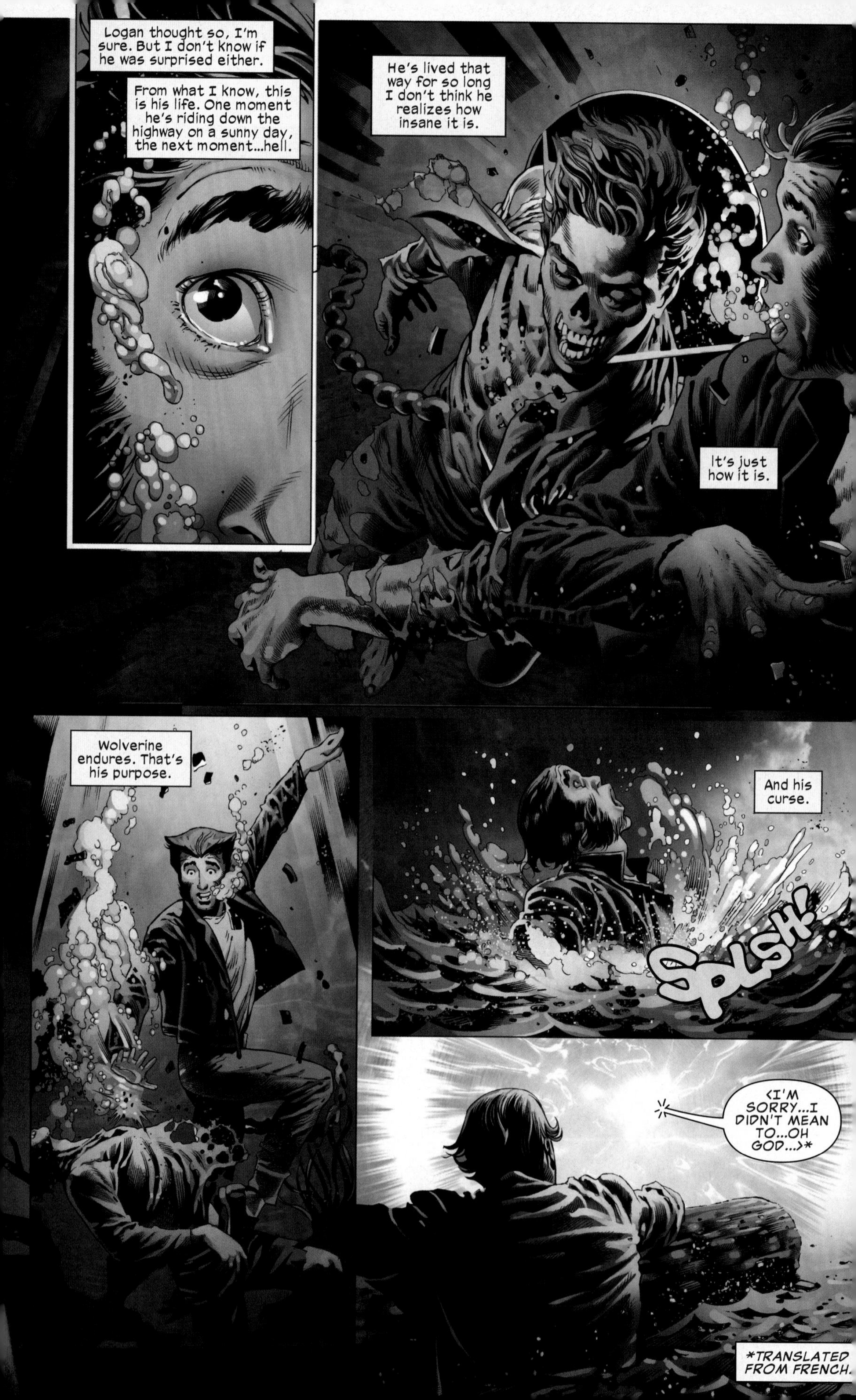

Logan thought so, I'm sure. But I don't know if he was surprised either.
From what I know, this is his life. One moment he's riding down the highway on a sunny day, the next moment...hell.
He's lived that way for so long I don't think he realizes how insane it is.
It's just how it is.
Wolverine endures. That's his purpose.
And his curse.
SPLSH!
<I'M SORRY...I DIDN'T MEAN TO...OH GOD...>*
*TRANSLATED FROM FRENCH.

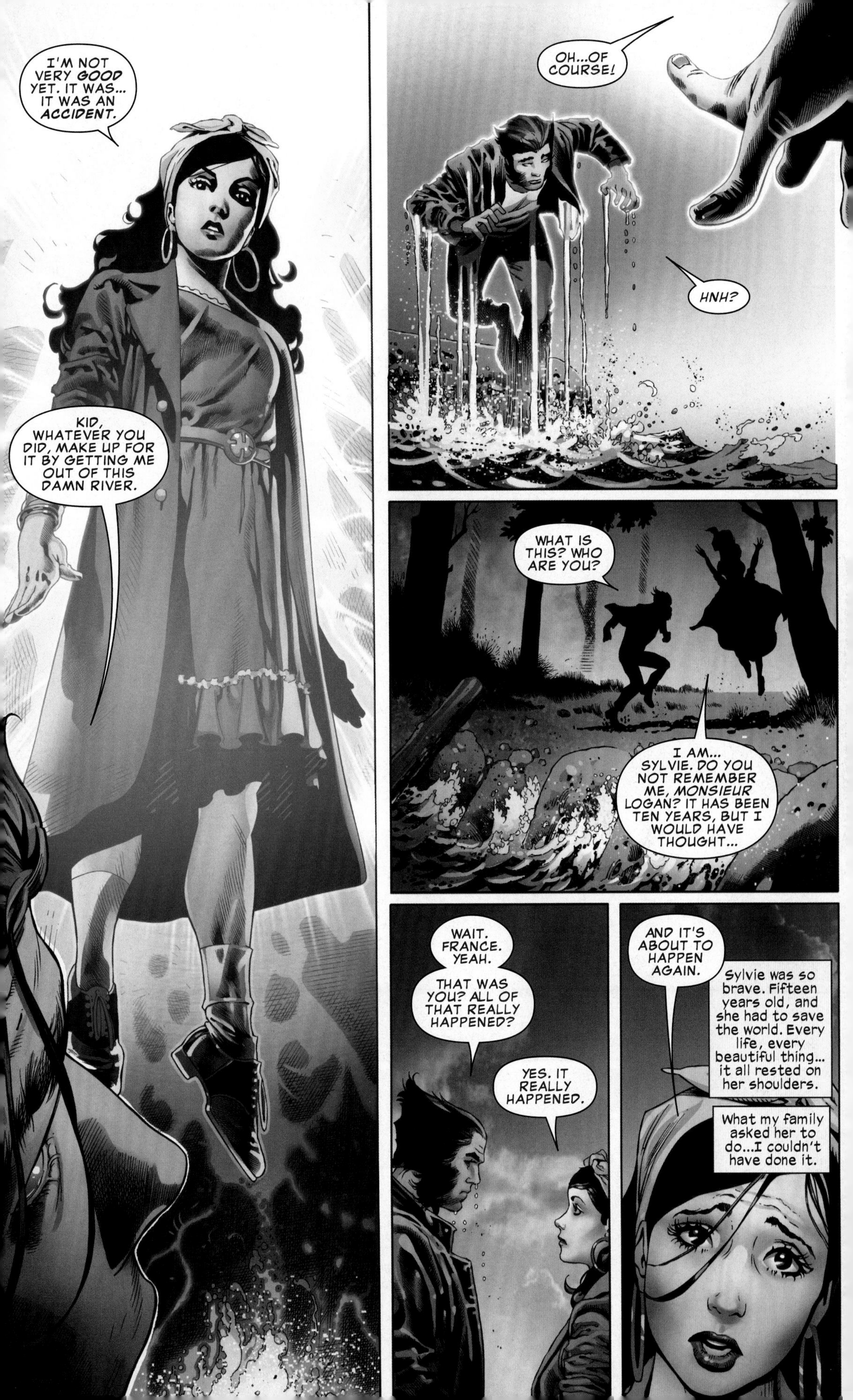
I'M NOT VERY GOOD YET. IT WAS... IT WAS AN ACCIDENT.
KID, WHATEVER YOU DID, MAKE UP FOR IT BY GETTING ME OUT OF THIS DAMN RIVER.
OH...OF COURSE!
HNH?
WHAT IS THIS? WHO ARE YOU?
I AM... SYLVIE. DO YOU NOT REMEMBER ME, MONSIEUR LOGAN? IT HAS BEEN TEN YEARS, BUT I WOULD HAVE THOUGHT...
WAIT. FRANCE. YEAH.
THAT WAS YOU? ALL OF THAT REALLY HAPPENED?
YES. IT REALLY HAPPENED.
AND IT'S ABOUT TO HAPPEN AGAIN.
Sylvie was so brave. Fifteen years old, and she had to save the world. Every life, every beautiful thing... it all rested on her shoulders.
What my family asked her to do...I couldn't have done it.

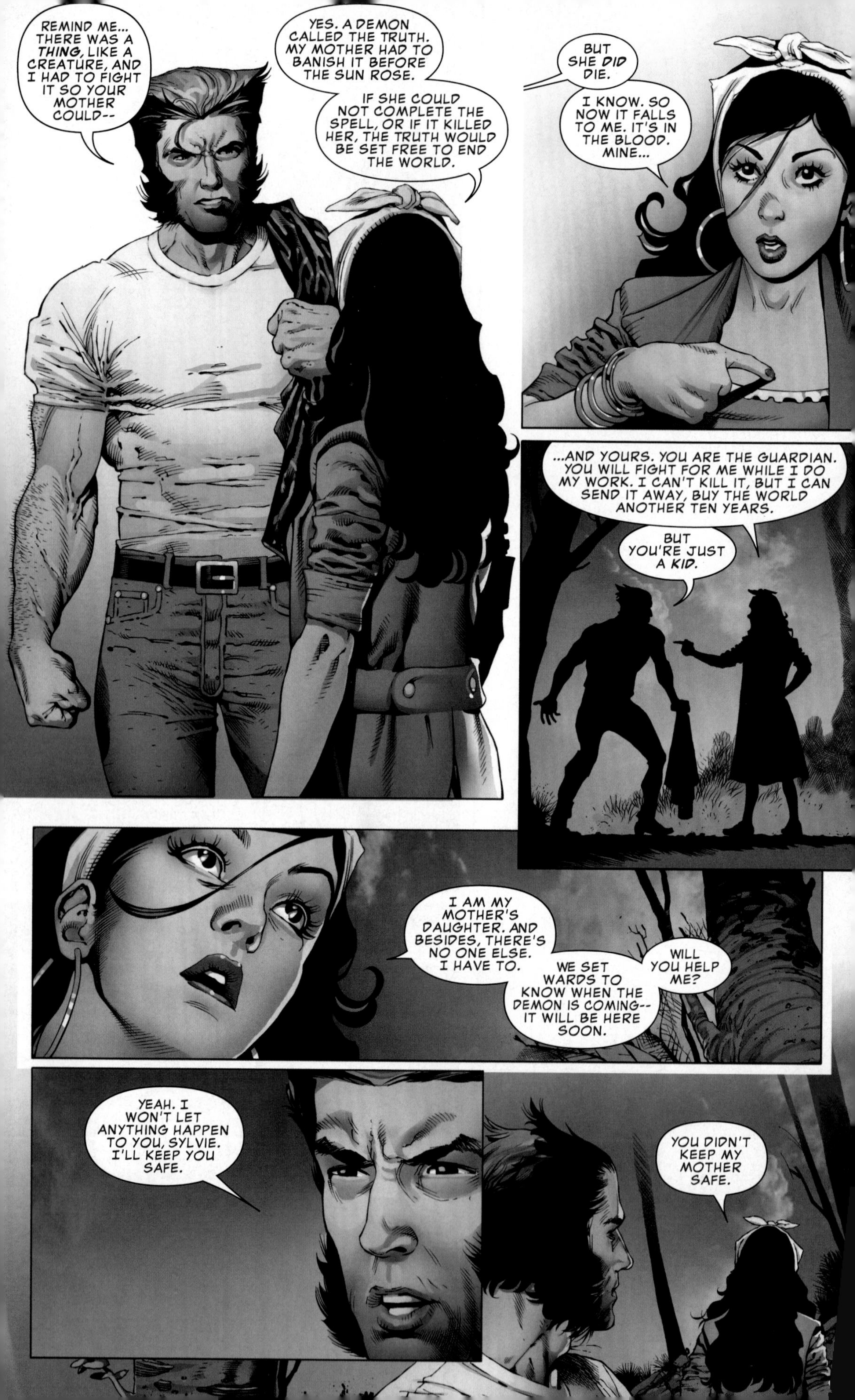
REMIND ME... THERE WAS A *THING*, LIKE A CREATURE, AND I HAD TO FIGHT IT SO YOUR MOTHER COULD--
YES. A DEMON CALLED THE TRUTH. MY MOTHER HAD TO BANISH IT BEFORE THE SUN ROSE.
IF SHE COULD NOT COMPLETE THE SPELL, OR IF IT KILLED HER, THE TRUTH WOULD BE SET FREE TO END THE WORLD.
BUT SHE *DID* DIE.
I KNOW. SO NOW IT FALLS TO ME. IT'S IN THE BLOOD. MINE...
...AND YOURS. YOU ARE THE GUARDIAN. YOU WILL FIGHT FOR ME WHILE I DO MY WORK. I CAN'T KILL IT, BUT I CAN SEND IT AWAY, BUY THE WORLD ANOTHER TEN YEARS.
BUT YOU'RE JUST A *KID*.
I AM MY MOTHER'S DAUGHTER. AND BESIDES, THERE'S NO ONE ELSE. I HAVE TO.
WE SET WARDS TO KNOW WHEN THE DEMON IS COMING-- IT WILL BE HERE SOON.
WILL YOU HELP ME?
YEAH. I WON'T LET ANYTHING HAPPEN TO YOU, SYLVIE. I'LL KEEP YOU SAFE.
YOU DIDN'T KEEP MY MOTHER SAFE.

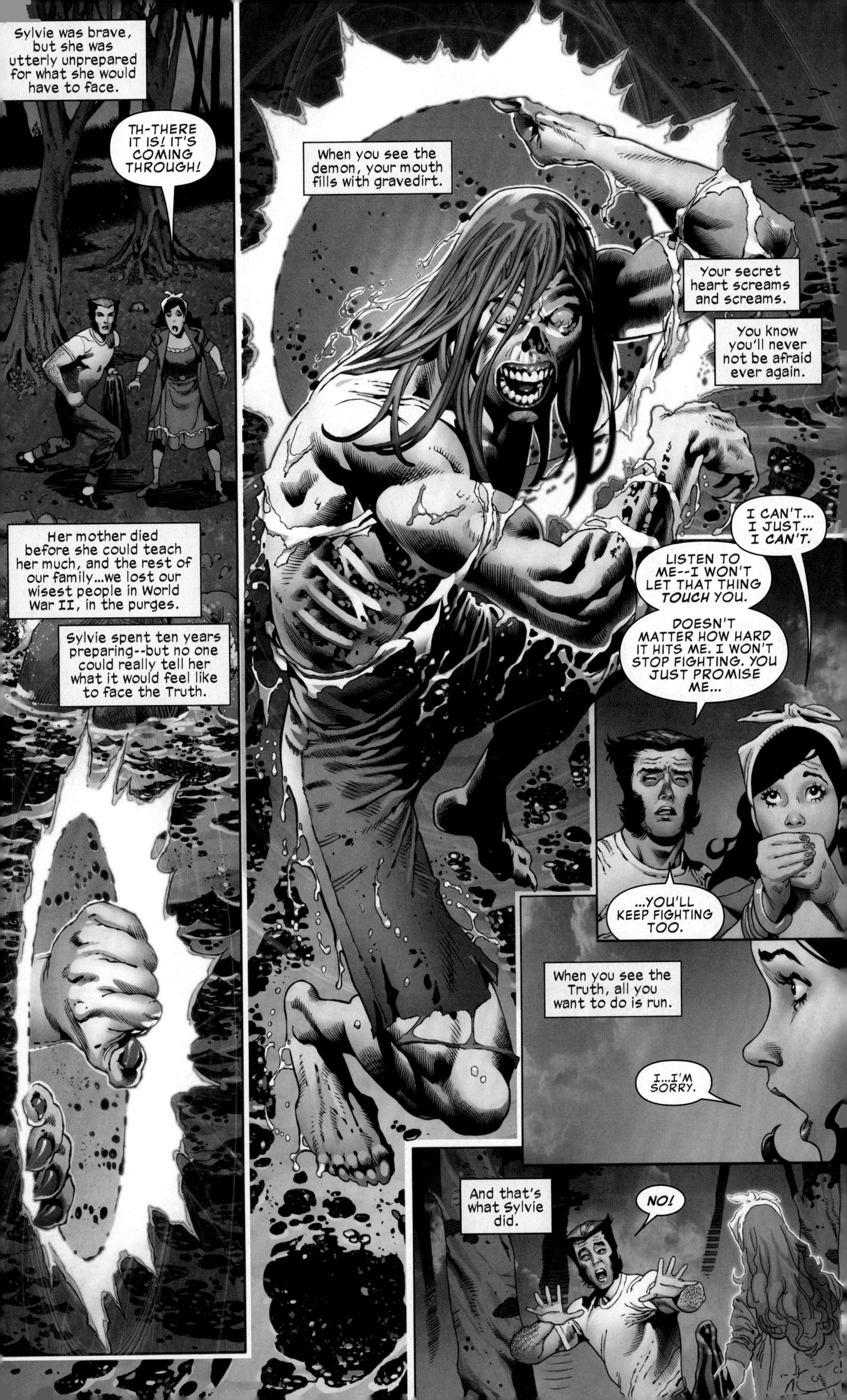
Sylvie was brave, but she was utterly unprepared for what she would have to face.
TH-THERE IT IS! IT'S COMING THROUGH!
Her mother died before she could teach her much, and the rest of our family...we lost our wisest people in World War II, in the purges.
Sylvie spent ten years preparing--but no one could really tell her what it would feel like to face the Truth.
When you see the demon, your mouth fills with gravedirt.
Your secret heart screams and screams.
You know you'll never not be afraid ever again.
I CAN'T... I JUST... I CAN'T.
LISTEN TO ME--I WON'T LET THAT THING TOUCH YOU.
DOESN'T MATTER HOW HARD IT HITS ME. I WON'T STOP FIGHTING. YOU JUST PROMISE ME...
...YOU'LL KEEP FIGHTING TOO.
When you see the Truth, all you want to do is run.
I...I'M SORRY.
And that's what Sylvie did.
NO!

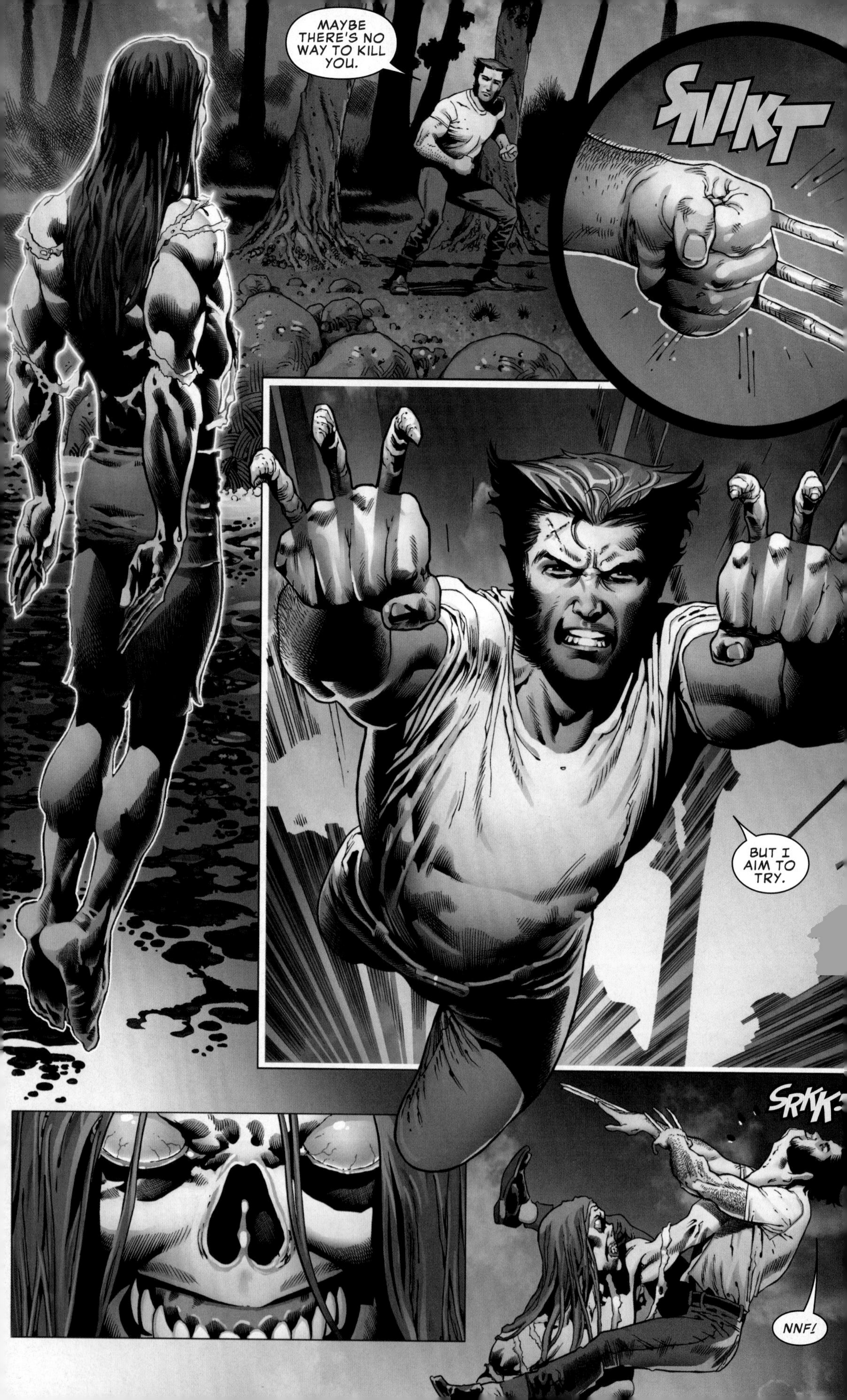
MAYBE THERE'S NO WAY TO KILL YOU.
SNIKT
BUT I AIM TO TRY.
SRKK
NNF!

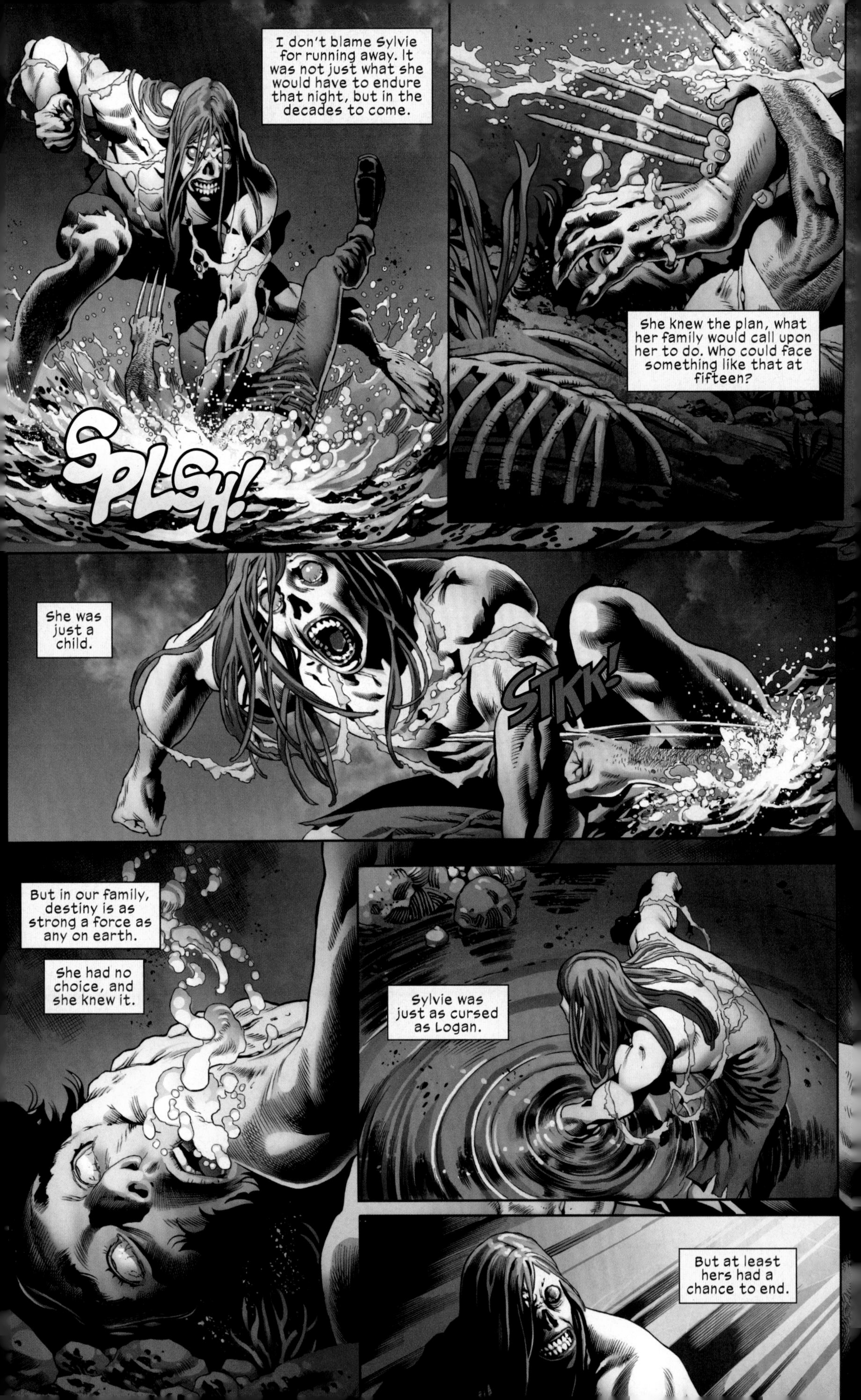

I don't blame Sylvie for running away. It was not just what she would have to endure that night, but in the decades to come.
SPLSH!
She knew the plan, what her family would call upon her to do. Who could face something like that at fifteen?
She was just a child.
STKK!
But in our family, destiny is as strong a force as any on earth.
She had no choice, and she knew it.
Sylvie was just as cursed as Logan.
But at least hers had a chance to end.

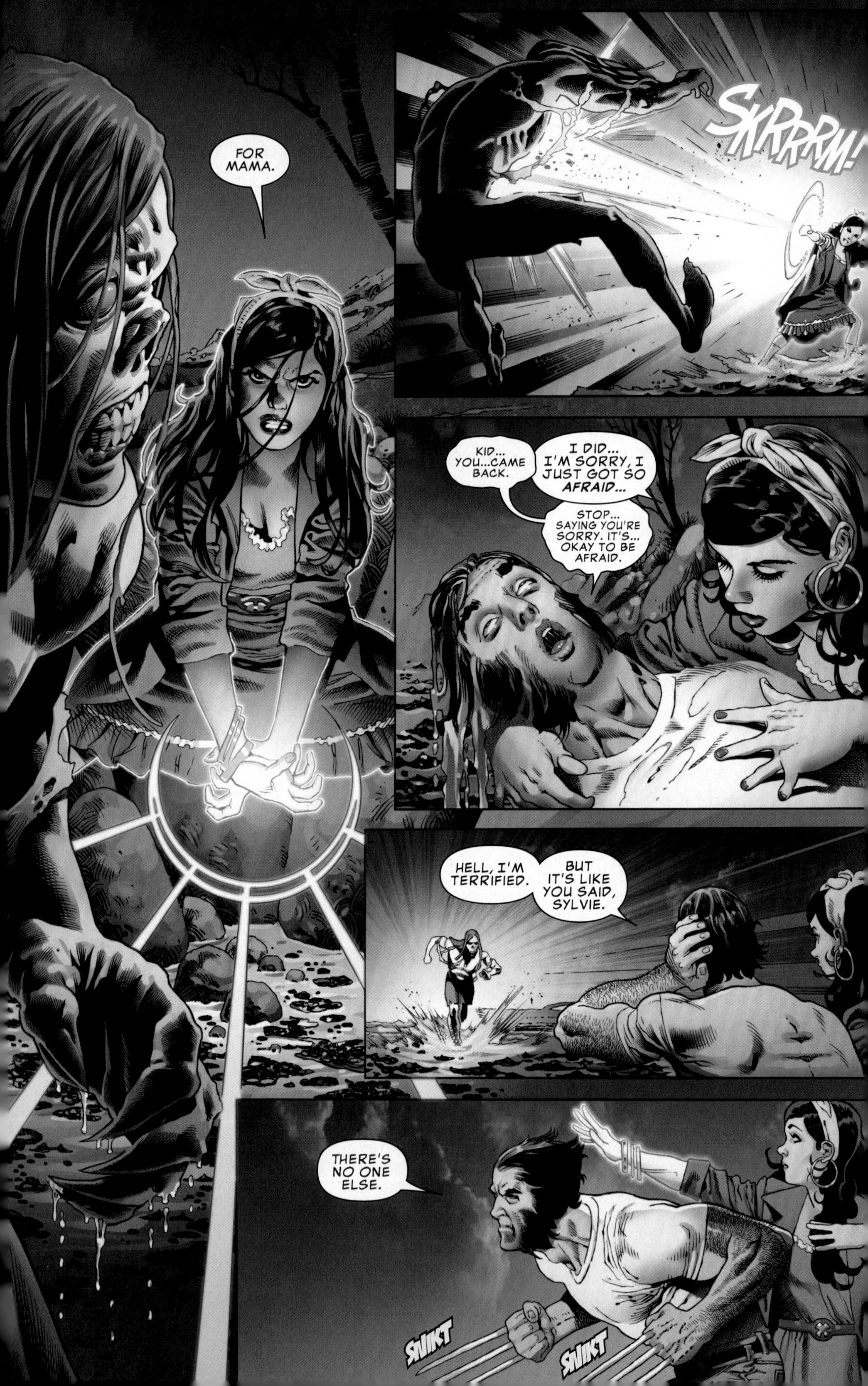
FOR MAMA.
SKRRRM!
KID... YOU...CAME BACK.
I DID... I'M SORRY, I JUST GOT SO AFRAID...
STOP... SAYING YOU'RE SORRY. IT'S... OKAY TO BE AFRAID.
HELL, I'M TERRIFIED.
BUT IT'S LIKE YOU SAID, SYLVIE.
THERE'S NO ONE ELSE.
SNIKT
SNIKT

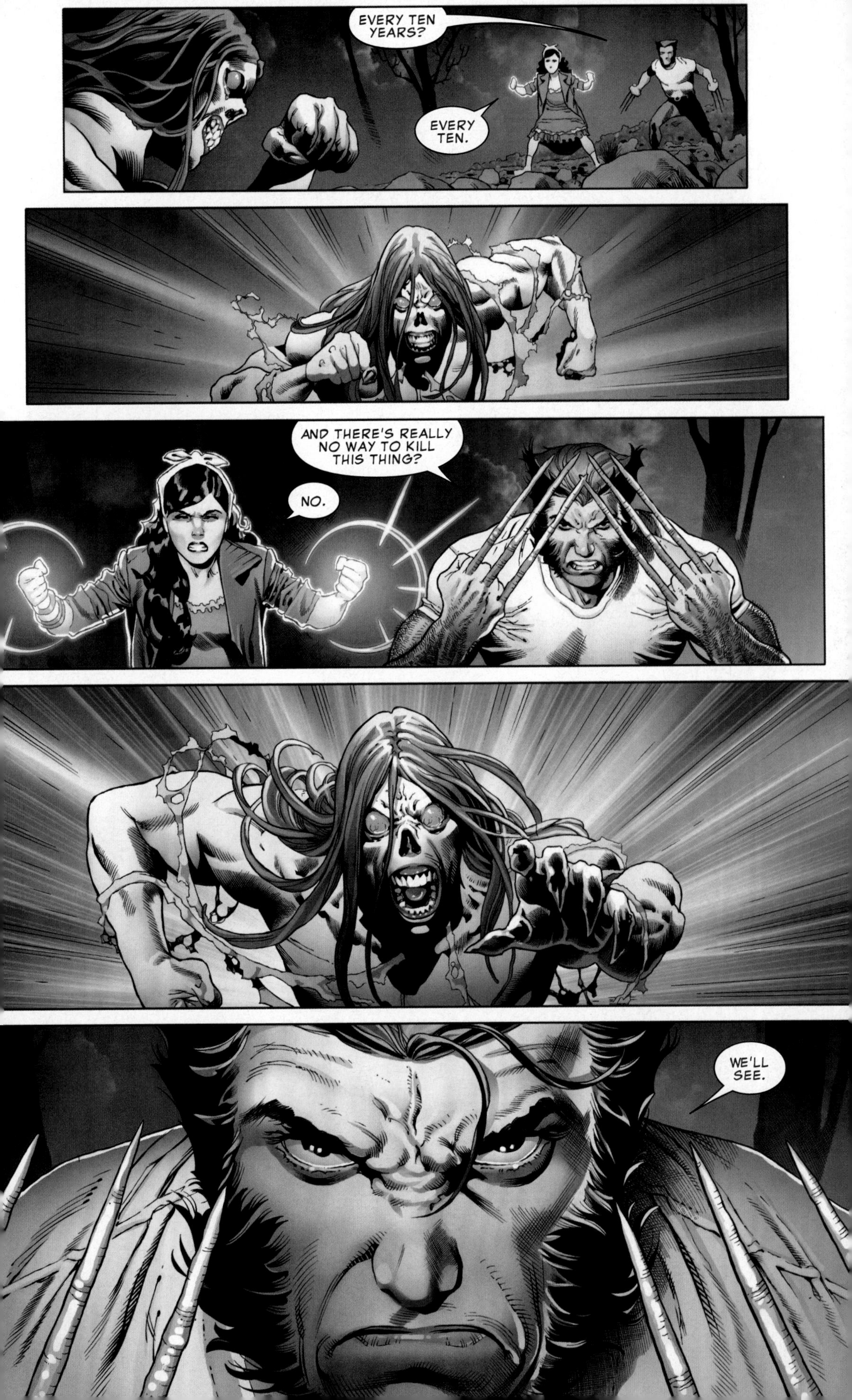
EVERY TEN YEARS?
EVERY TEN.
AND THERE'S REALLY NO WAY TO KILL THIS THING?
NO.
WE'LL SEE.

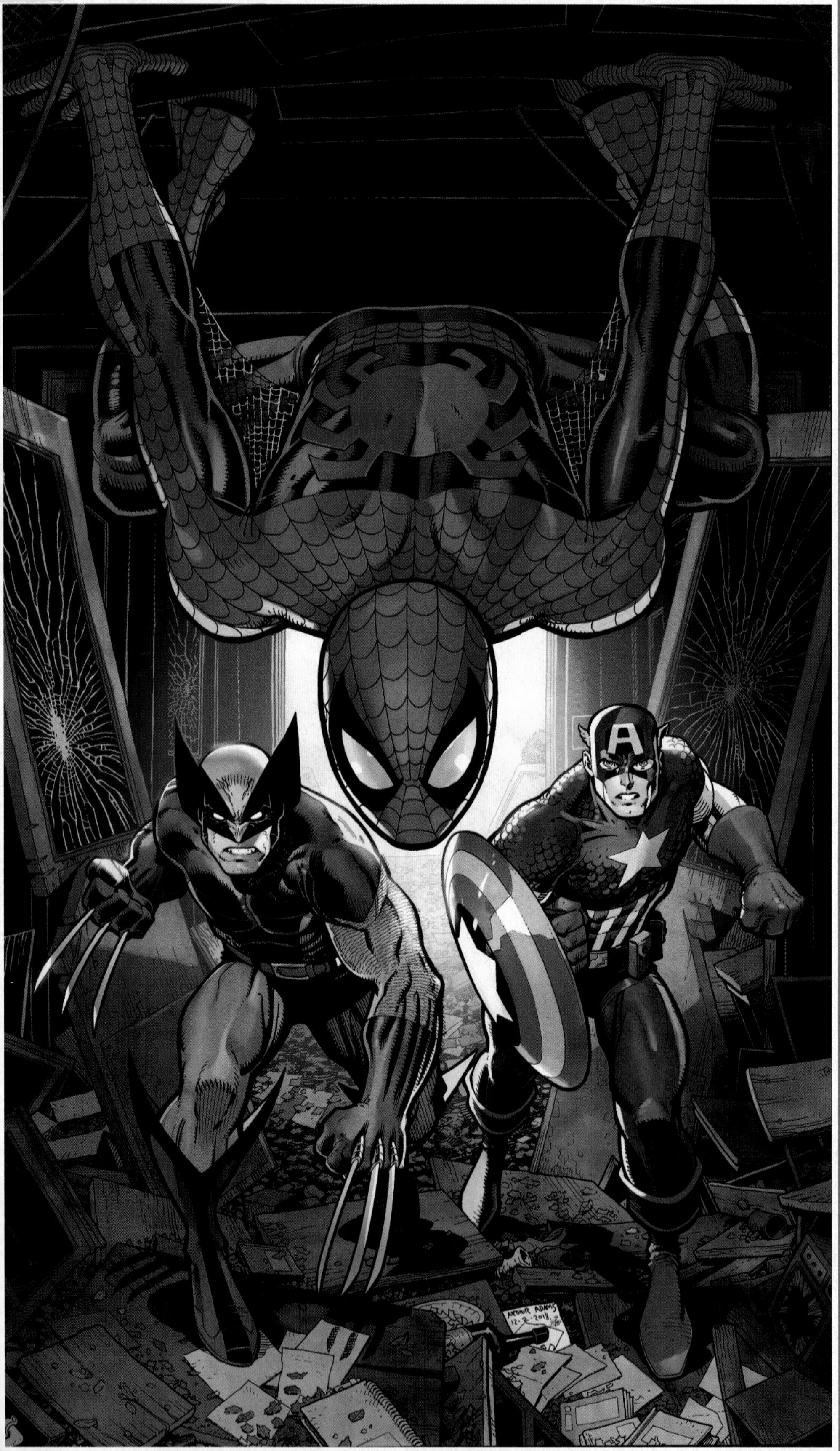
ARTHUR ADAMS

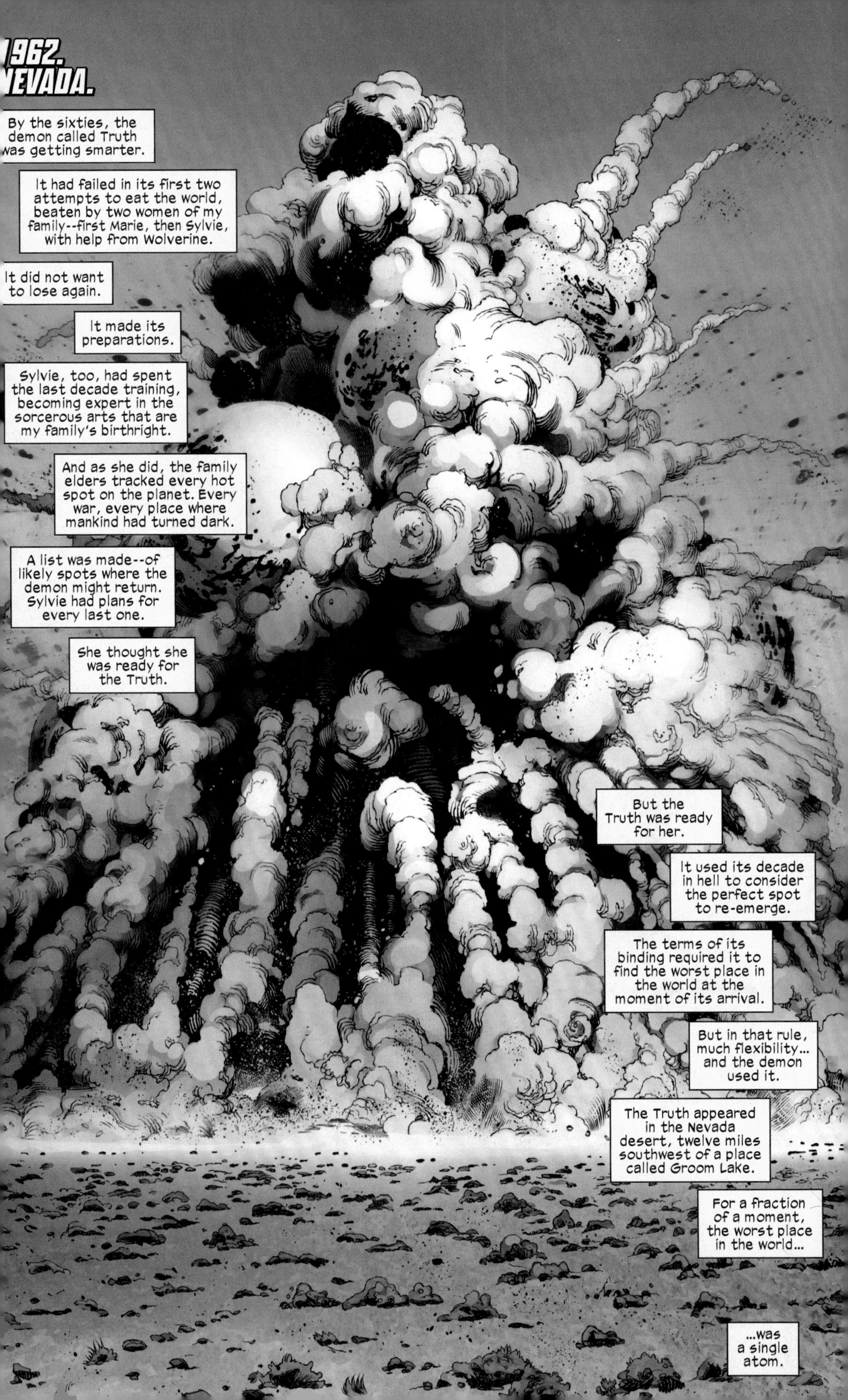
1962.
NEVADA.
By the sixties, the demon called Truth was getting smarter.
It had failed in its first two attempts to eat the world, beaten by two women of my family--first Marie, then Sylvie, with help from Wolverine.
It did not want to lose again.
It made its preparations.
Sylvie, too, had spent the last decade training, becoming expert in the sorcerous arts that are my family's birthright.
And as she did, the family elders tracked every hot spot on the planet. Every war, every place where mankind had turned dark.
A list was made--of likely spots where the demon might return. Sylvie had plans for every last one.
She thought she was ready for the Truth.
But the Truth was ready for her.
It used its decade in hell to consider the perfect spot to re-emerge.
The terms of its binding required it to find the worst place in the world at the moment of its arrival.
But in that rule, much flexibility... and the demon used it.
The Truth appeared in the Nevada desert, twelve miles southwest of a place called Groom Lake.
For a fraction of a moment, the worst place in the world...
...was a single atom.

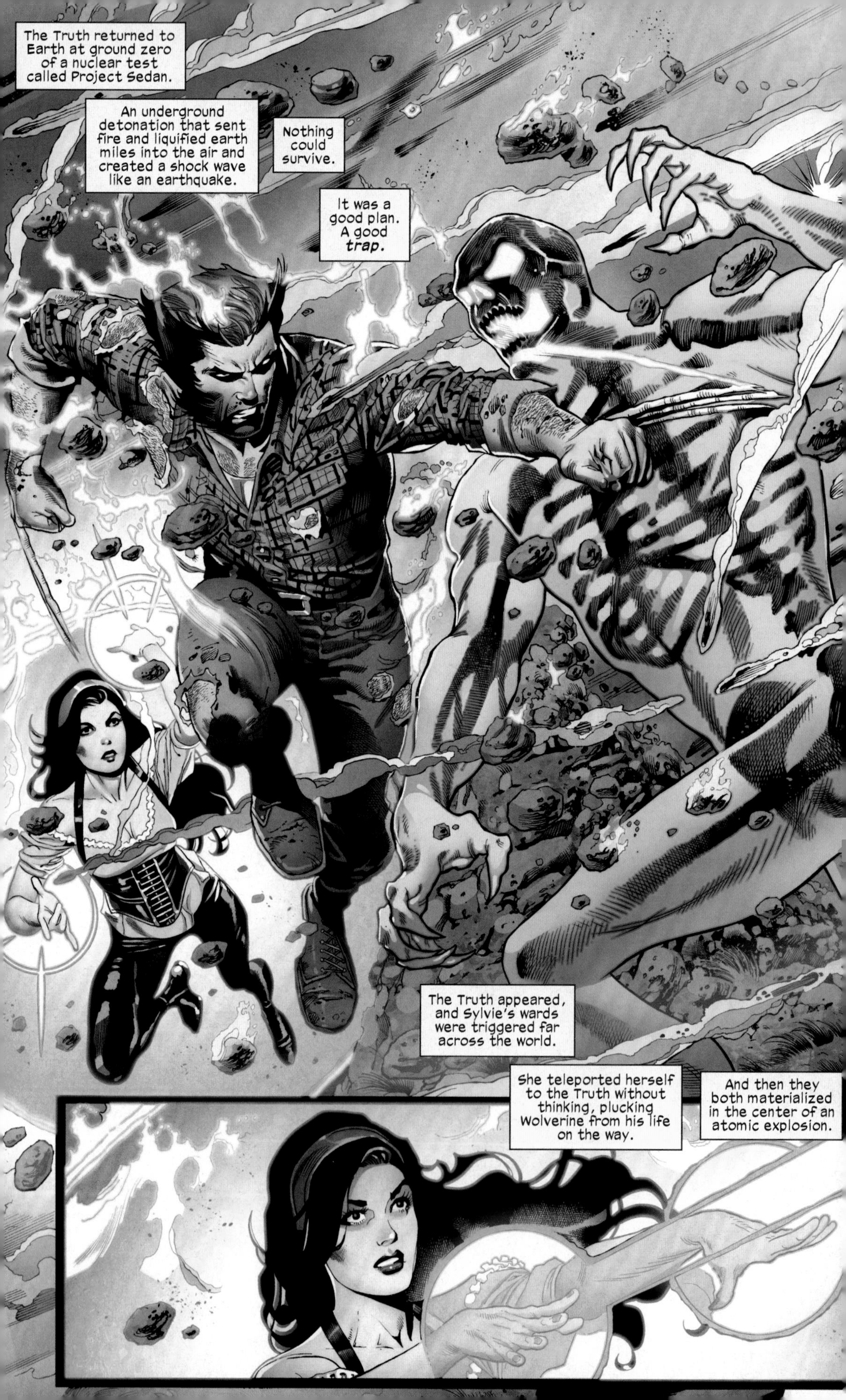
The Truth returned to Earth at ground zero of a nuclear test called Project Sedan.
An underground detonation that sent fire and liquified earth miles into the air and created a shock wave like an earthquake.
Nothing could survive.
It was a good plan. A good *trap.*
The Truth appeared, and Sylvie's wards were triggered far across the world.
She teleported herself to the Truth without thinking, plucking Wolverine from his life on the way.
And then they both materialized in the center of an atomic explosion.

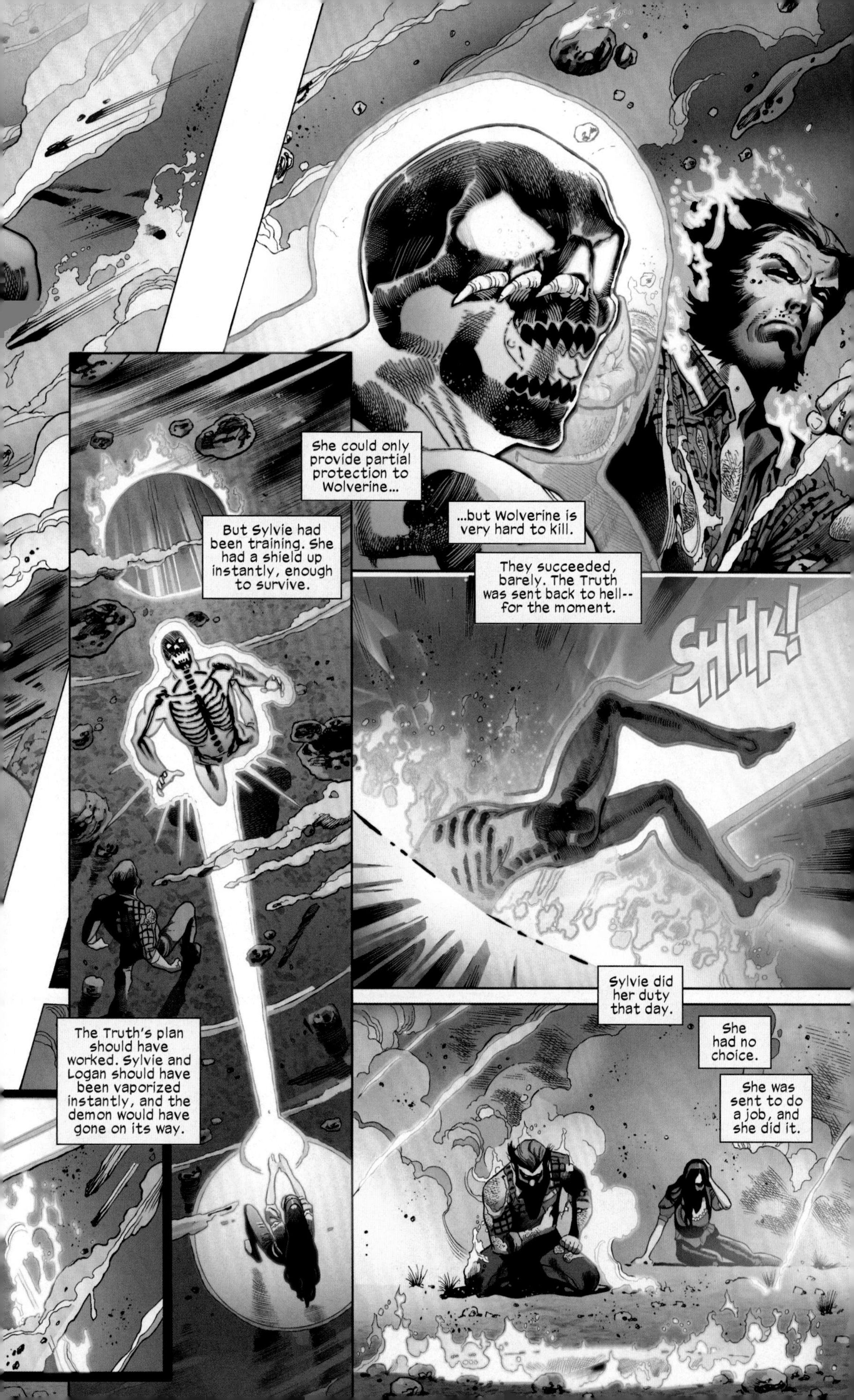

She could only provide partial protection to Wolverine...
But Sylvie had been training. She had a shield up instantly, enough to survive.
...but Wolverine is very hard to kill.
The Truth's plan should have worked. Sylvie and Logan should have been vaporized instantly, and the demon would have gone on its way.
They succeeded, barely. The Truth was sent back to hell-- for the moment.
SHHK!
Sylvie did her duty that day.
She had no choice.
She was sent to do a job, and she did it.

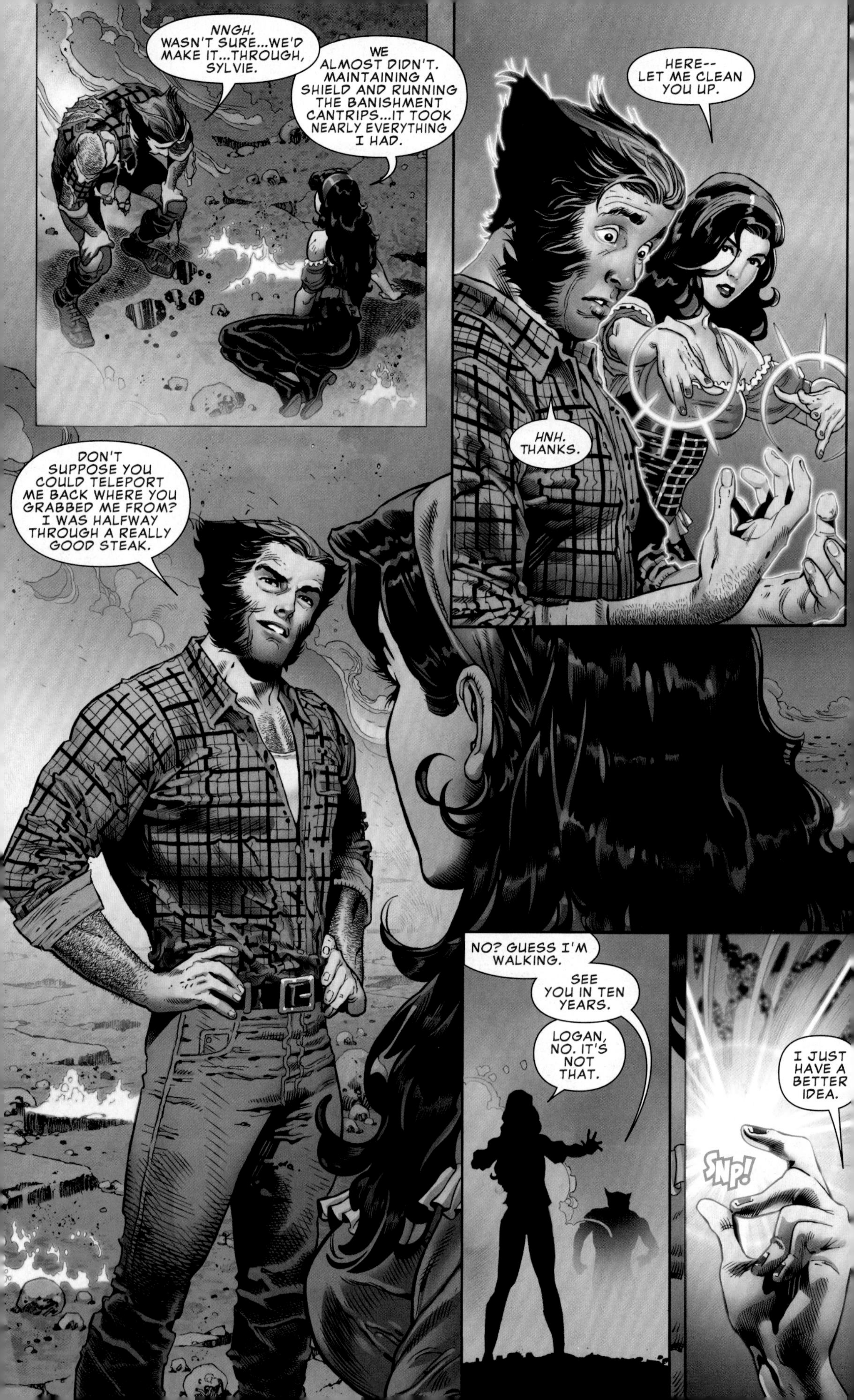
NNGH. WASN'T SURE...WE'D MAKE IT...THROUGH, SYLVIE.
WE ALMOST DIDN'T. MAINTAINING A SHIELD AND RUNNING THE BANISHMENT CANTRIPS...IT TOOK NEARLY EVERYTHING I HAD.
HERE-- LET ME CLEAN YOU UP.
HNH. THANKS.
DON'T SUPPOSE YOU COULD TELEPORT ME BACK WHERE YOU GRABBED ME FROM? I WAS HALFWAY THROUGH A REALLY GOOD STEAK.
NO? GUESS I'M WALKING.
SEE YOU IN TEN YEARS.
LOGAN, NO. IT'S NOT THAT.
I JUST HAVE A BETTER IDEA.
SNP!

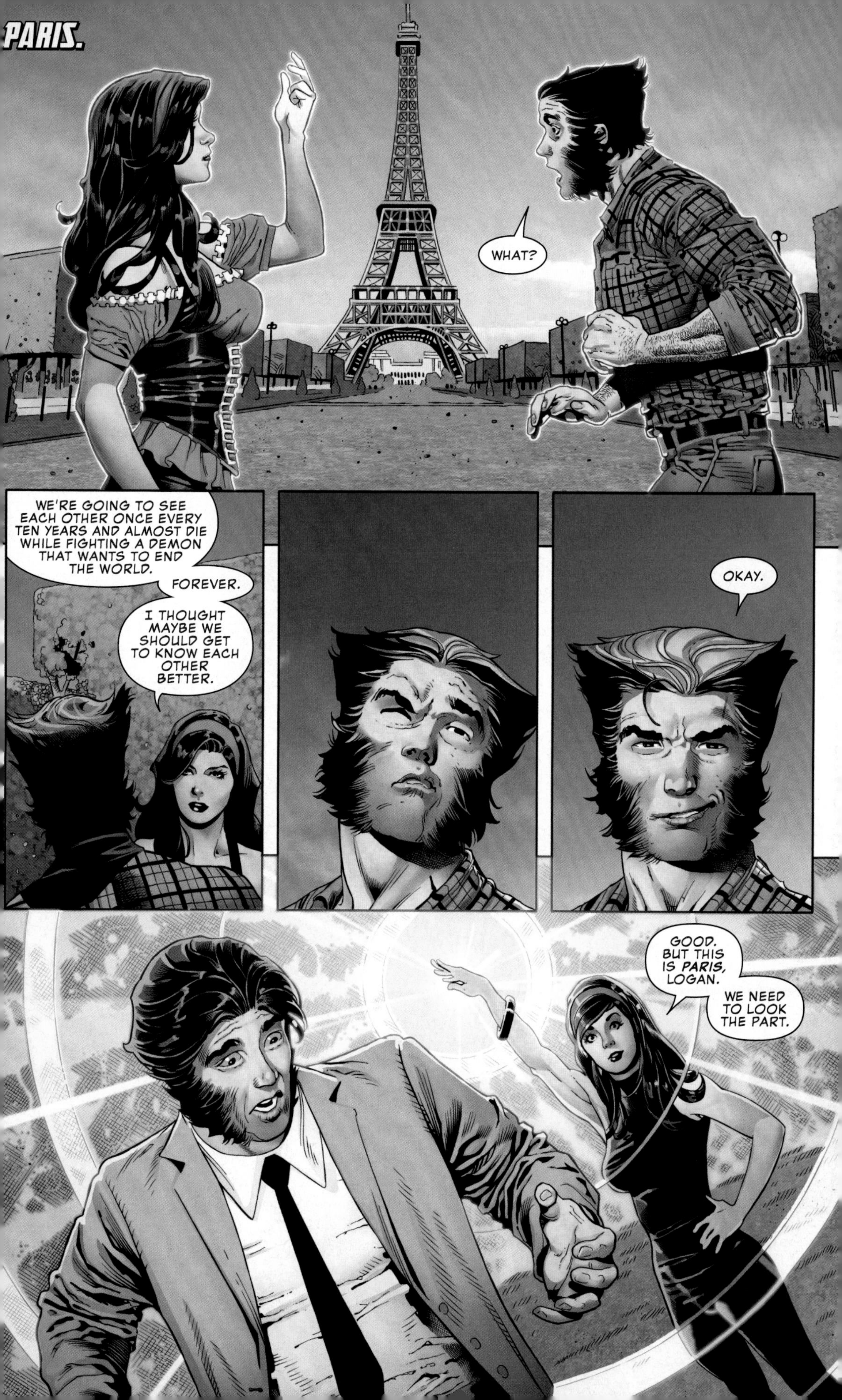
PARIS.
WHAT?
WE'RE GOING TO SEE EACH OTHER ONCE EVERY TEN YEARS AND ALMOST DIE WHILE FIGHTING A DEMON THAT WANTS TO END THE WORLD.
FOREVER.
I THOUGHT MAYBE WE SHOULD GET TO KNOW EACH OTHER BETTER.
OKAY.
GOOD. BUT THIS IS PARIS, LOGAN.
WE NEED TO LOOK THE PART.

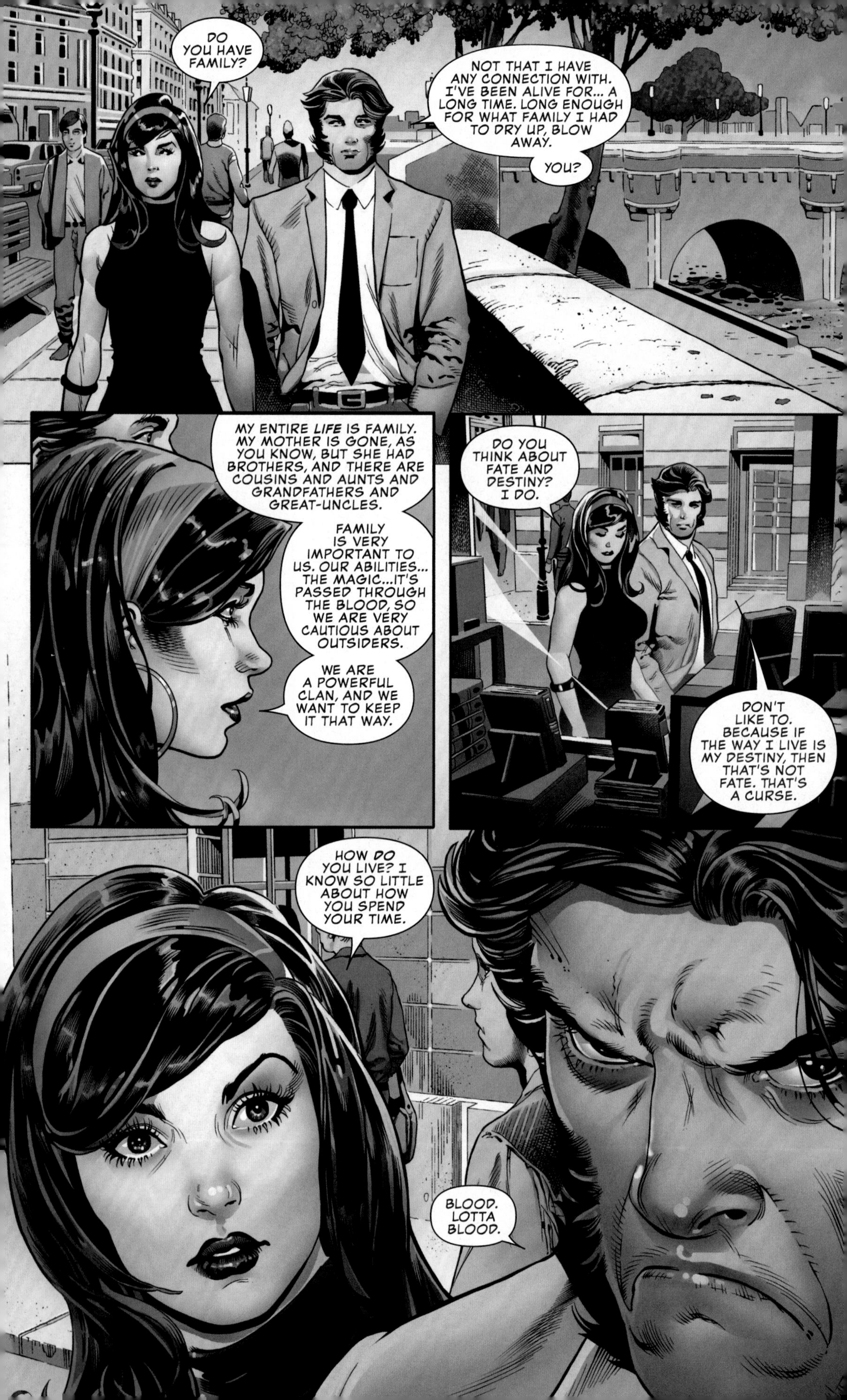
DO YOU HAVE FAMILY?
NOT THAT I HAVE ANY CONNECTION WITH. I'VE BEEN ALIVE FOR... A LONG TIME. LONG ENOUGH FOR WHAT FAMILY I HAD TO DRY UP, BLOW AWAY.
YOU?
MY ENTIRE LIFE IS FAMILY. MY MOTHER IS GONE, AS YOU KNOW, BUT SHE HAD BROTHERS, AND THERE ARE COUSINS AND AUNTS AND GRANDFATHERS AND GREAT-UNCLES.
FAMILY IS VERY IMPORTANT TO US. OUR ABILITIES... THE MAGIC...IT'S PASSED THROUGH THE BLOOD, SO WE ARE VERY CAUTIOUS ABOUT OUTSIDERS.
WE ARE A POWERFUL CLAN, AND WE WANT TO KEEP IT THAT WAY.
DO YOU THINK ABOUT FATE AND DESTINY? I DO.
DON'T LIKE TO. BECAUSE IF THE WAY I LIVE IS MY DESTINY, THEN THAT'S NOT FATE. THAT'S A CURSE.
HOW DO YOU LIVE? I KNOW SO LITTLE ABOUT HOW YOU SPEND YOUR TIME.
BLOOD. LOTTA BLOOD.

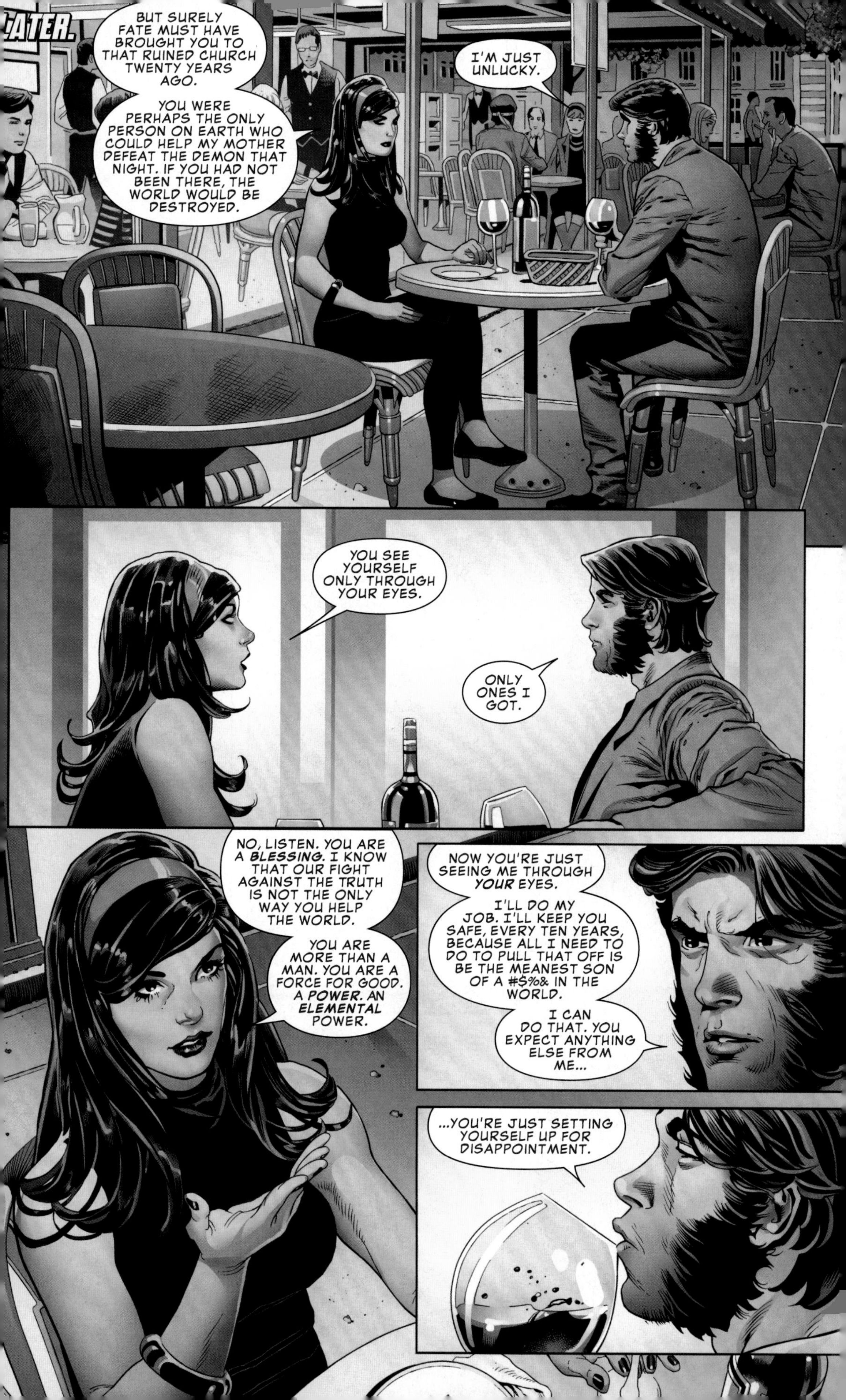
LATER.
BUT SURELY FATE MUST HAVE BROUGHT YOU TO THAT RUINED CHURCH TWENTY YEARS AGO.
YOU WERE PERHAPS THE ONLY PERSON ON EARTH WHO COULD HELP MY MOTHER DEFEAT THE DEMON THAT NIGHT. IF YOU HAD NOT BEEN THERE, THE WORLD WOULD BE DESTROYED.
I'M JUST UNLUCKY.
YOU SEE YOURSELF ONLY THROUGH YOUR EYES.
ONLY ONES I GOT.
NO, LISTEN. YOU ARE A ***BLESSING.*** I KNOW THAT OUR FIGHT AGAINST THE TRUTH IS NOT THE ONLY WAY YOU HELP THE WORLD.
YOU ARE MORE THAN A MAN. YOU ARE A FORCE FOR GOOD. A ***POWER.*** AN ***ELEMENTAL*** POWER.
NOW YOU'RE JUST SEEING ME THROUGH ***YOUR*** EYES.
I'LL DO MY JOB. I'LL KEEP YOU SAFE, EVERY TEN YEARS, BECAUSE ALL I NEED TO DO TO PULL THAT OFF IS BE THE MEANEST SON OF A #$%& IN THE WORLD.
I CAN DO THAT. YOU EXPECT ANYTHING ELSE FROM ME...
...YOU'RE JUST SETTING YOURSELF UP FOR DISAPPOINTMENT.

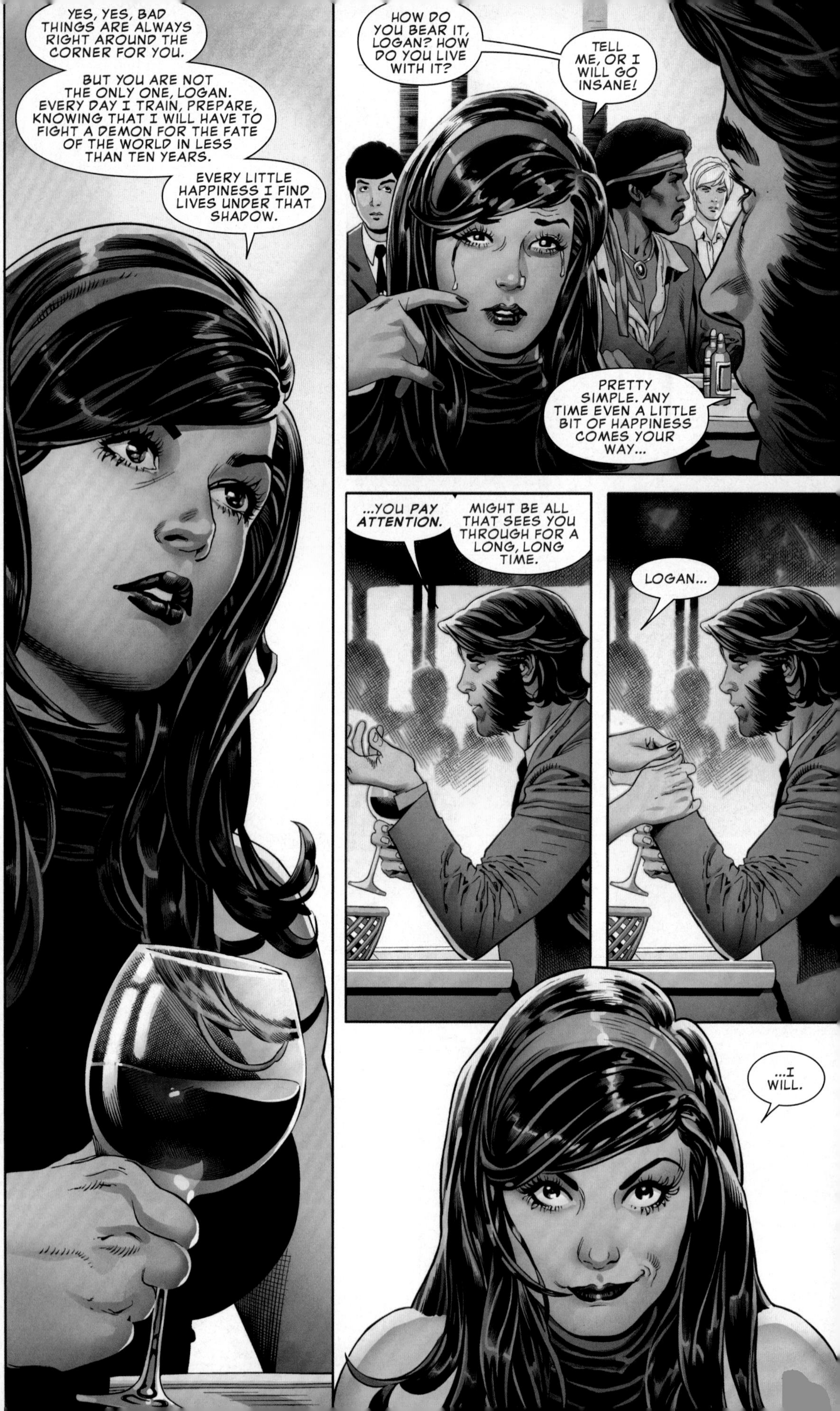
YES, YES, BAD THINGS ARE ALWAYS RIGHT AROUND THE CORNER FOR YOU.
BUT YOU ARE NOT THE ONLY ONE, LOGAN. EVERY DAY I TRAIN, PREPARE, KNOWING THAT I WILL HAVE TO FIGHT A DEMON FOR THE FATE OF THE WORLD IN LESS THAN TEN YEARS.
EVERY LITTLE HAPPINESS I FIND LIVES UNDER THAT SHADOW.
HOW DO YOU BEAR IT, LOGAN? HOW DO YOU LIVE WITH IT?
TELL ME, OR I WILL GO INSANE!
PRETTY SIMPLE. ANY TIME EVEN A LITTLE BIT OF HAPPINESS COMES YOUR WAY...
...YOU PAY ATTENTION.
MIGHT BE ALL THAT SEES YOU THROUGH FOR A LONG, LONG TIME.
LOGAN...
...I WILL.

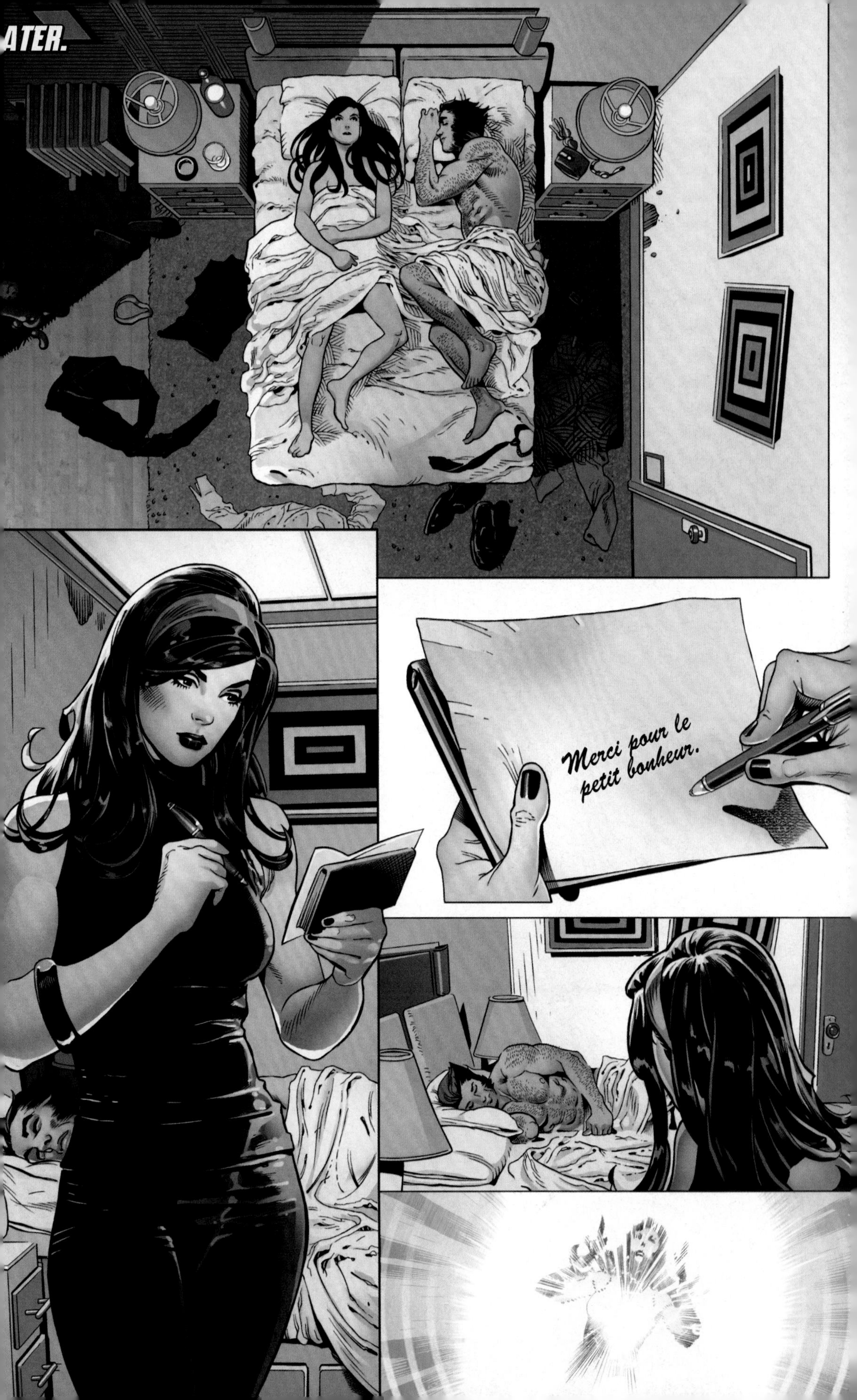
ATER.
Merci pour le petit bonheur.

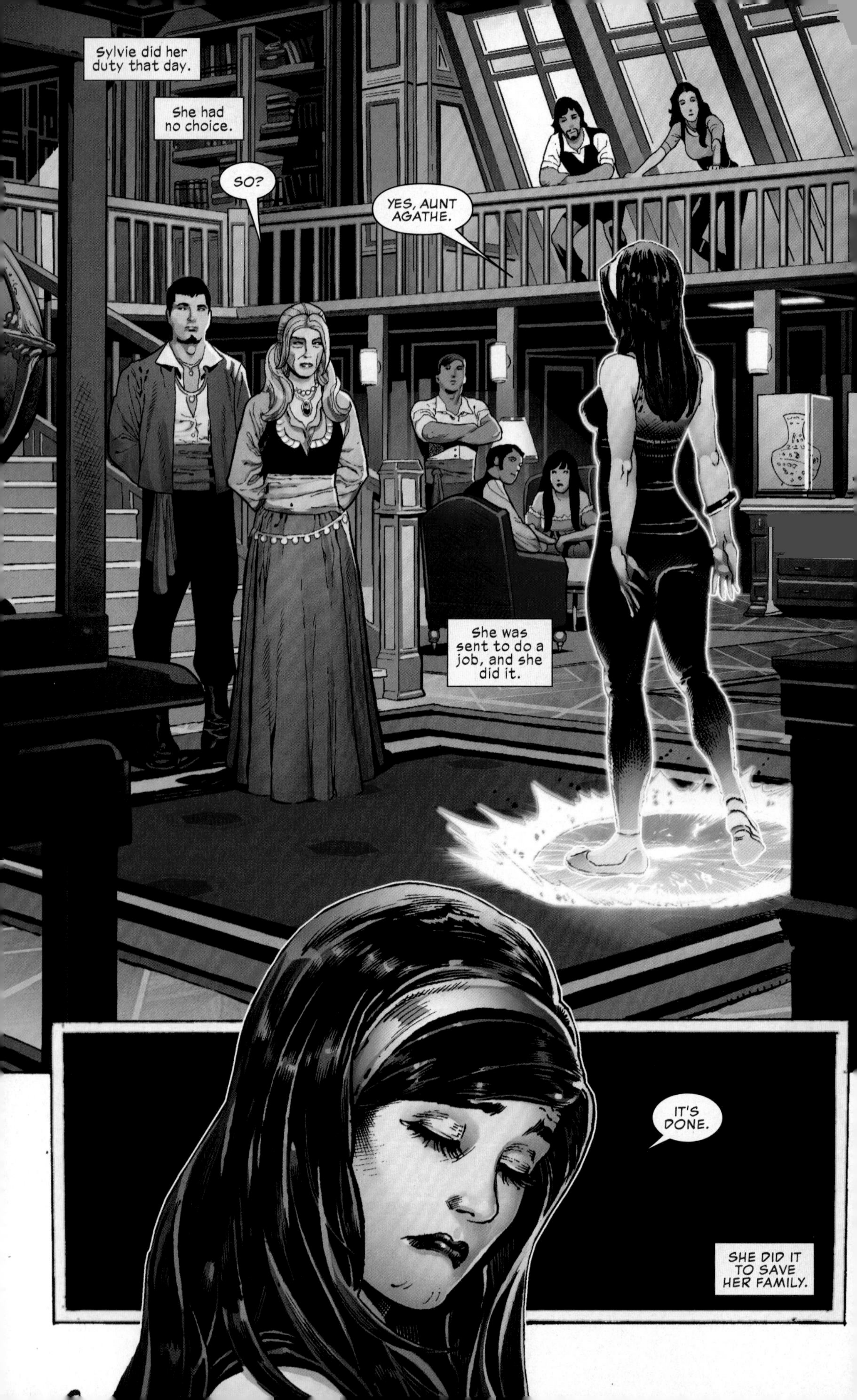

Sylvie did her duty that day.
She had no choice.
SO?
YES, AUNT AGATHE.
She was sent to do a job, and she did it.
IT'S DONE.
SHE DID IT TO SAVE HER FAMILY.

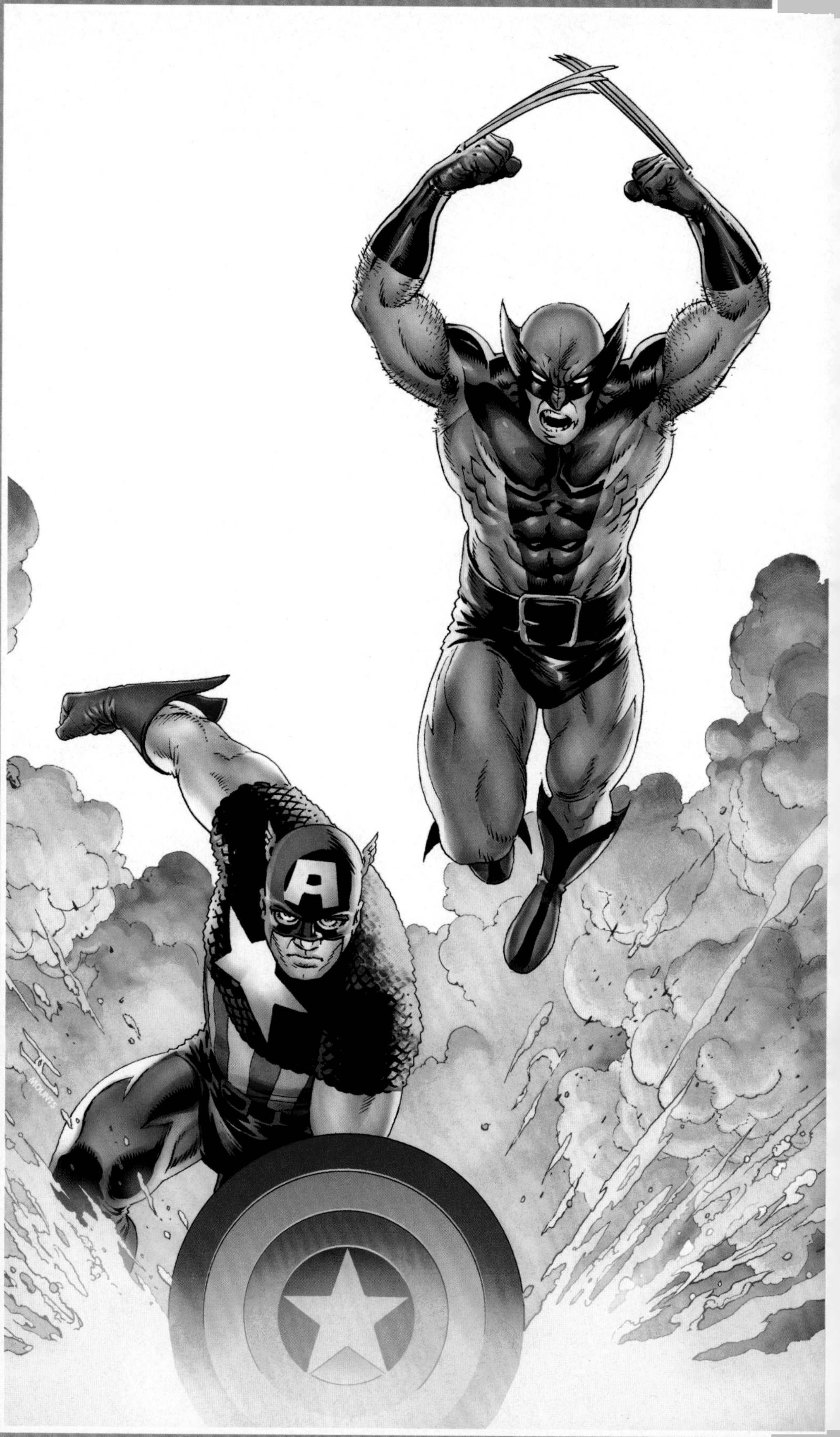
MOUNTS

#1 variant by **JOHN CASSADAY** & **PAUL MOUNTS**

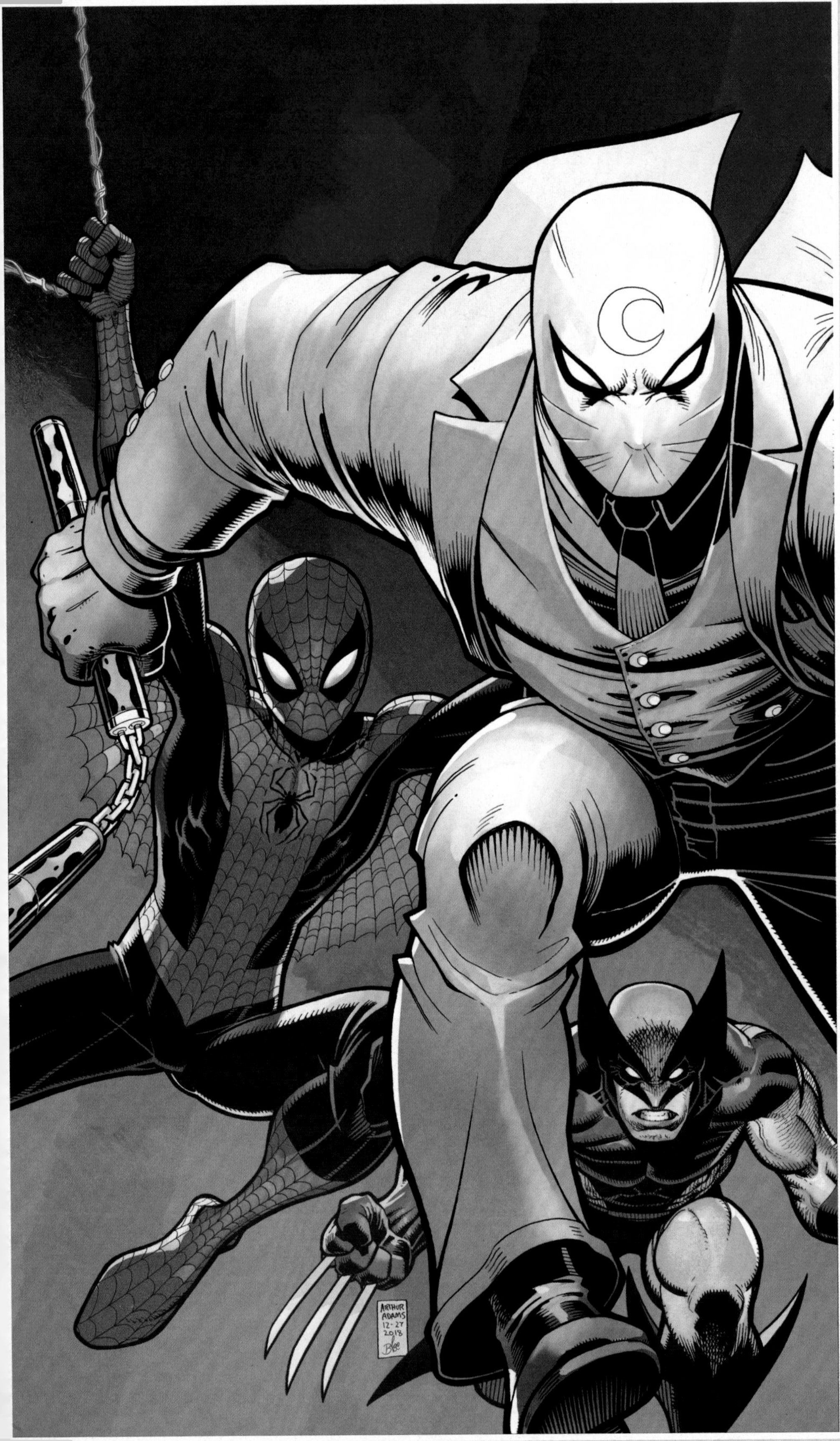
ARTHUR ADAMS
12-27
2018

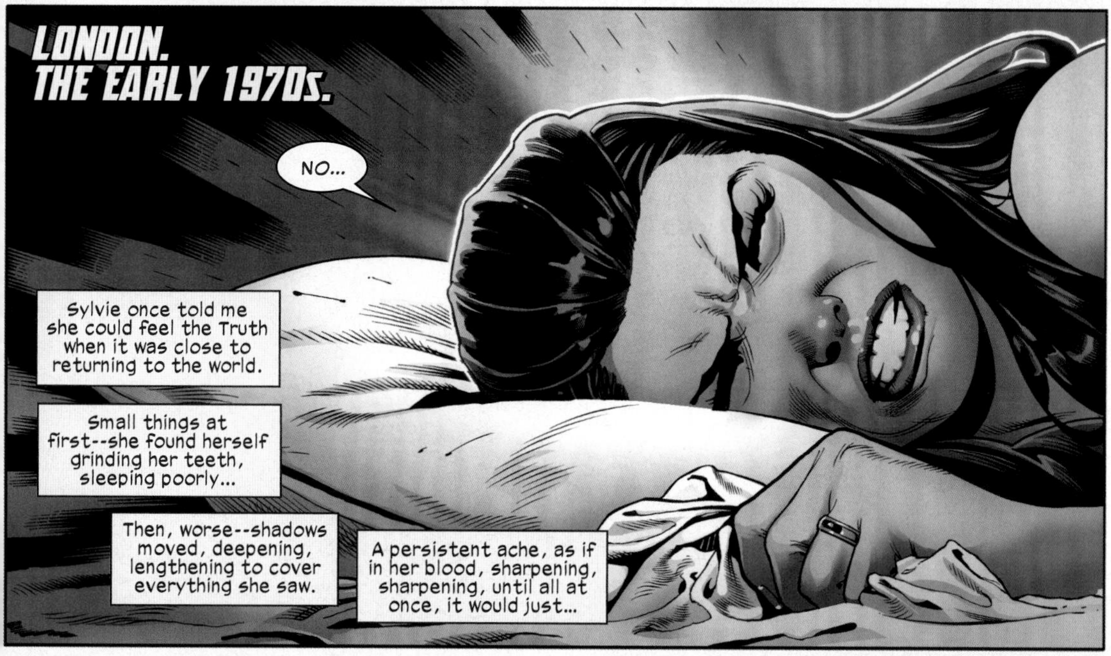
LONDON.
THE EARLY 1970s.
NO...
Sylvie once told me she could feel the Truth when it was close to returning to the world.
Small things at first--she found herself grinding her teeth, sleeping poorly...
Then, worse--shadows moved, deepening, lengthening to cover everything she saw.
A persistent ache, as if in her blood, sharpening, sharpening, until all at once, it would just...

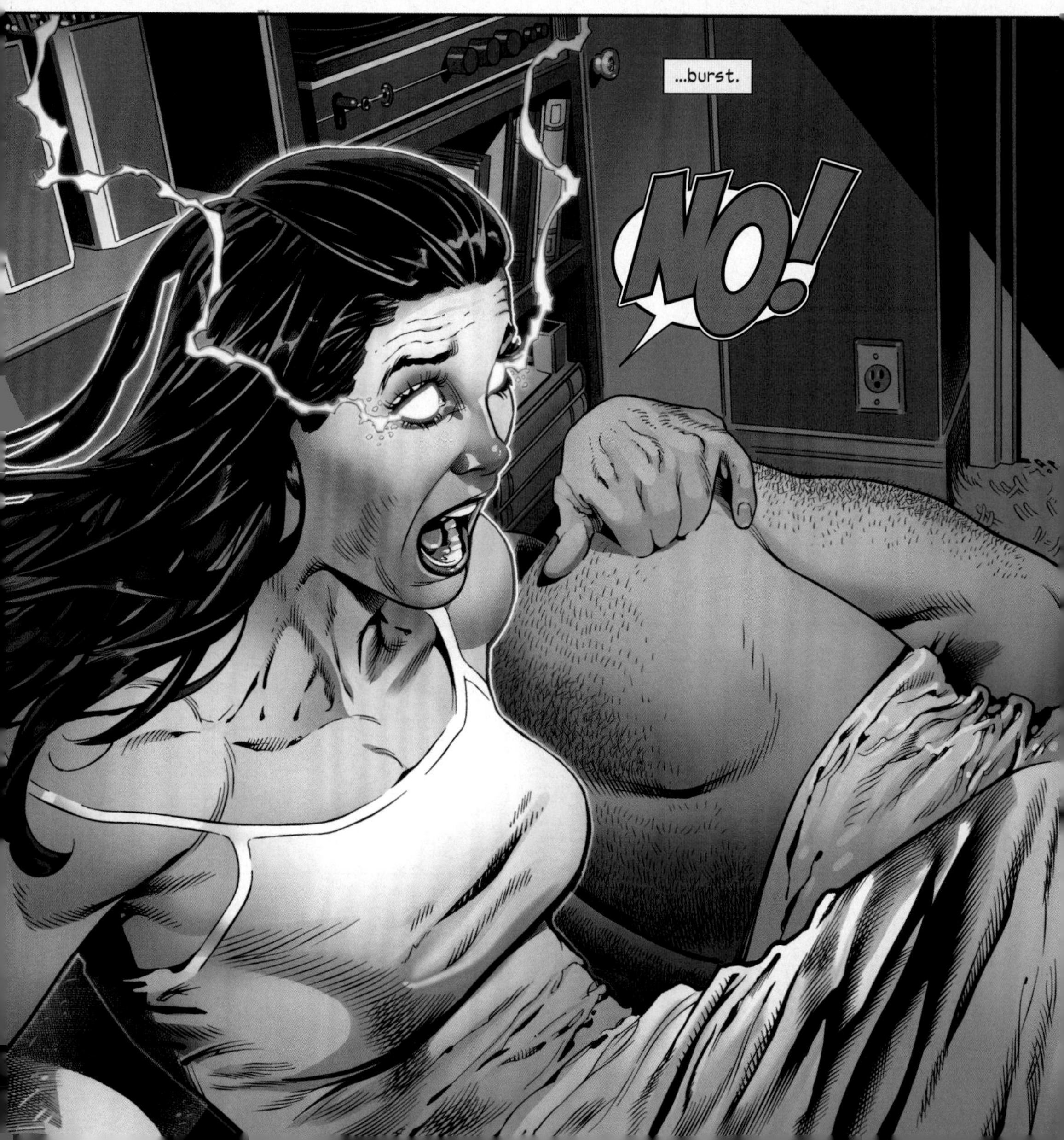
...burst.
NO!

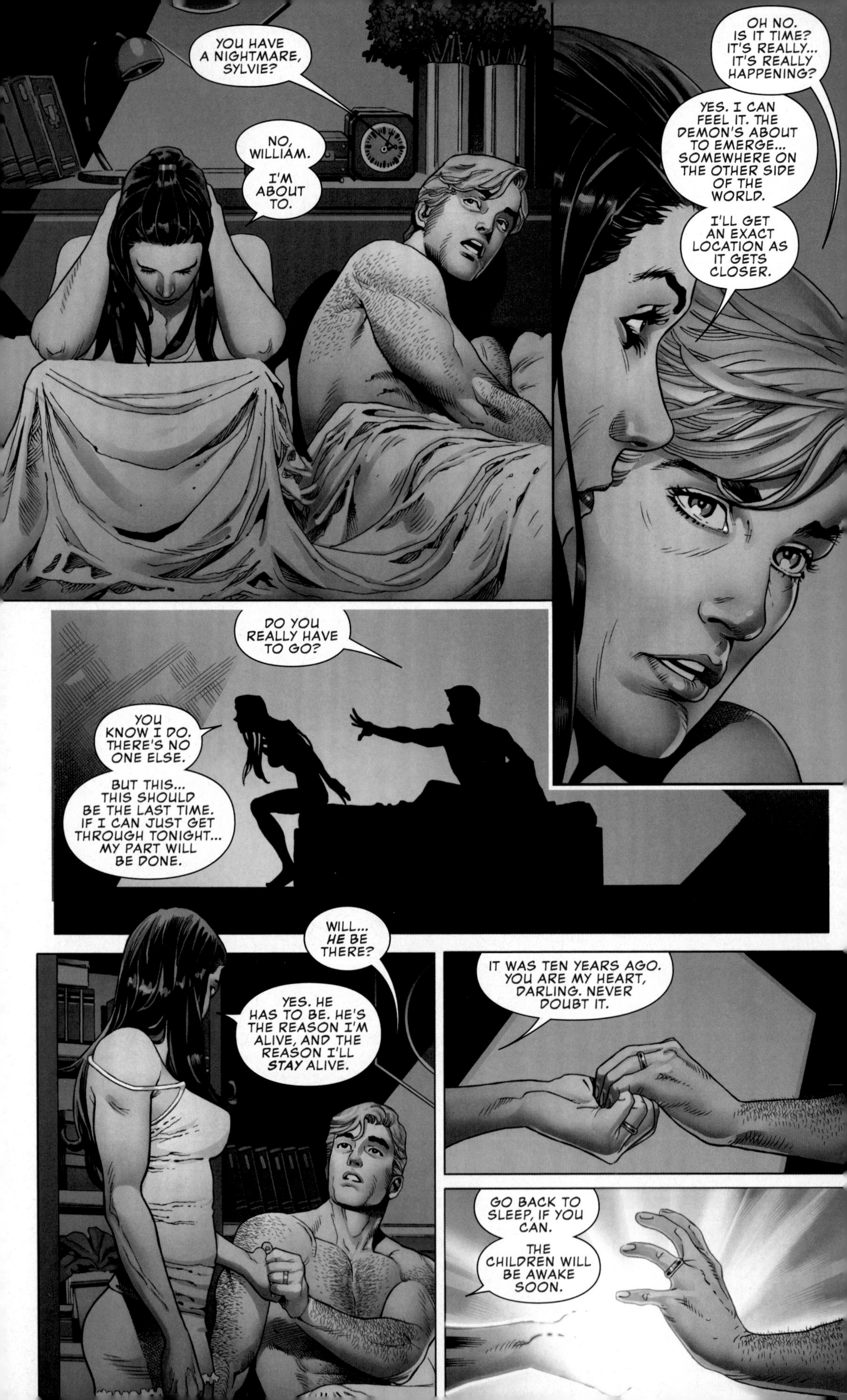
YOU HAVE A NIGHTMARE, SYLVIE?
NO, WILLIAM.
I'M ABOUT TO.
OH NO. IS IT TIME? IT'S REALLY... IT'S REALLY HAPPENING?
YES. I CAN FEEL IT. THE DEMON'S ABOUT TO EMERGE... SOMEWHERE ON THE OTHER SIDE OF THE WORLD.
I'LL GET AN EXACT LOCATION AS IT GETS CLOSER.
DO YOU REALLY HAVE TO GO?
YOU KNOW I DO. THERE'S NO ONE ELSE.
BUT THIS... THIS SHOULD BE THE LAST TIME. IF I CAN JUST GET THROUGH TONIGHT... MY PART WILL BE DONE.
WILL... *HE* BE THERE?
YES. HE HAS TO BE. HE'S THE REASON I'M ALIVE, AND THE REASON I'LL *STAY* ALIVE.
IT WAS TEN YEARS AGO. YOU ARE MY HEART, DARLING. NEVER DOUBT IT.
GO BACK TO SLEEP, IF YOU CAN.
THE CHILDREN WILL BE AWAKE SOON.

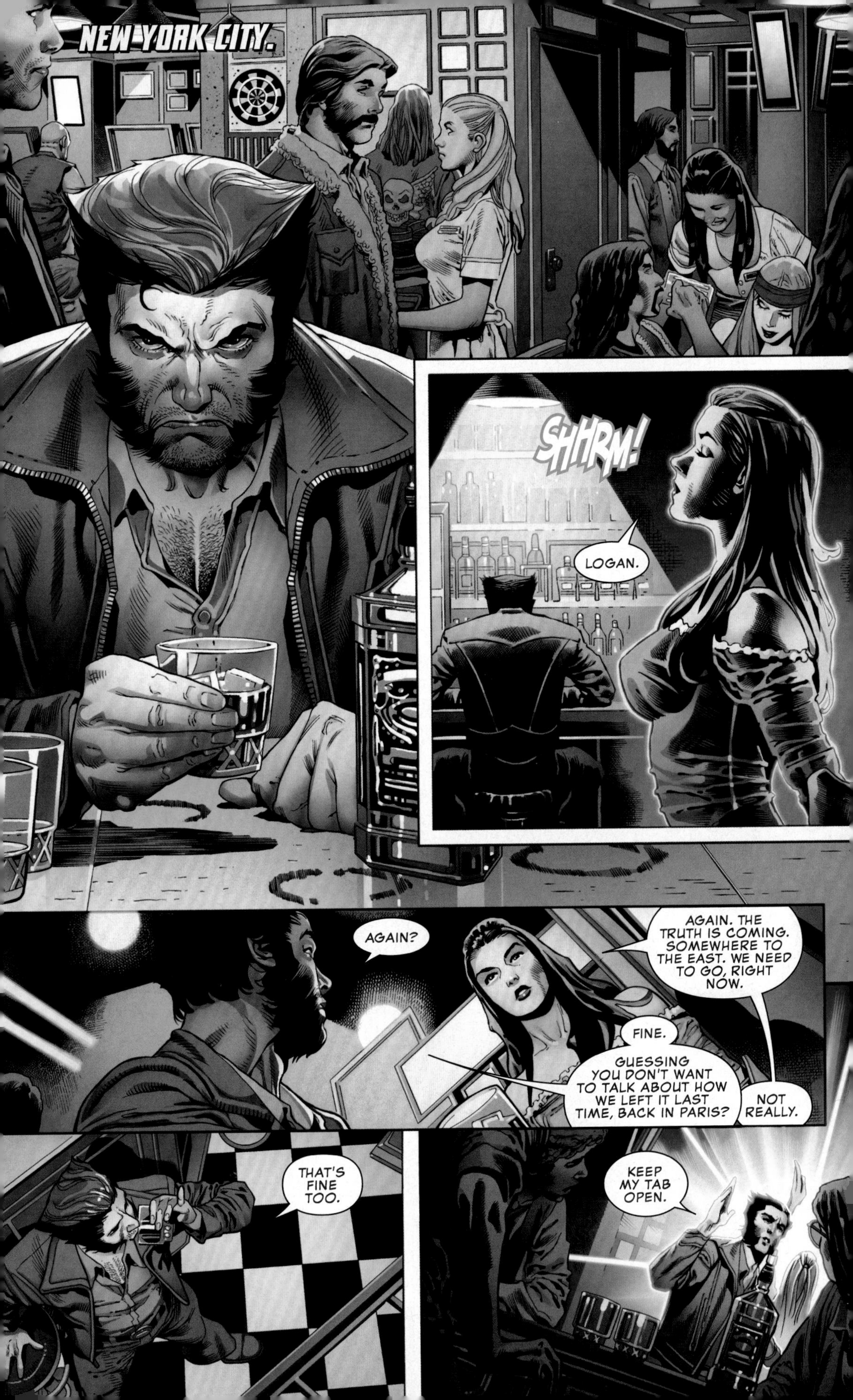
NEW YORK CITY.
SHHRM!
LOGAN.
AGAIN?
AGAIN. THE TRUTH IS COMING. SOMEWHERE TO THE EAST. WE NEED TO GO, RIGHT NOW.
FINE.
GUESSING YOU DON'T WANT TO TALK ABOUT HOW WE LEFT IT LAST TIME, BACK IN PARIS?
NOT REALLY.
THAT'S FINE TOO.
KEEP MY TAB OPEN.

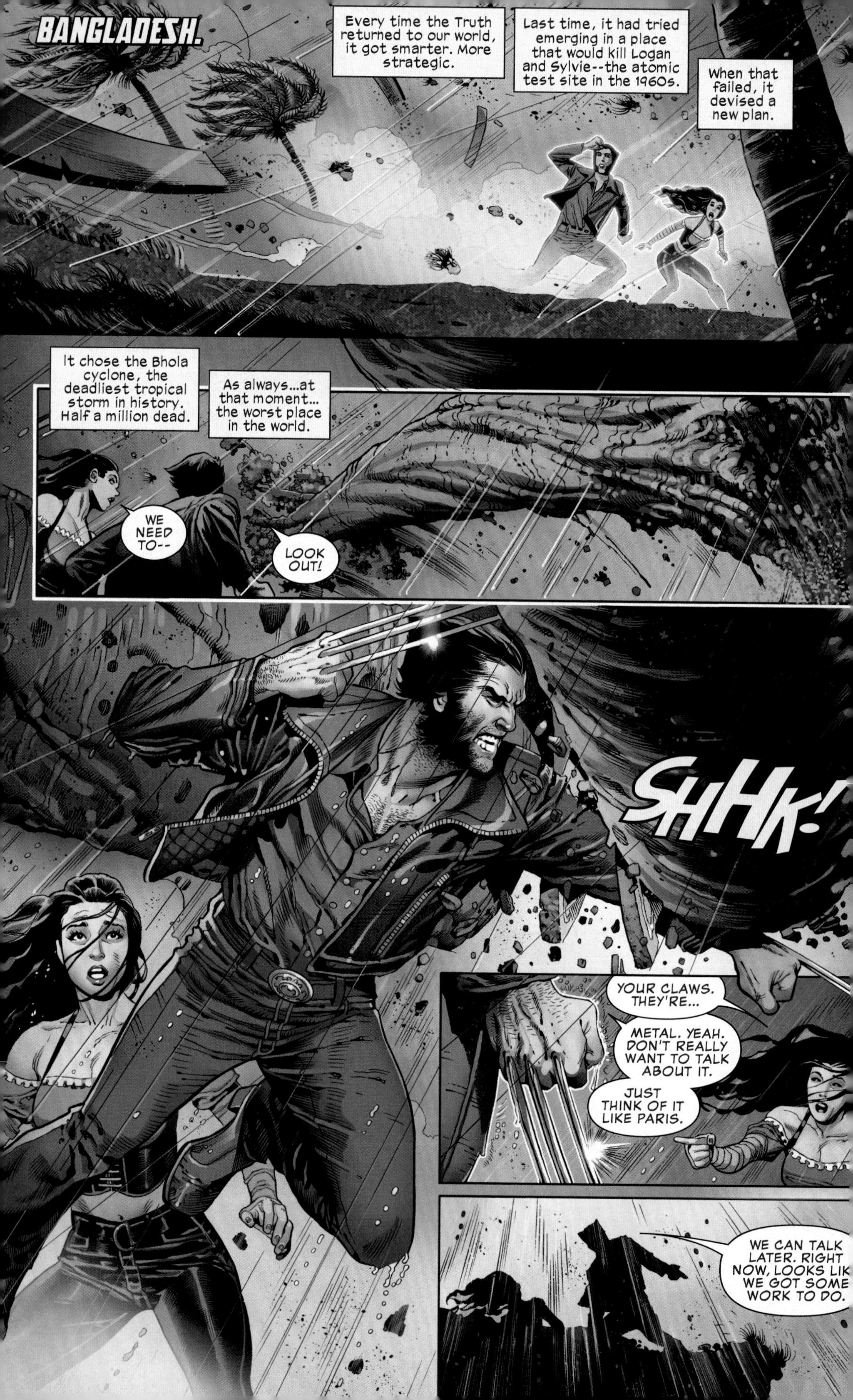
BANGLADESH.
Every time the Truth returned to our world, it got smarter. More strategic.
Last time, it had tried emerging in a place that would kill Logan and Sylvie--the atomic test site in the 1960s.
When that failed, it devised a new plan.
It chose the Bhola cyclone, the deadliest tropical storm in history. Half a million dead.
As always...at that moment... the worst place in the world.
WE NEED TO--
LOOK OUT!
SHHK!
YOUR CLAWS. THEY'RE...
METAL. YEAH. DON'T REALLY WANT TO TALK ABOUT IT.
JUST THINK OF IT LIKE PARIS.
WE CAN TALK LATER. RIGHT NOW, LOOKS LIK WE GOT SOME WORK TO DO.

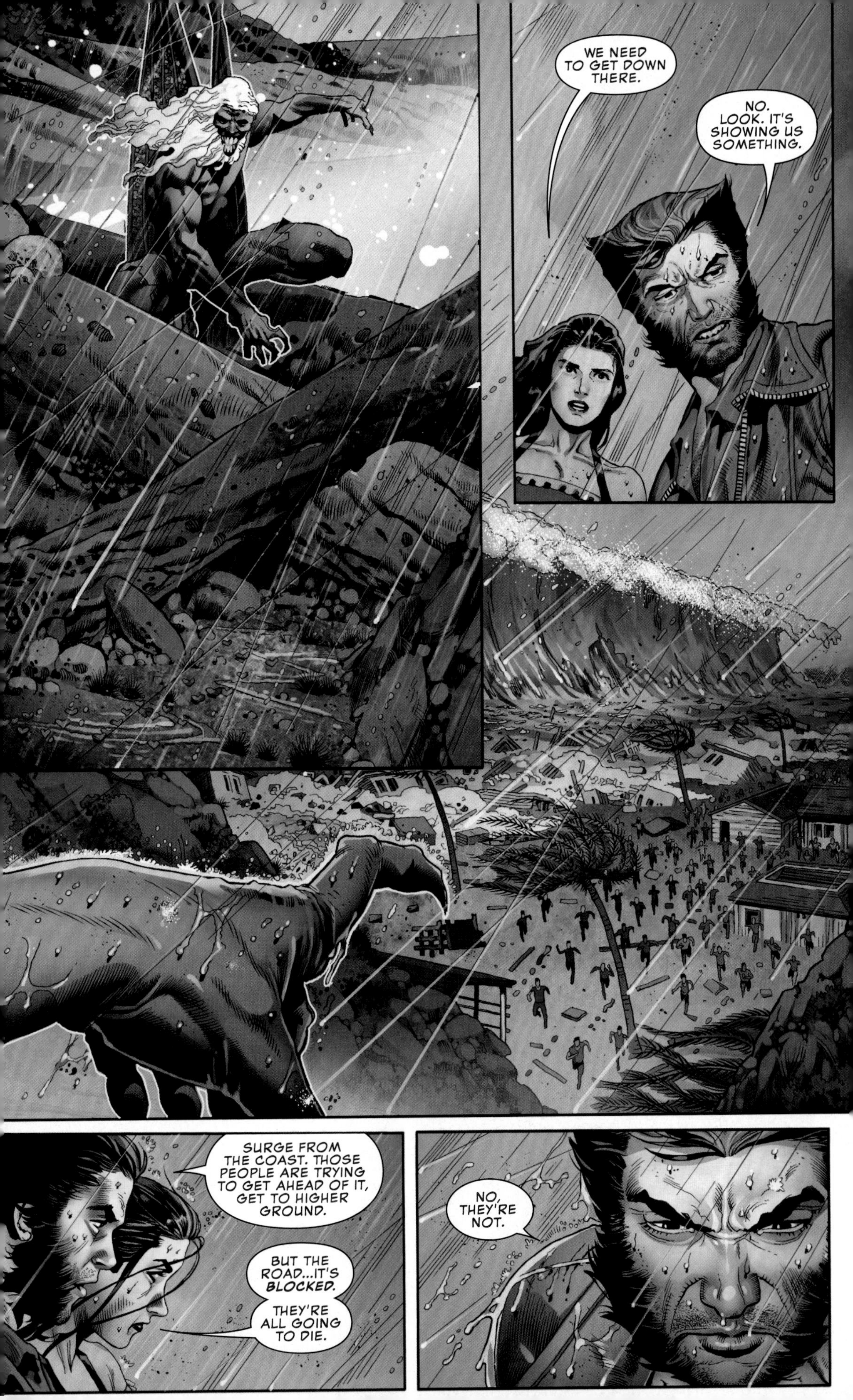
WE NEED TO GET DOWN THERE.
NO. LOOK. IT'S SHOWING US SOMETHING.
SURGE FROM THE COAST. THOSE PEOPLE ARE TRYING TO GET AHEAD OF IT, GET TO HIGHER GROUND.
BUT THE ROAD...IT'S *BLOCKED.*
THEY'RE ALL GOING TO DIE.
NO, THEY'RE NOT.

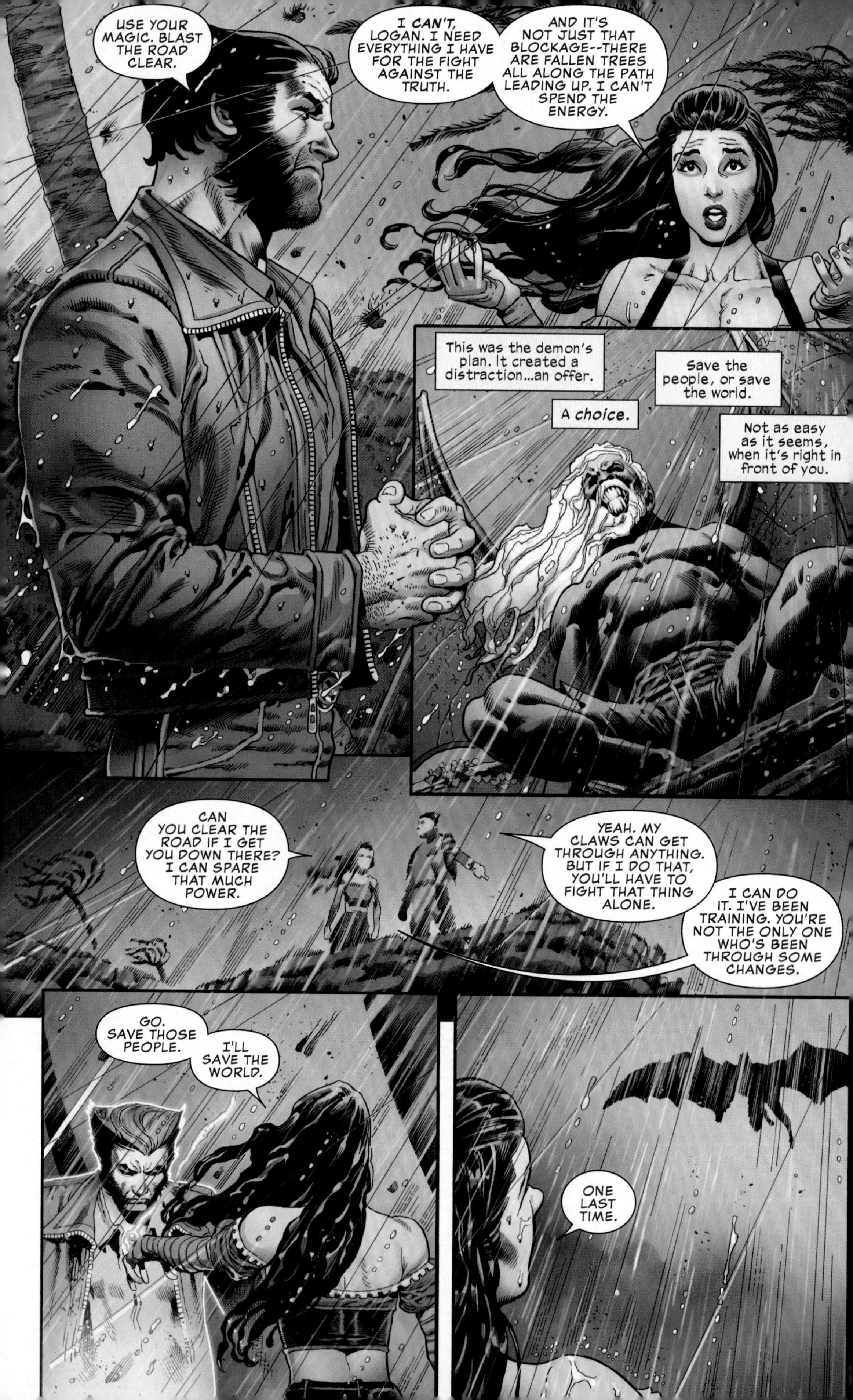
USE YOUR MAGIC. BLAST THE ROAD CLEAR.
I *CAN'T*, LOGAN. I NEED EVERYTHING I HAVE FOR THE FIGHT AGAINST THE TRUTH.
AND IT'S NOT JUST THAT BLOCKAGE--THERE ARE FALLEN TREES ALL ALONG THE PATH LEADING UP. I CAN'T SPEND THE ENERGY.
This was the demon's plan. It created a distraction...an offer.
Save the people, or save the world.
A *choice*.
Not as easy as it seems, when it's right in front of you.
CAN YOU CLEAR THE ROAD IF I GET YOU DOWN THERE? I CAN SPARE THAT MUCH POWER.
YEAH. MY CLAWS CAN GET THROUGH ANYTHING. BUT IF I DO THAT, YOU'LL HAVE TO FIGHT THAT THING ALONE.
I CAN DO IT. I'VE BEEN TRAINING. YOU'RE NOT THE ONLY ONE WHO'S BEEN THROUGH SOME CHANGES.
GO. SAVE THOSE PEOPLE.
I'LL SAVE THE WORLD.
ONE LAST TIME.

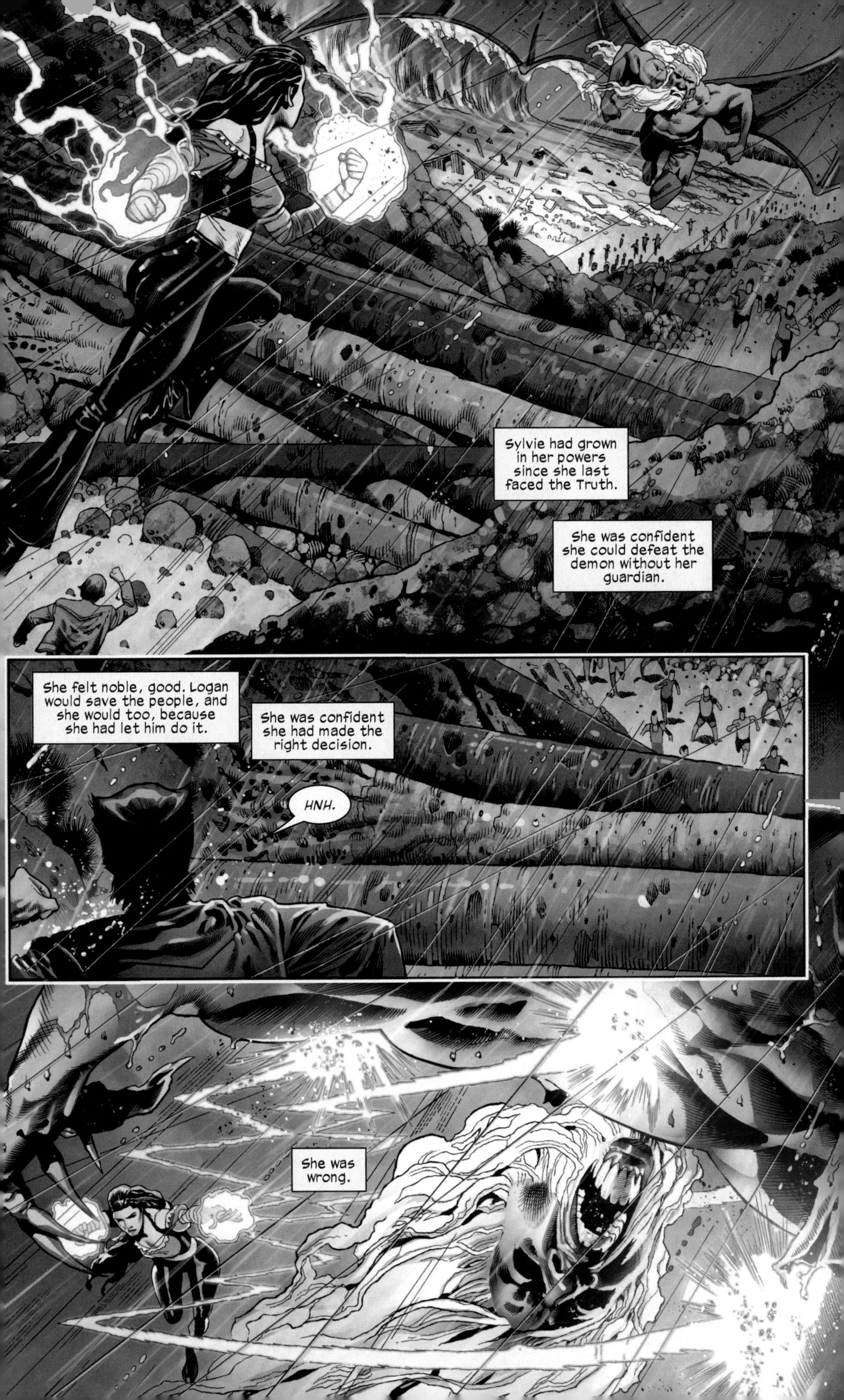
Sylvie had grown in her powers since she last faced the Truth.
She was confident she could defeat the demon without her guardian.
She felt noble, good. Logan would save the people, and she would too, because she had let him do it.
She was confident she had made the right decision.
HNH.
She was wrong.

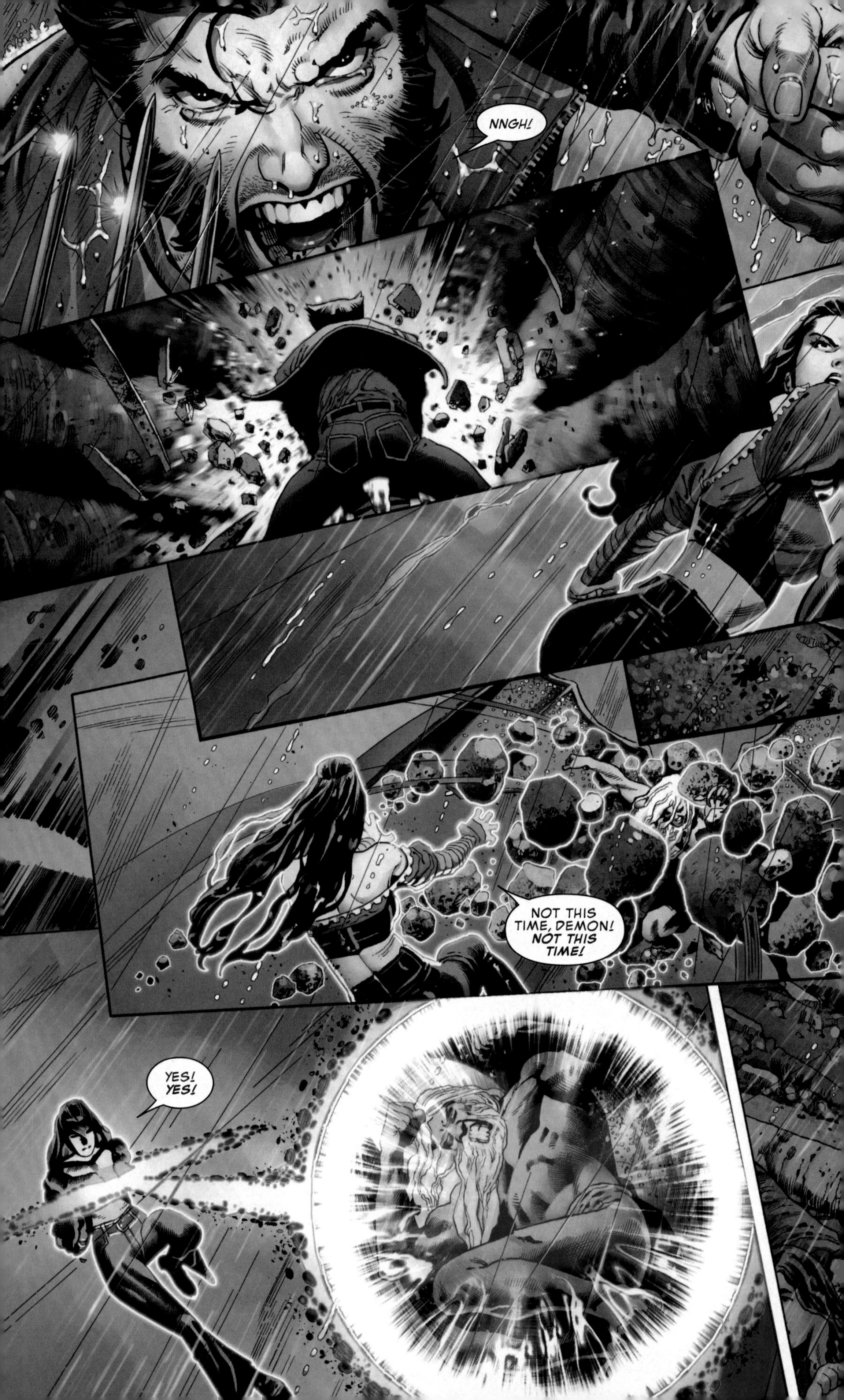
NNGH!
NOT THIS TIME, DEMON! NOT THIS TIME!
YES! YES!

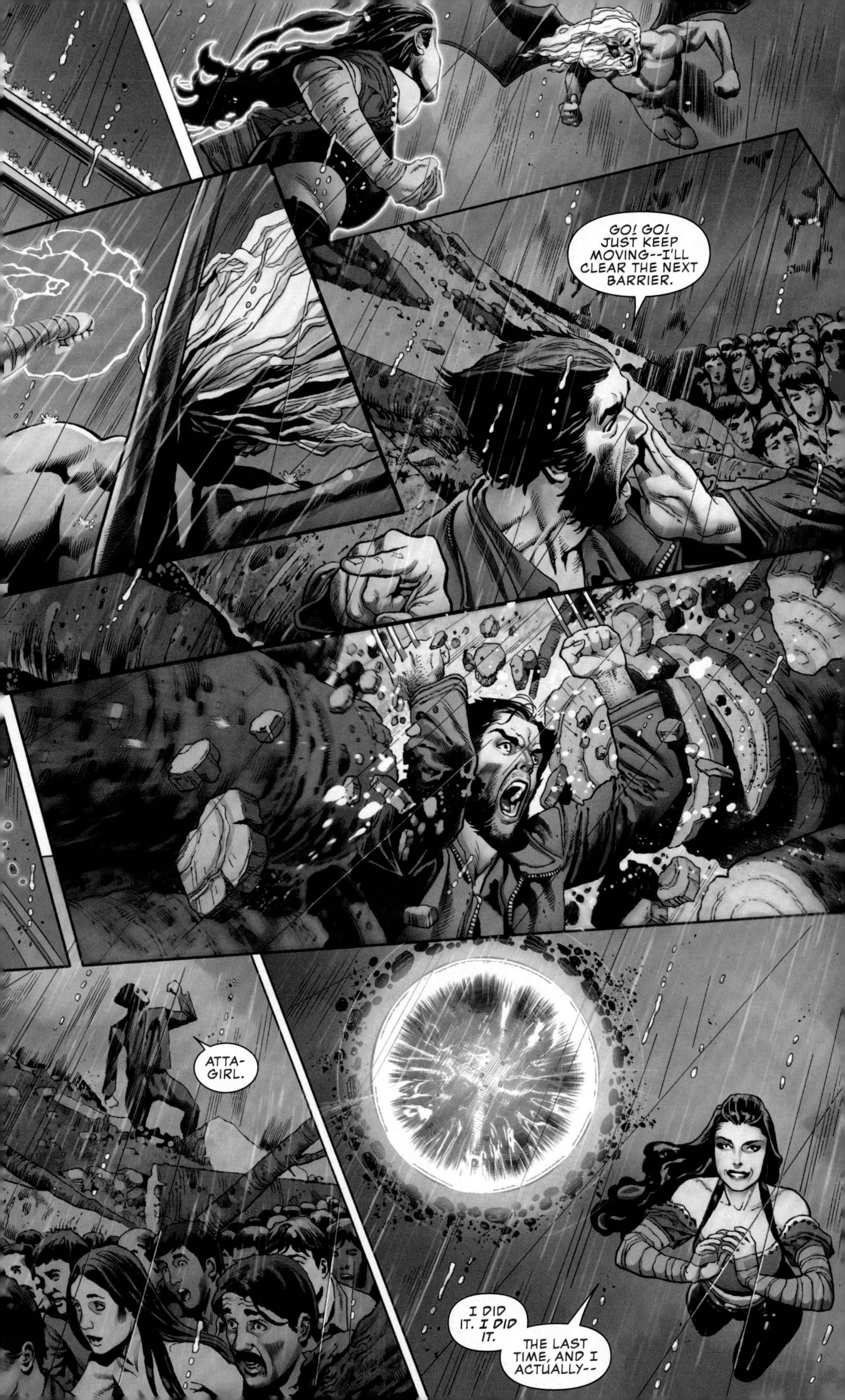
GO! GO! JUST KEEP MOVING--I'LL CLEAR THE NEXT BARRIER.
ATTA-GIRL.
I DID IT. I DID IT.
THE LAST TIME, AND I ACTUALLY--

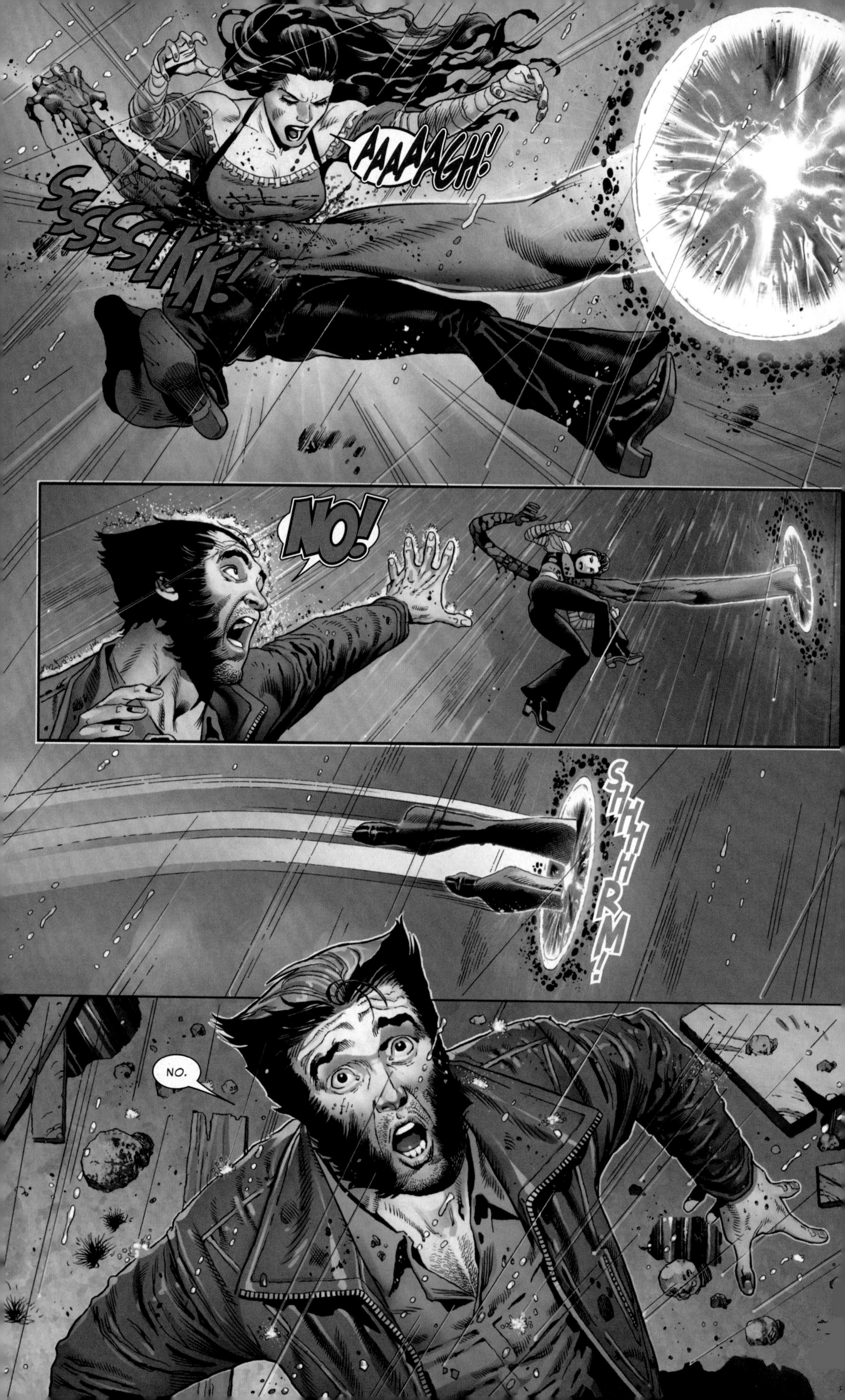

AAAAAGH!
SSSSSLIKK!
NO!
SHHHHHRRM!
NO.

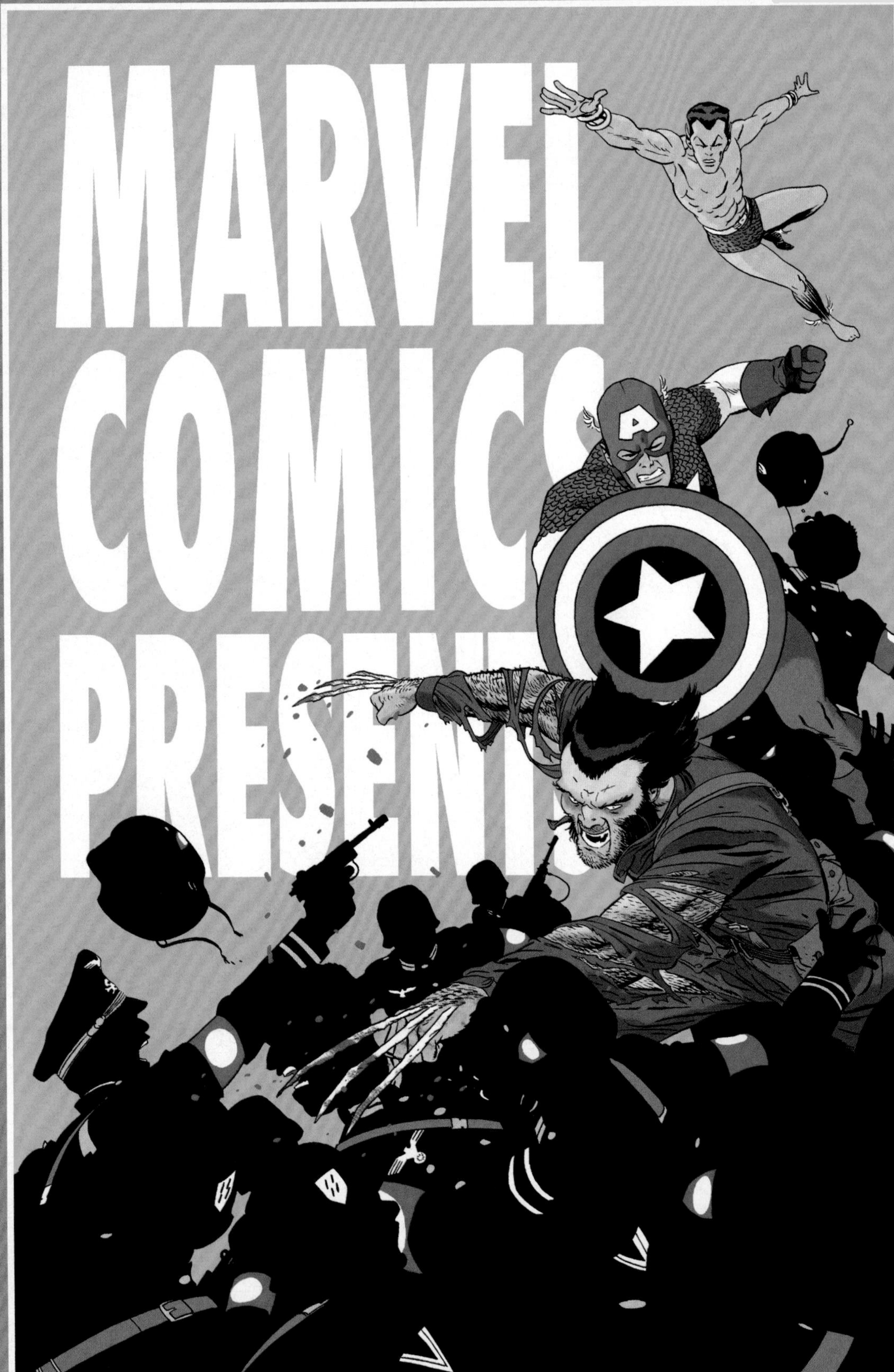
MARVEL
COMICS
PRESENTS

#1 variant by **MARCOS MARTIN**

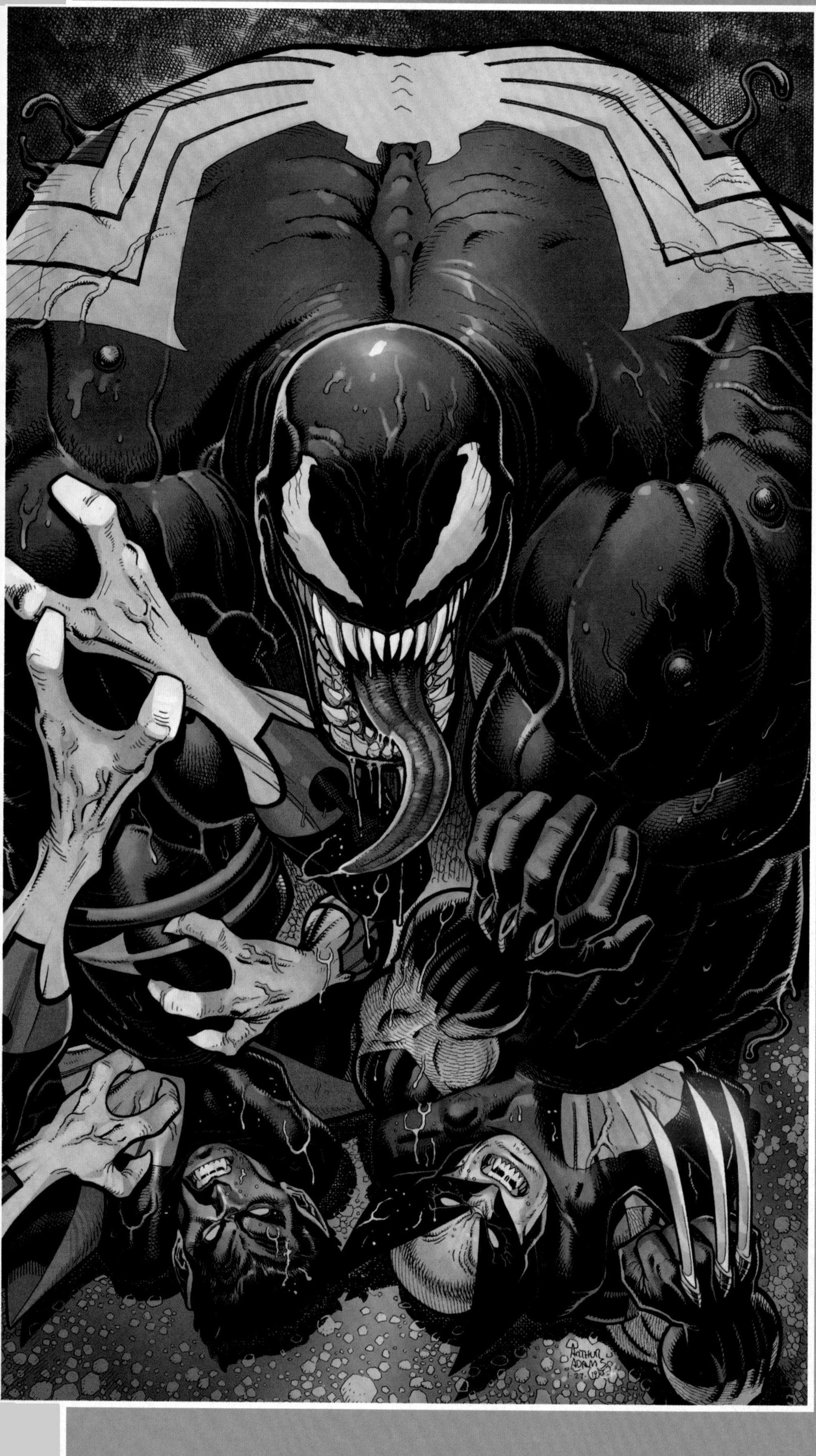

ARTHUR ADAMS

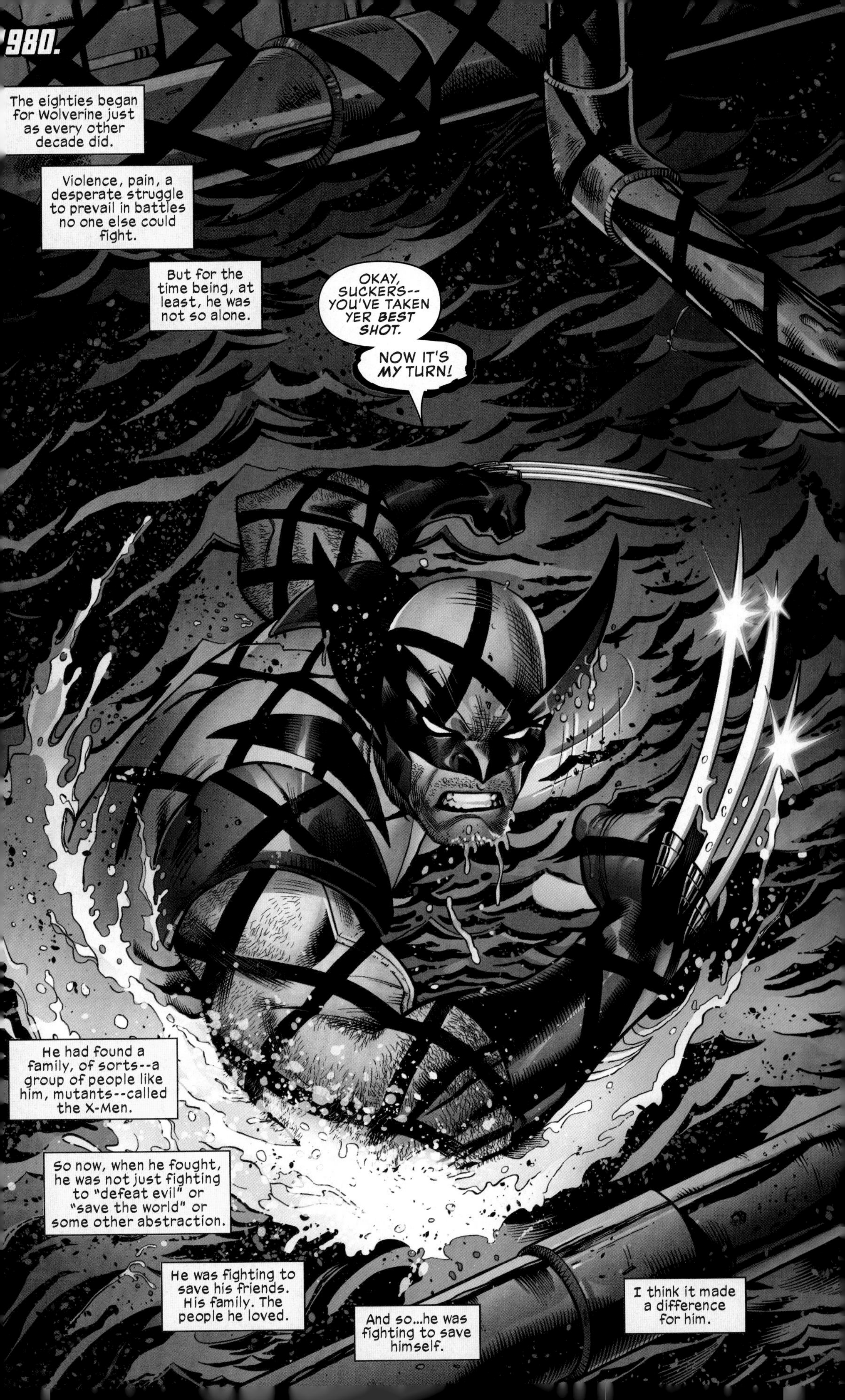
1980.
The eighties began for Wolverine just as every other decade did.
Violence, pain, a desperate struggle to prevail in battles no one else could fight.
But for the time being, at least, he was not so alone.
OKAY, SUCKERS-- YOU'VE TAKEN YER BEST SHOT.
NOW IT'S MY TURN!
He had found a family, of sorts--a group of people like him, mutants--called the X-Men.
So now, when he fought, he was not just fighting to "defeat evil" or "save the world" or some other abstraction.
He was fighting to save his friends. His family. The people he loved.
And so...he was fighting to save himself.
I think it made a difference for him.

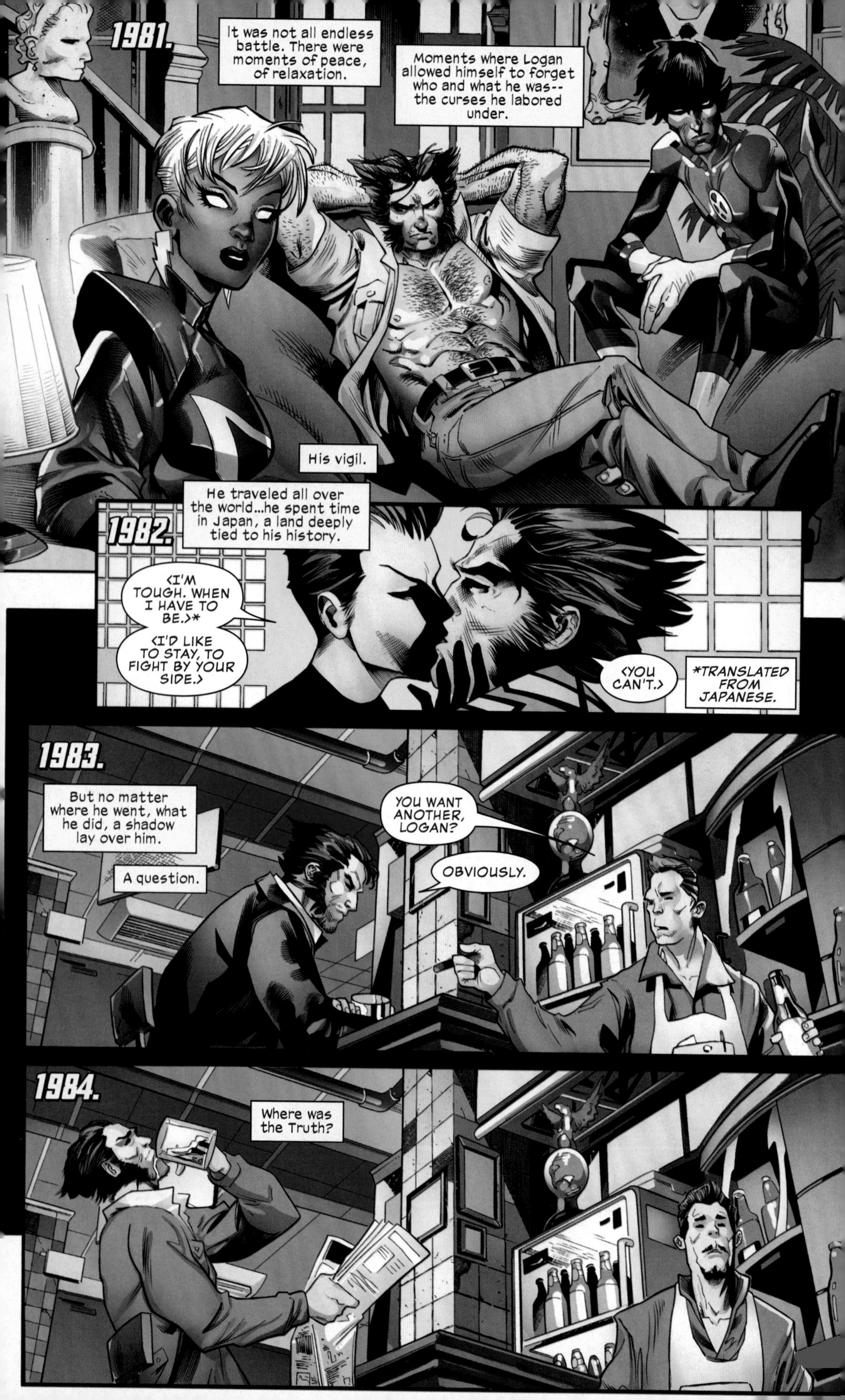
1981.
It was not all endless battle. There were moments of peace, of relaxation.
Moments where Logan allowed himself to forget who and what he was-- the curses he labored under.
His vigil.
He traveled all over the world...he spent time in Japan, a land deeply tied to his history.
1982.
<I'M TOUGH. WHEN I HAVE TO BE.>*
<I'D LIKE TO STAY, TO FIGHT BY YOUR SIDE.>
<YOU CAN'T.>
*TRANSLATED FROM JAPANESE.
1983.
But no matter where he went, what he did, a shadow lay over him.
A question.
YOU WANT ANOTHER, LOGAN?
OBVIOUSLY.
1984.
Where was the Truth?

985.

The demon would return to our world to destroy it at some point in the 1980s. That was the rule Logan had been given.

And he had seen it kill Sylvie--the witch with whom he had entered into a strange partnership to defend the world once per decade.

She had banished it even as she died... But who, now, would fight it? Logan's claws alone were not enough.

1986.

Magic was required. To find the Truth as it began to re-emerge, to bring Logan and Sylvie to that location...

...and then for Sylvie to cast the banishment spell while Logan defended her.

But with the witch dead...who would do these things?

Wolverine went through a great deal in the 1980s... but these questions were never far from his mind.

1987.

With every year that passed without him being called to fight the Truth, the shadow on Wolverine's mind grew deeper and darker.

He scoured the news, looking for the worst places in the world, the spots the demon preferred to emerge, looking for signs.

If the Truth appeared, Logan would go to fight it, even without Sylvie.

--THE BASQUE SEPARATIST GROUP ETA IS CLAIMING RESPONSIBILITY FOR THE BOMBINGS, WHICH LEFT 21 DEAD AND MORE THAN TWICE THAT WOUNDED--

HEY. TURN THAT UP.

1988.

But as the decade drew to a close, and the Truth had not yet emerged, Logan did something he is exceptionally good at.

He went looking for a fight.

HNH.

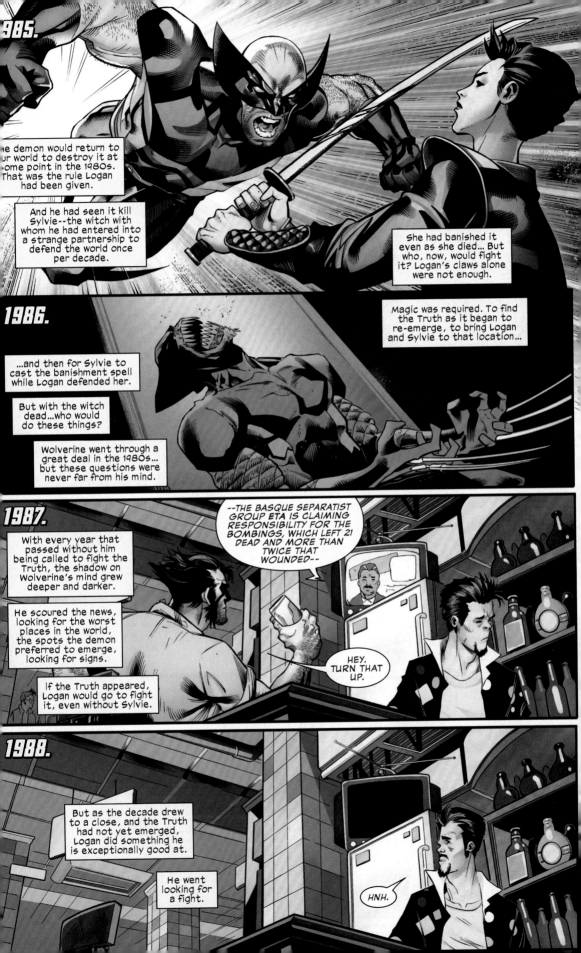

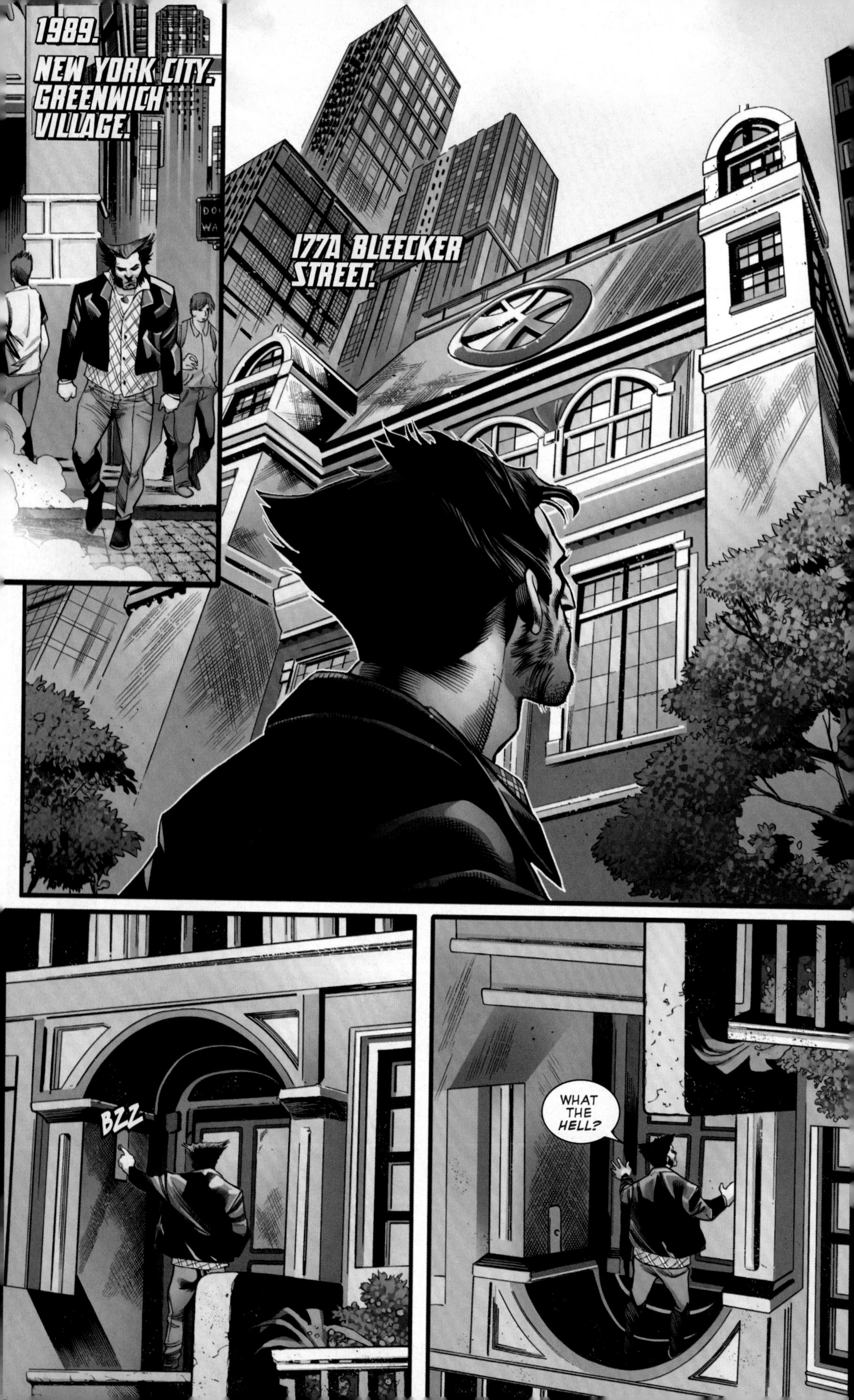
1989.
NEW YORK CITY. GREENWICH VILLAGE.
177A BLEECKER STREET.
BZZ
WHAT THE HELL?

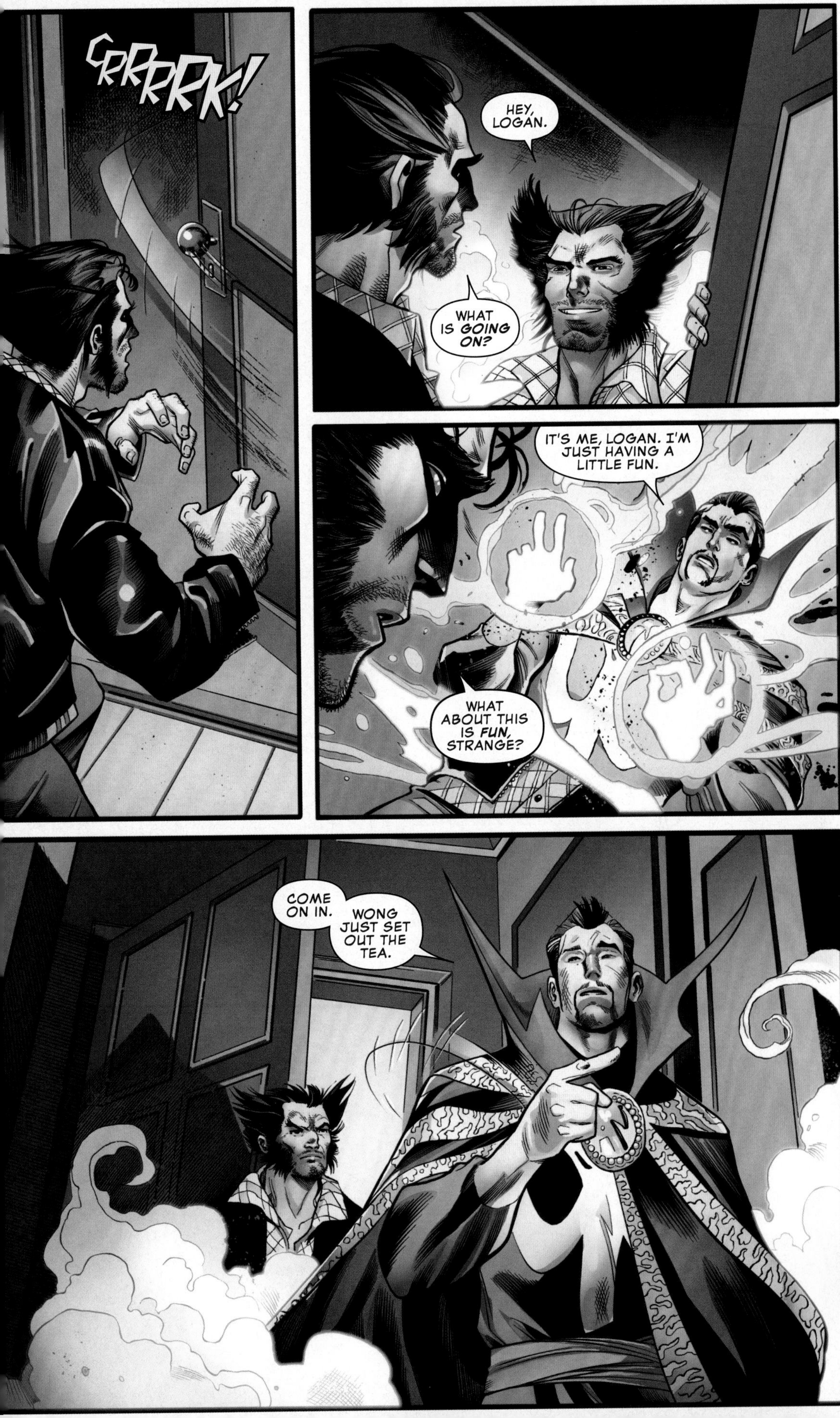
CRRRRK!
HEY, LOGAN.
WHAT IS *GOING* ON?
IT'S ME, LOGAN. I'M JUST HAVING A LITTLE FUN.
WHAT ABOUT THIS IS *FUN*, STRANGE?
COME ON IN.
WONG JUST SET OUT THE TEA.

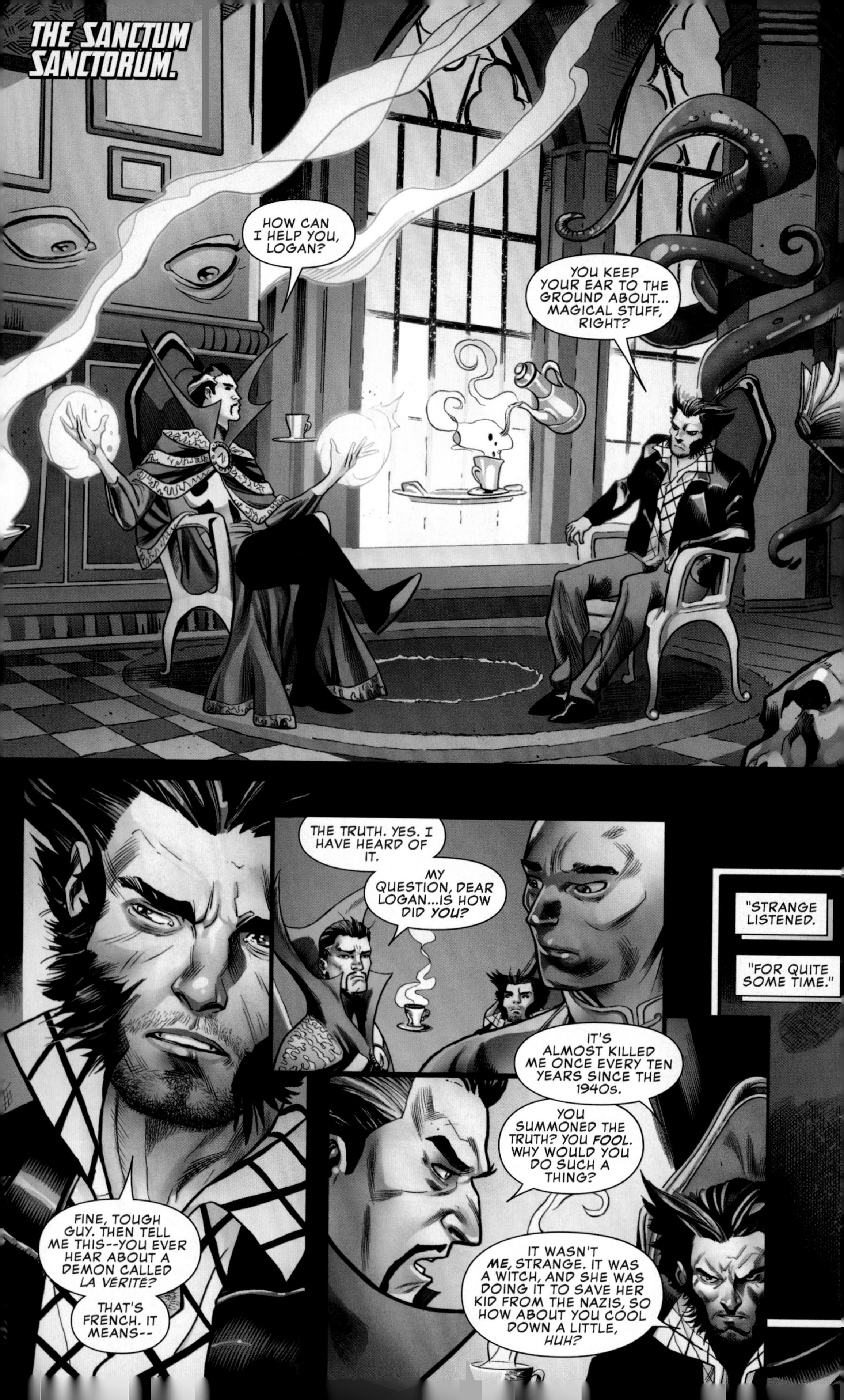
THE SANCTUM SANCTORUM.
HOW CAN I HELP YOU, LOGAN?
YOU KEEP YOUR EAR TO THE GROUND ABOUT... MAGICAL STUFF, RIGHT?
FINE, TOUGH GUY. THEN TELL ME THIS--YOU EVER HEAR ABOUT A DEMON CALLED LA VÉRITÉ?
THAT'S FRENCH. IT MEANS--
THE TRUTH. YES. I HAVE HEARD OF IT.
MY QUESTION, DEAR LOGAN...IS HOW DID YOU?
"STRANGE LISTENED.
"FOR QUITE SOME TIME."
IT'S ALMOST KILLED ME ONCE EVERY TEN YEARS SINCE THE 1940s.
YOU SUMMONED THE TRUTH? YOU FOOL. WHY WOULD YOU DO SUCH A THING?
IT WASN'T ME, STRANGE. IT WAS A WITCH, AND SHE WAS DOING IT TO SAVE HER KID FROM THE NAZIS, SO HOW ABOUT YOU COOL DOWN A LITTLE, HUH?

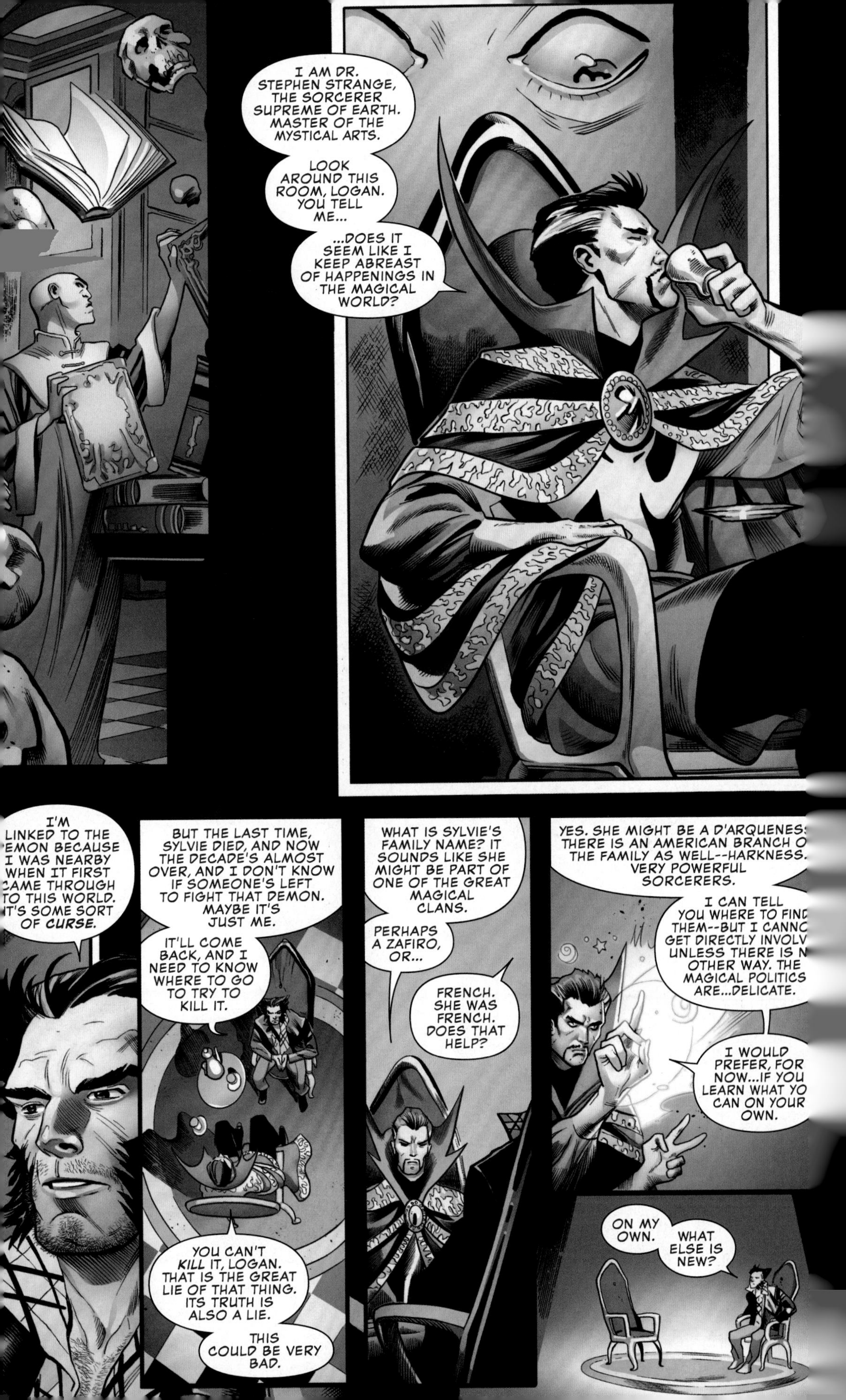
I AM DR. STEPHEN STRANGE, THE SORCERER SUPREME OF EARTH. MASTER OF THE MYSTICAL ARTS.
LOOK AROUND THIS ROOM, LOGAN. YOU TELL ME...
...DOES IT SEEM LIKE I KEEP ABREAST OF HAPPENINGS IN THE MAGICAL WORLD?
I'M LINKED TO THE EMON BECAUSE I WAS NEARBY WHEN IT FIRST CAME THROUGH TO THIS WORLD. IT'S SOME SORT OF CURSE.
BUT THE LAST TIME, SYLVIE DIED, AND NOW THE DECADE'S ALMOST OVER, AND I DON'T KNOW IF SOMEONE'S LEFT TO FIGHT THAT DEMON. MAYBE IT'S JUST ME.
IT'LL COME BACK, AND I NEED TO KNOW WHERE TO GO TO TRY TO KILL IT.
YOU CAN'T KILL IT, LOGAN. THAT IS THE GREAT LIE OF THAT THING. ITS TRUTH IS ALSO A LIE.
THIS COULD BE VERY BAD.
WHAT IS SYLVIE'S FAMILY NAME? IT SOUNDS LIKE SHE MIGHT BE PART OF ONE OF THE GREAT MAGICAL CLANS.
PERHAPS A ZAFIRO, OR...
FRENCH. SHE WAS FRENCH. DOES THAT HELP?
YES. SHE MIGHT BE A D'ARQUENES THERE IS AN AMERICAN BRANCH O THE FAMILY AS WELL--HARKNESS. VERY POWERFUL SORCERERS.
I CAN TELL YOU WHERE TO FIND THEM--BUT I CANNO GET DIRECTLY INVOLV UNLESS THERE IS N OTHER WAY. THE MAGICAL POLITICS ARE...DELICATE.
I WOULD PREFER, FOR NOW...IF YOU LEARN WHAT YO CAN ON YOUR OWN.
ON MY OWN.
WHAT ELSE IS NEW?

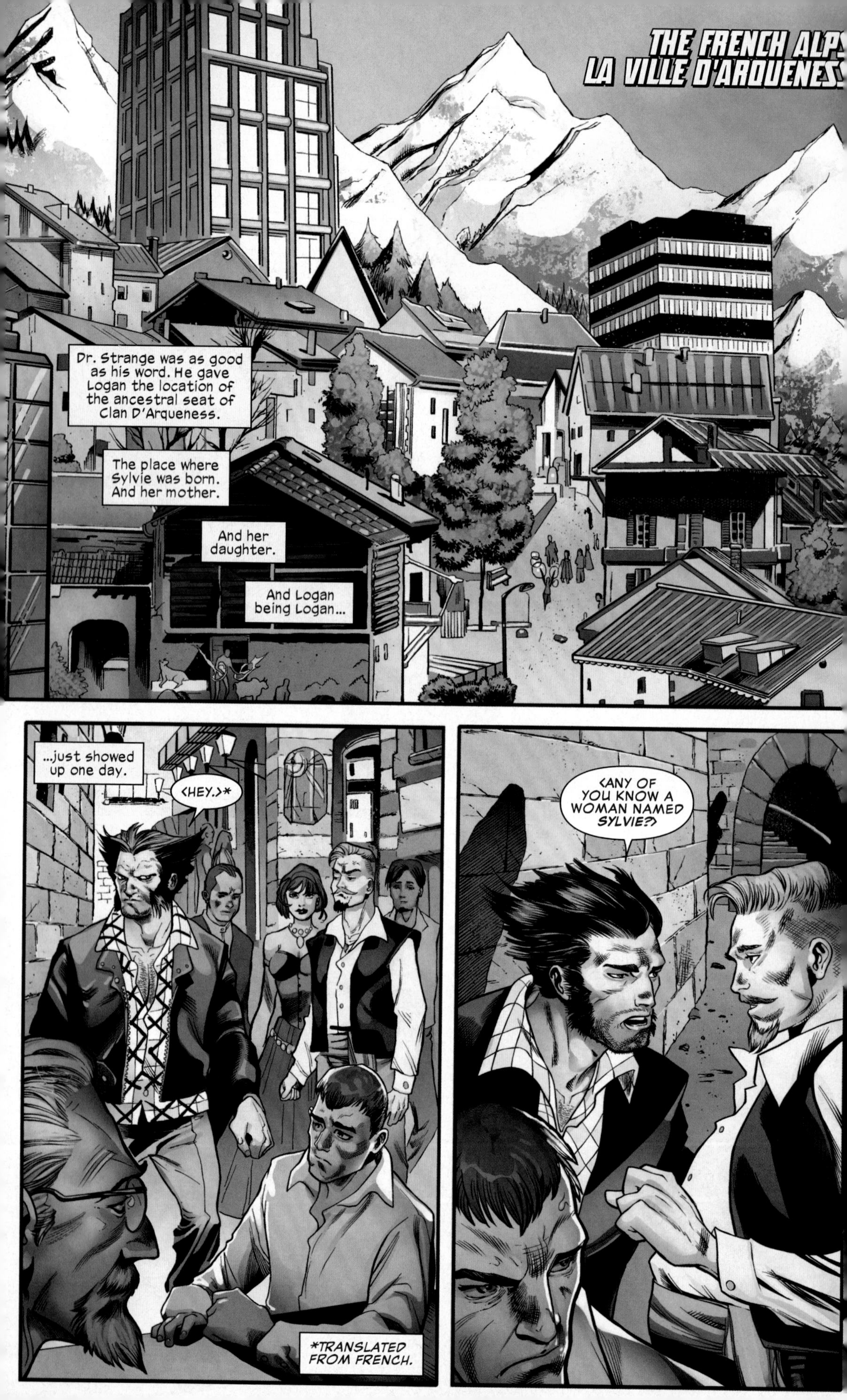
THE FRENCH ALPS
LA VILLE D'ARQUENES
Dr. Strange was as good as his word. He gave Logan the location of the ancestral seat of Clan D'Arqueness.
The place where Sylvie was born. And her mother.
And her daughter.
And Logan being Logan...
...just showed up one day.
<HEY.>*
*TRANSLATED FROM FRENCH.
<ANY OF YOU KNOW A WOMAN NAMED SYLVIE?>

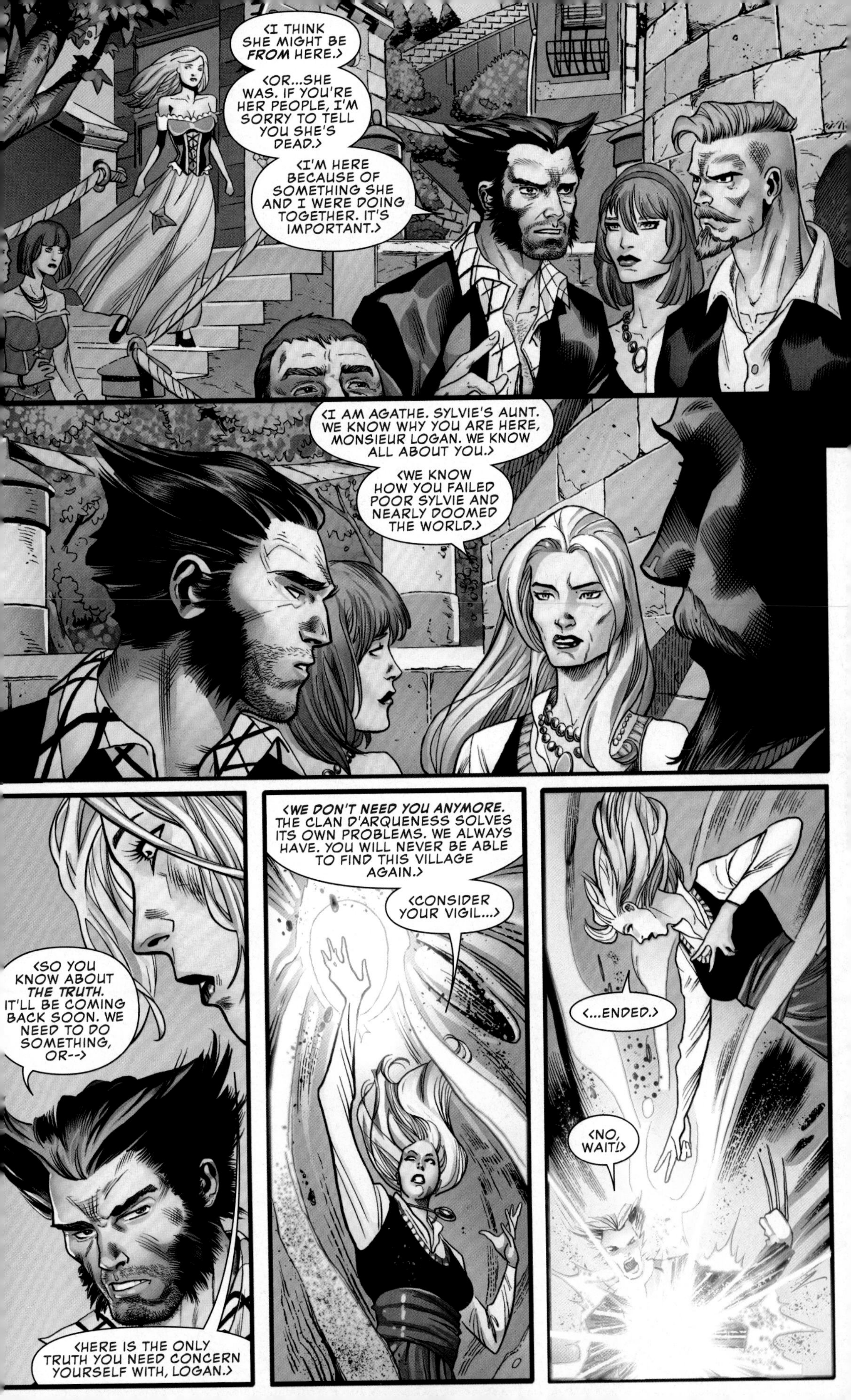

<I THINK SHE MIGHT BE *FROM* HERE.>
<OR...SHE WAS. IF YOU'RE HER PEOPLE, I'M SORRY TO TELL YOU SHE'S DEAD.>
<I'M HERE BECAUSE OF SOMETHING SHE AND I WERE DOING TOGETHER. IT'S IMPORTANT.>
<I AM AGATHE. SYLVIE'S AUNT. WE KNOW WHY YOU ARE HERE, MONSIEUR LOGAN. WE KNOW ALL ABOUT YOU.>
<WE KNOW HOW YOU FAILED POOR SYLVIE AND NEARLY DOOMED THE WORLD.>
<SO YOU KNOW ABOUT *THE TRUTH*. IT'LL BE COMING BACK SOON. WE NEED TO DO SOMETHING, OR-->
<HERE IS THE ONLY TRUTH YOU NEED CONCERN YOURSELF WITH, LOGAN.>
<*WE DON'T NEED YOU ANYMORE.* THE CLAN D'ARQUENESS SOLVES ITS OWN PROBLEMS. WE ALWAYS HAVE. YOU WILL NEVER BE ABLE TO FIND THIS VILLAGE AGAIN.>
<CONSIDER YOUR VIGIL...>
<...ENDED.>
<NO, WAIT!>

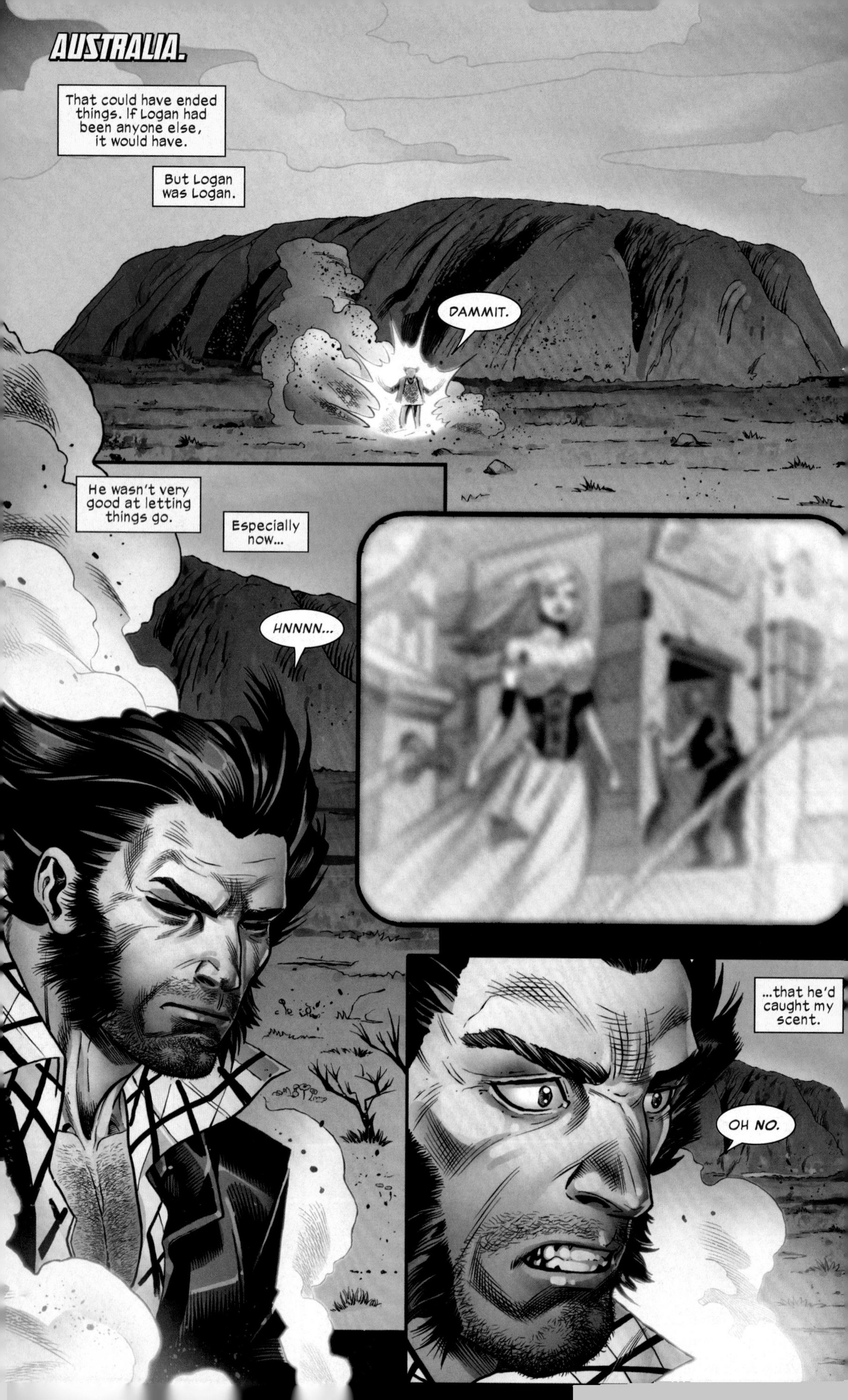
AUSTRALIA.
That could have ended things. If Logan had been anyone else, it would have.
But Logan was Logan.
DAMMIT.
He wasn't very good at letting things go.
Especially now...
HNNNN...
...that he'd caught my scent.
OH NO.

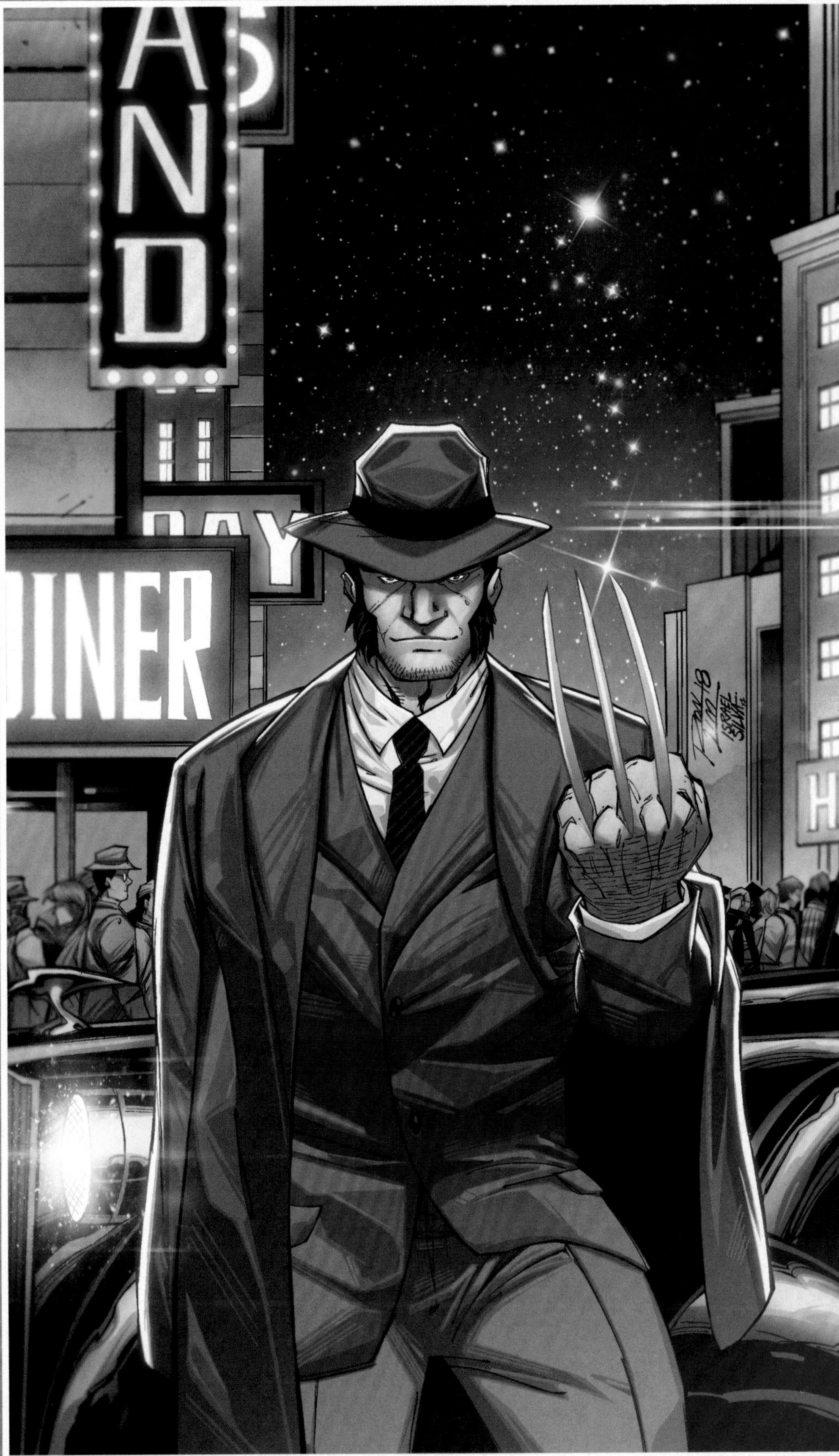
AND
DINER

#1 variant by **RON LIM** & **ISRAEL SILVA**

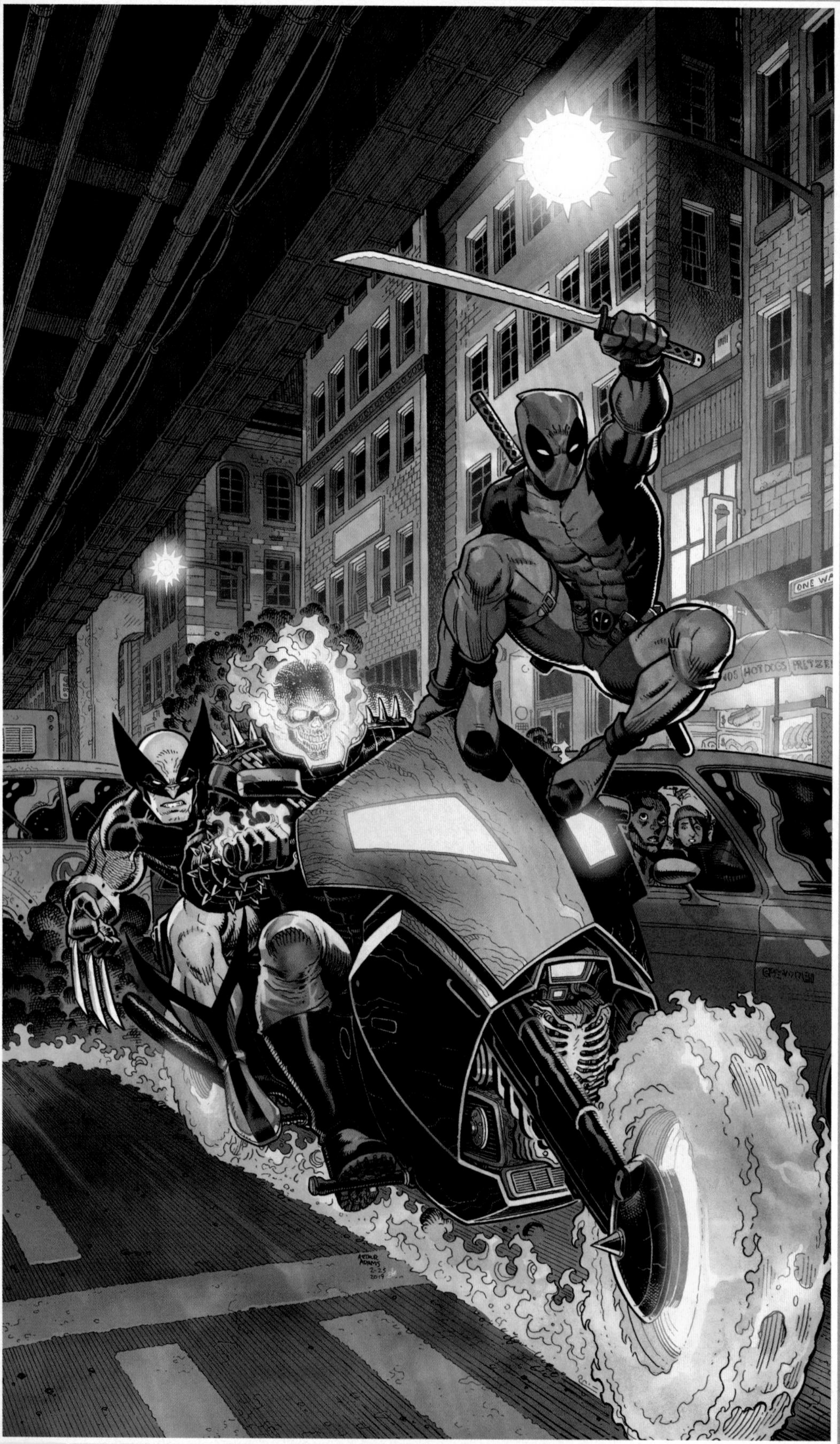
ONE WA
HOT DOGS

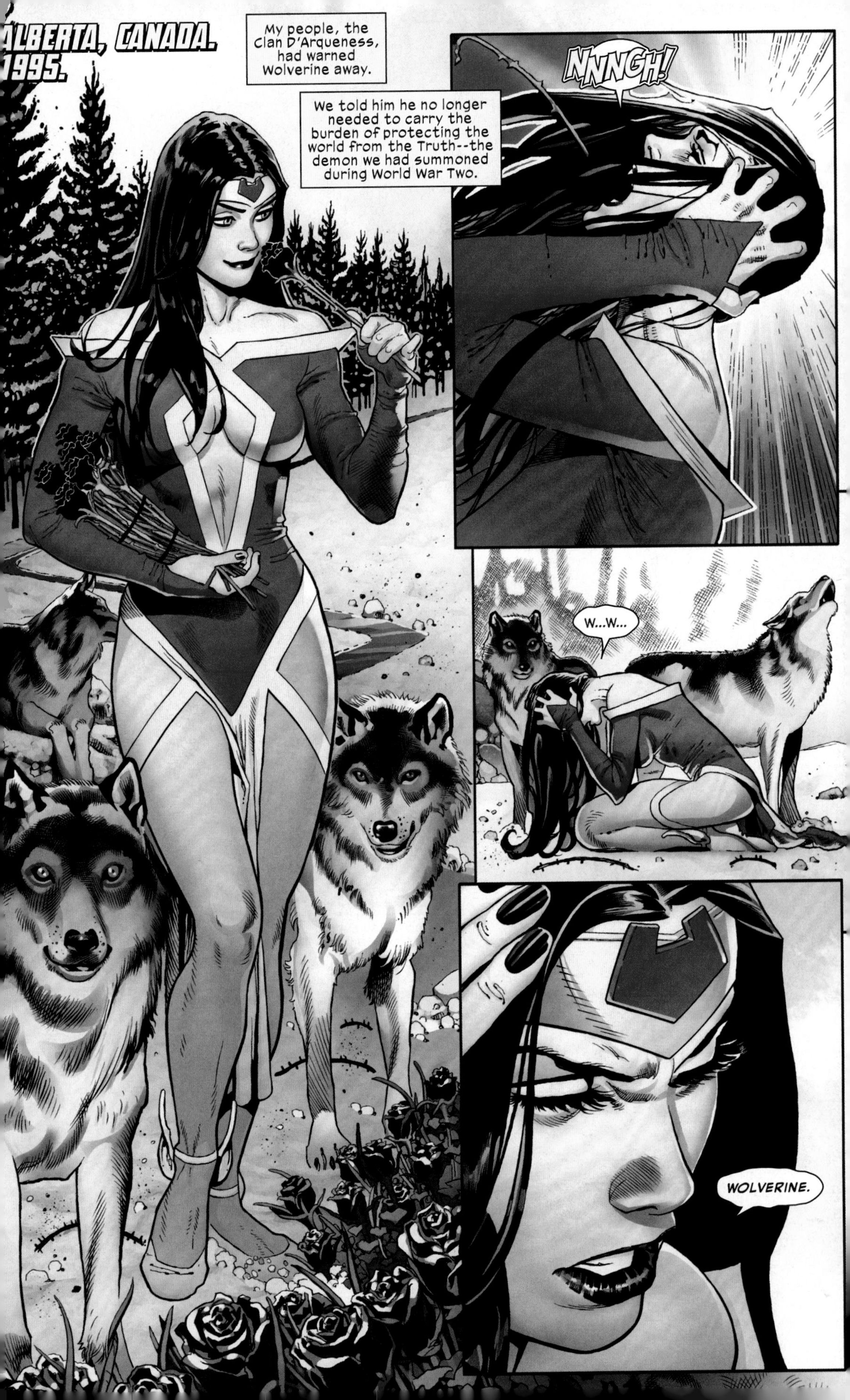
ALBERTA, CANADA. 1995.
My people, the Clan D'Arqueness, had warned Wolverine away.
We told him he no longer needed to carry the burden of protecting the world from the Truth--the demon we had summoned during World War Two.
NNNGH!
W...W...
WOLVERINE.

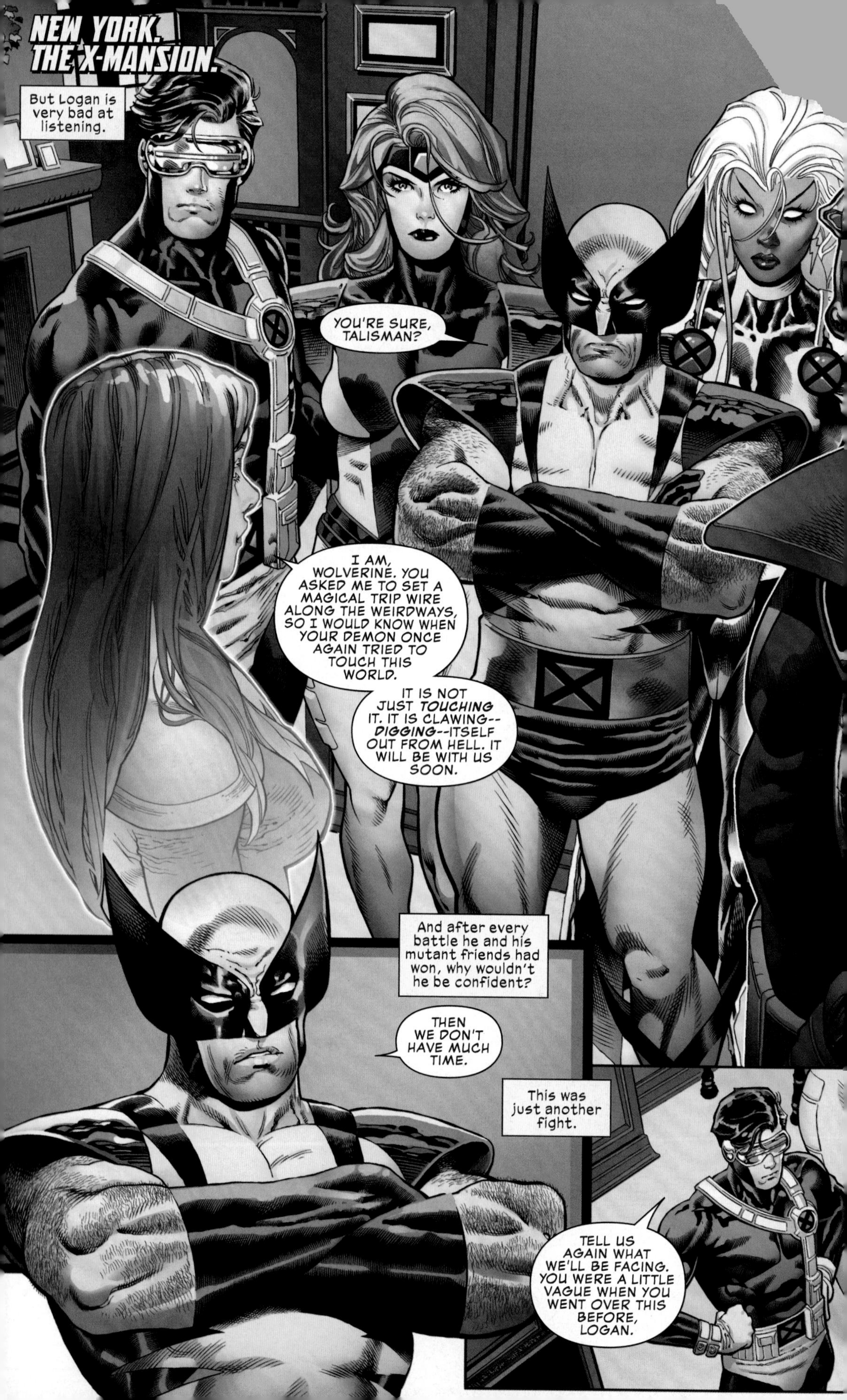
NEW YORK.
THE X-MANSION.
But Logan is very bad at listening.
YOU'RE SURE, TALISMAN?
I AM, WOLVERINE. YOU ASKED ME TO SET A MAGICAL TRIP WIRE ALONG THE WEIRDWAYS, SO I WOULD KNOW WHEN YOUR DEMON ONCE AGAIN TRIED TO TOUCH THIS WORLD.
IT IS NOT JUST *TOUCHING* IT. IT IS CLAWING--*DIGGING*--ITSELF OUT FROM HELL. IT WILL BE WITH US SOON.
And after every battle he and his mutant friends had won, why wouldn't he be confident?
THEN WE DON'T HAVE MUCH TIME.
This was just another fight.
TELL US AGAIN WHAT WE'LL BE FACING. YOU WERE A LITTLE VAGUE WHEN YOU WENT OVER THIS BEFORE, LOGAN.

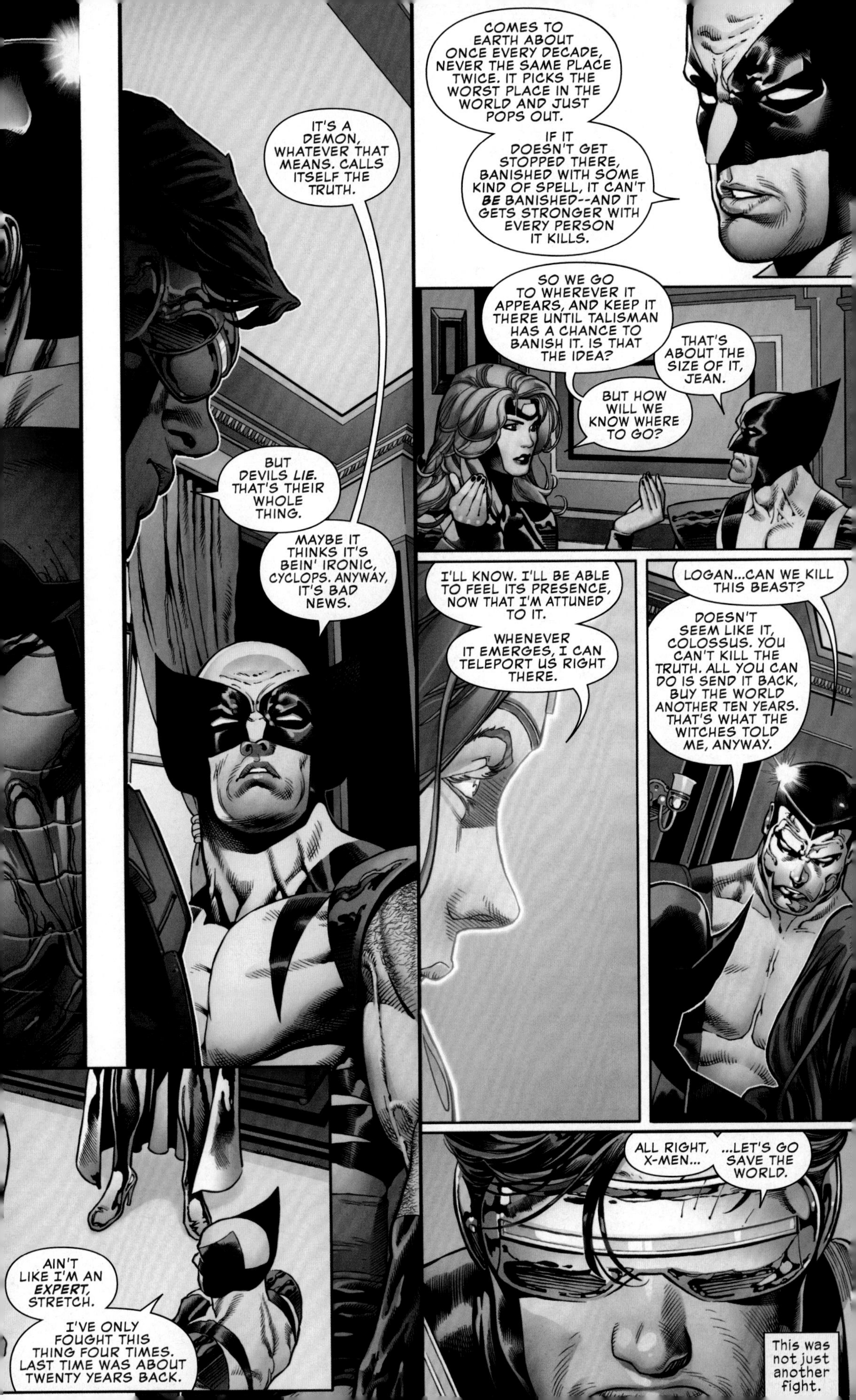
IT'S A DEMON, WHATEVER THAT MEANS. CALLS ITSELF THE TRUTH.
BUT DEVILS LIE. THAT'S THEIR WHOLE THING.
MAYBE IT THINKS IT'S BEIN' IRONIC, CYCLOPS. ANYWAY, IT'S BAD NEWS.
AIN'T LIKE I'M AN EXPERT, STRETCH.
I'VE ONLY FOUGHT THIS THING FOUR TIMES. LAST TIME WAS ABOUT TWENTY YEARS BACK.
COMES TO EARTH ABOUT ONCE EVERY DECADE, NEVER THE SAME PLACE TWICE. IT PICKS THE WORST PLACE IN THE WORLD AND JUST POPS OUT.
IF IT DOESN'T GET STOPPED THERE, BANISHED WITH SOME KIND OF SPELL, IT CAN'T BE BANISHED--AND IT GETS STRONGER WITH EVERY PERSON IT KILLS.
SO WE GO TO WHEREVER IT APPEARS, AND KEEP IT THERE UNTIL TALISMAN HAS A CHANCE TO BANISH IT. IS THAT THE IDEA?
THAT'S ABOUT THE SIZE OF IT, JEAN.
BUT HOW WILL WE KNOW WHERE TO GO?
I'LL KNOW. I'LL BE ABLE TO FEEL ITS PRESENCE, NOW THAT I'M ATTUNED TO IT.
WHENEVER IT EMERGES, I CAN TELEPORT US RIGHT THERE.
LOGAN...CAN WE KILL THIS BEAST?
DOESN'T SEEM LIKE IT, COLOSSUS. YOU CAN'T KILL THE TRUTH. ALL YOU CAN DO IS SEND IT BACK, BUY THE WORLD ANOTHER TEN YEARS. THAT'S WHAT THE WITCHES TOLD ME, ANYWAY.
ALL RIGHT, X-MEN...
...LET'S GO SAVE THE WORLD.
This was not just another fight.

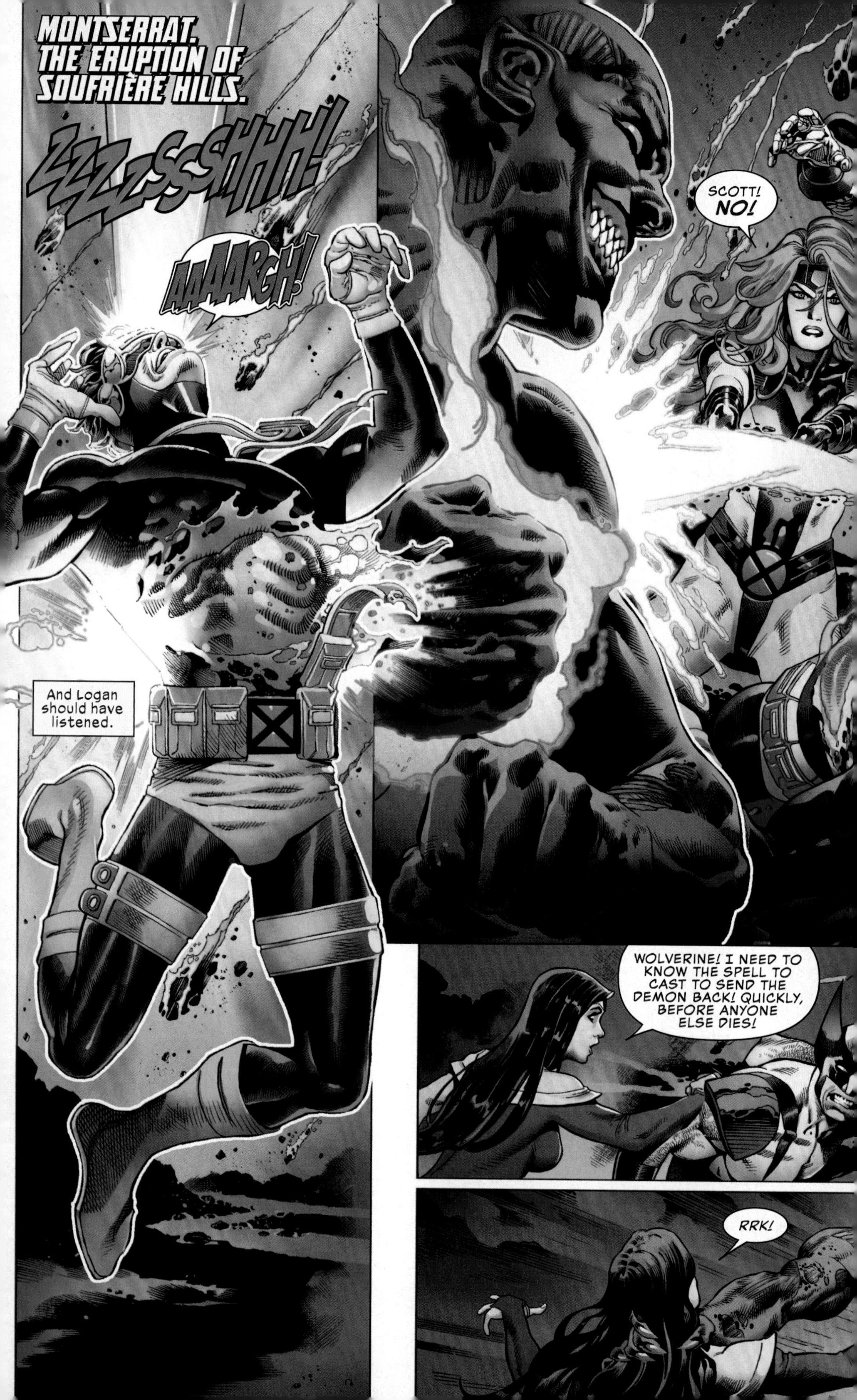
MONTSERRAT. THE ERUPTION OF SOUFRIÈRE HILLS.
ZZZZSSSHHH!
AAAARGH!
SCOTT! NO!
And Logan should have listened.
WOLVERINE! I NEED TO KNOW THE SPELL TO CAST TO SEND THE DEMON BACK! QUICKLY, BEFORE ANYONE ELSE DIES!
RRK!

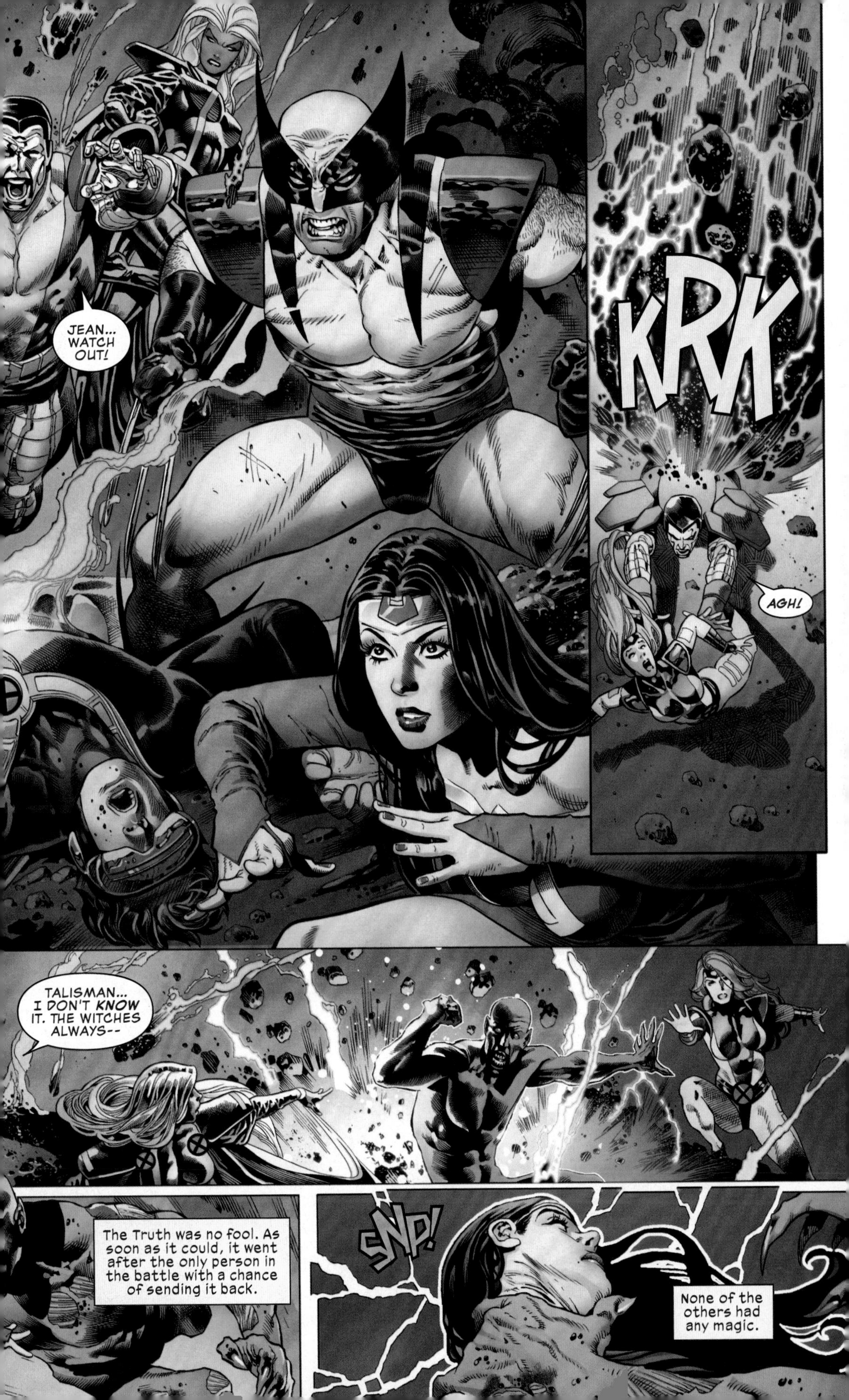
JEAN... WATCH OUT!
KRK
AGH!
TALISMAN... I DON'T KNOW IT. THE WITCHES ALWAYS--
The Truth was no fool. As soon as it could, it went after the only person in the battle with a chance of sending it back.
SNP!
None of the others had any magic.

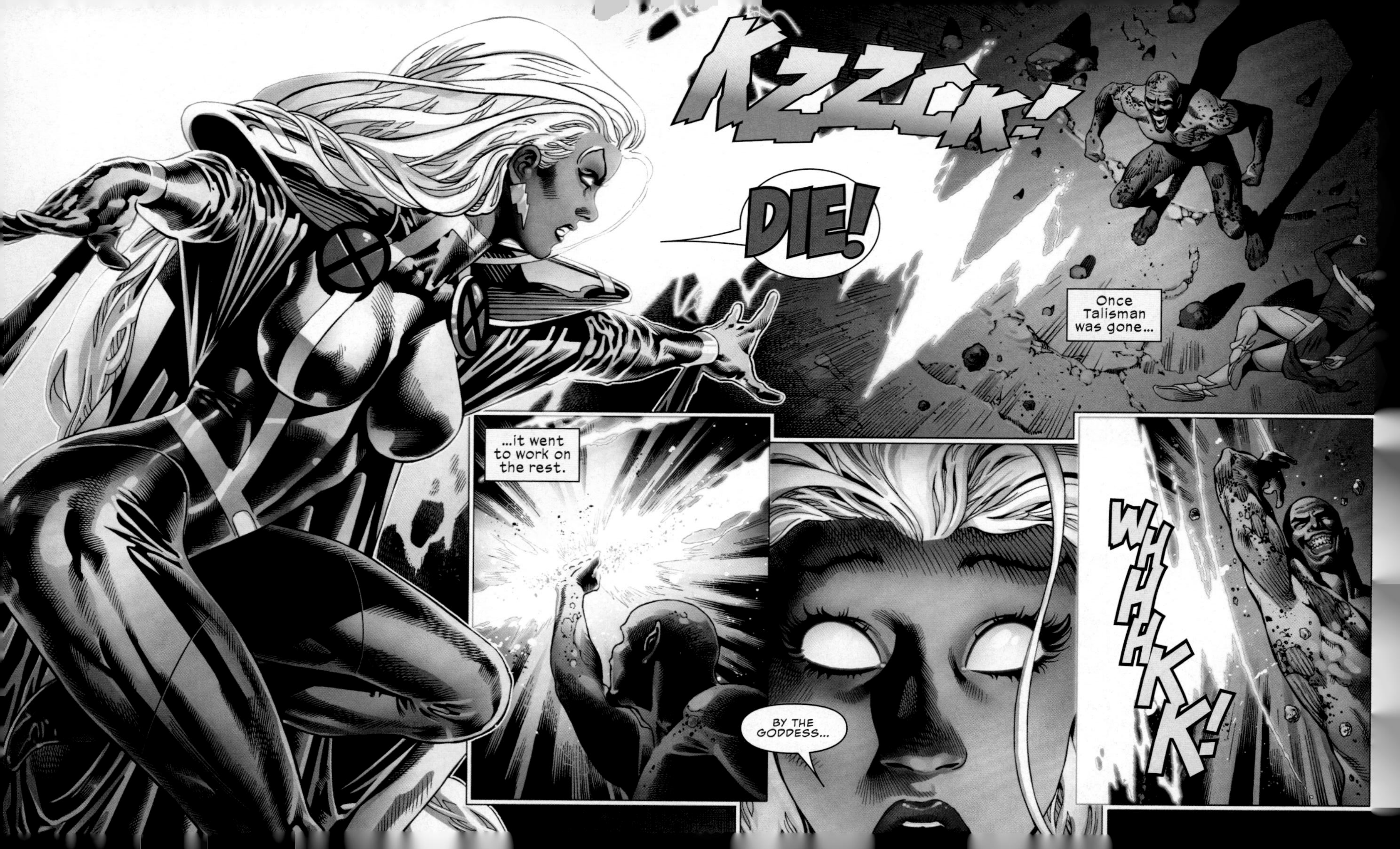
KZZZCK!
DIE!
Once Talisman was gone...
...it went to work on the rest.
BY THE GODDESS...
WHHHKK!

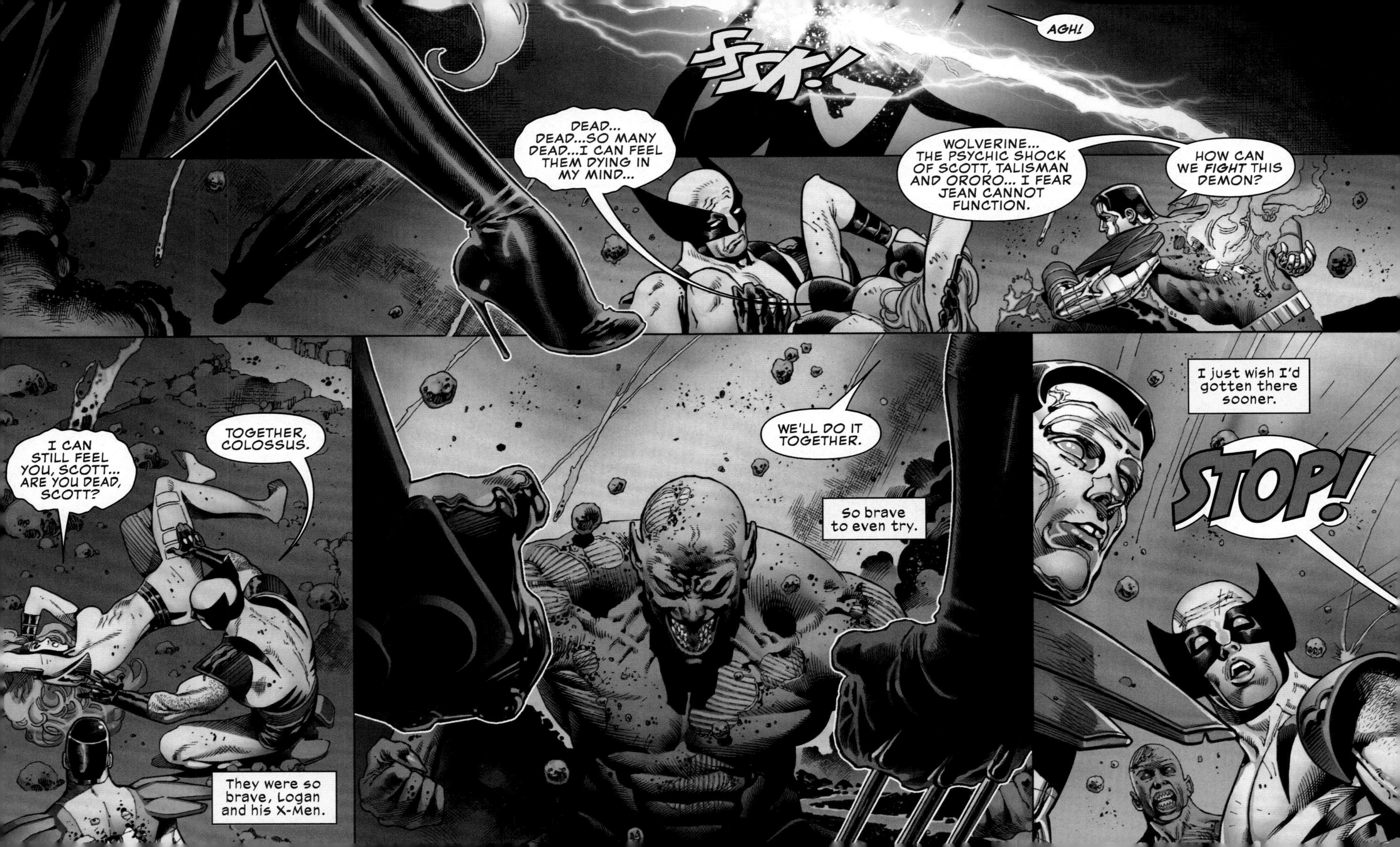
SSSK!
AGH!
DEAD... DEAD...SO MANY DEAD...I CAN FEEL THEM DYING IN MY MIND...
WOLVERINE... THE PSYCHIC SHOCK OF SCOTT, TALISMAN AND ORORO... I FEAR JEAN CANNOT FUNCTION.
HOW CAN WE *FIGHT* THIS DEMON?
I CAN STILL FEEL YOU, SCOTT... ARE YOU DEAD, SCOTT?
TOGETHER, COLOSSUS.
They were so brave, Logan and his X-Men.
WE'LL DO IT TOGETHER.
So brave to even try.
I just wish I'd gotten there sooner.
STOP!

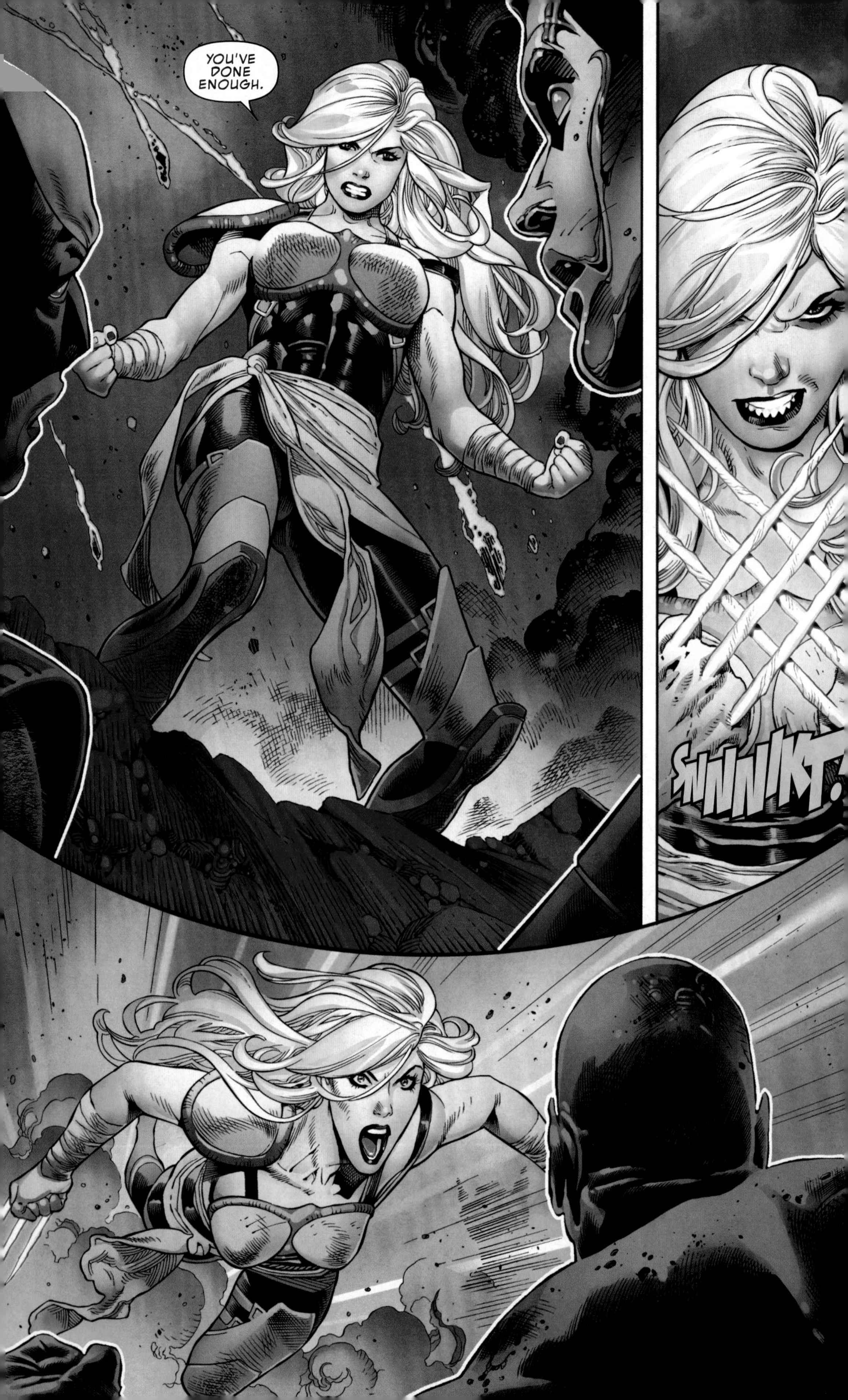
YOU'VE DONE ENOUGH.
SNNNIKT!

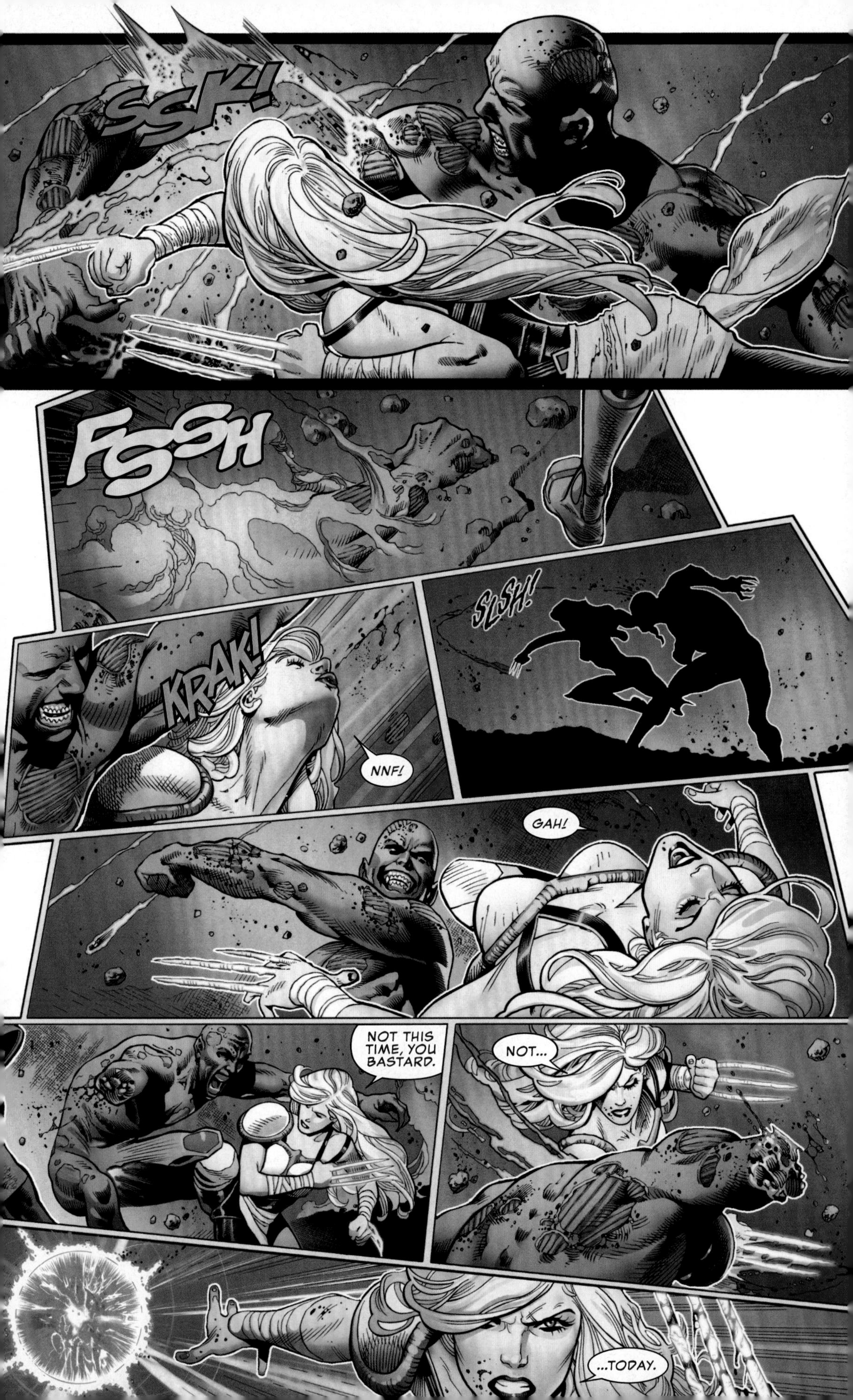
SSK!
FSSH
KRAK!
NNF!
SLSH!
GAH!
NOT THIS TIME, YOU BASTARD.
NOT...
...TODAY.

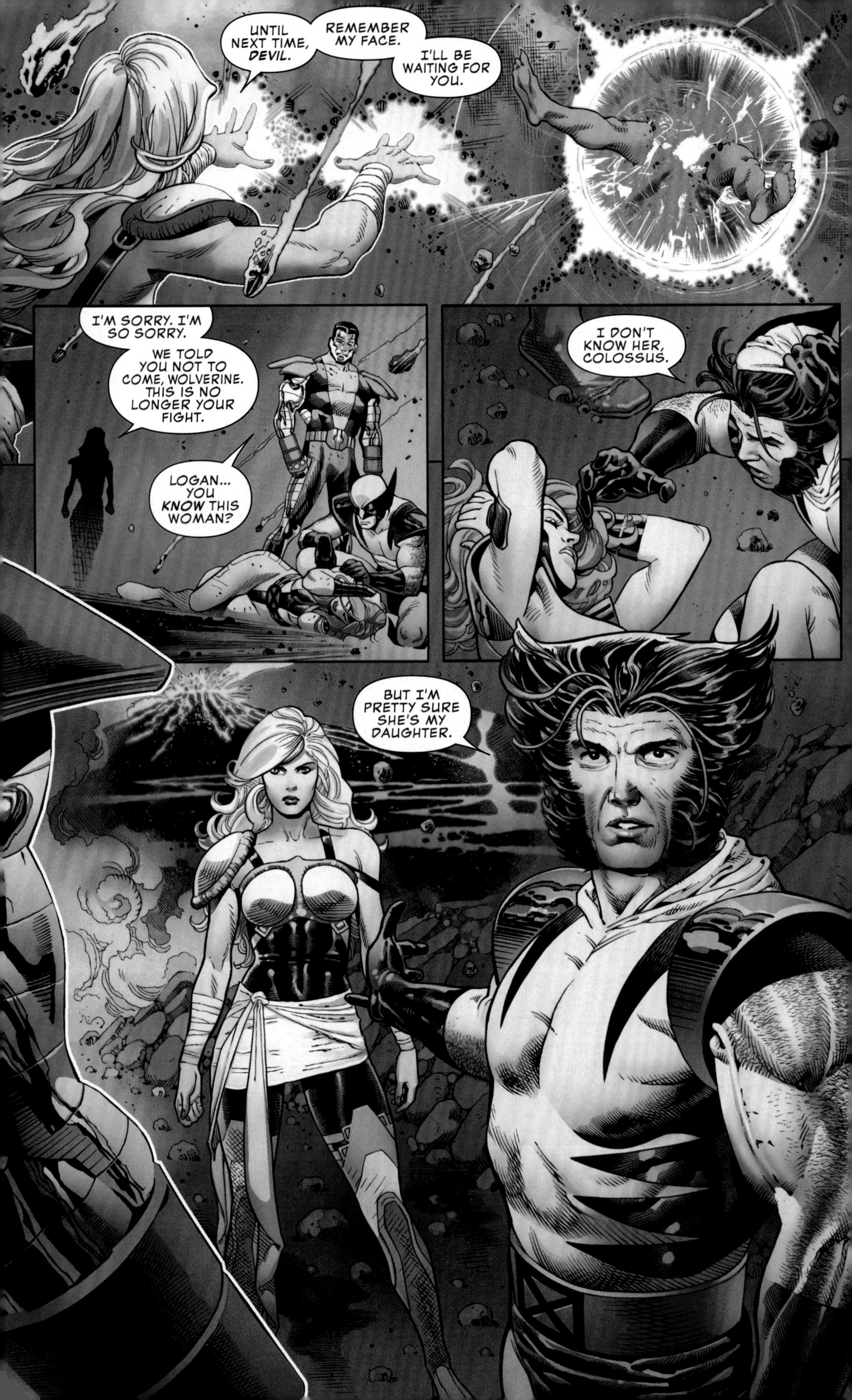
UNTIL NEXT TIME, DEVIL.
REMEMBER MY FACE.
I'LL BE WAITING FOR YOU.
I'M SORRY. I'M SO SORRY.
WE TOLD YOU NOT TO COME, WOLVERINE. THIS IS NO LONGER YOUR FIGHT.
LOGAN... YOU KNOW THIS WOMAN?
I DON'T KNOW HER, COLOSSUS.
BUT I'M PRETTY SURE SHE'S MY DAUGHTER.

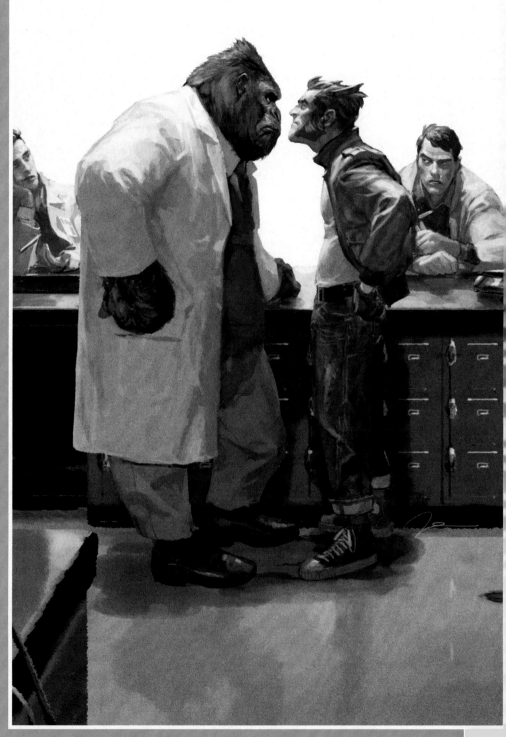

#2 variant by **GERALD PAREL**

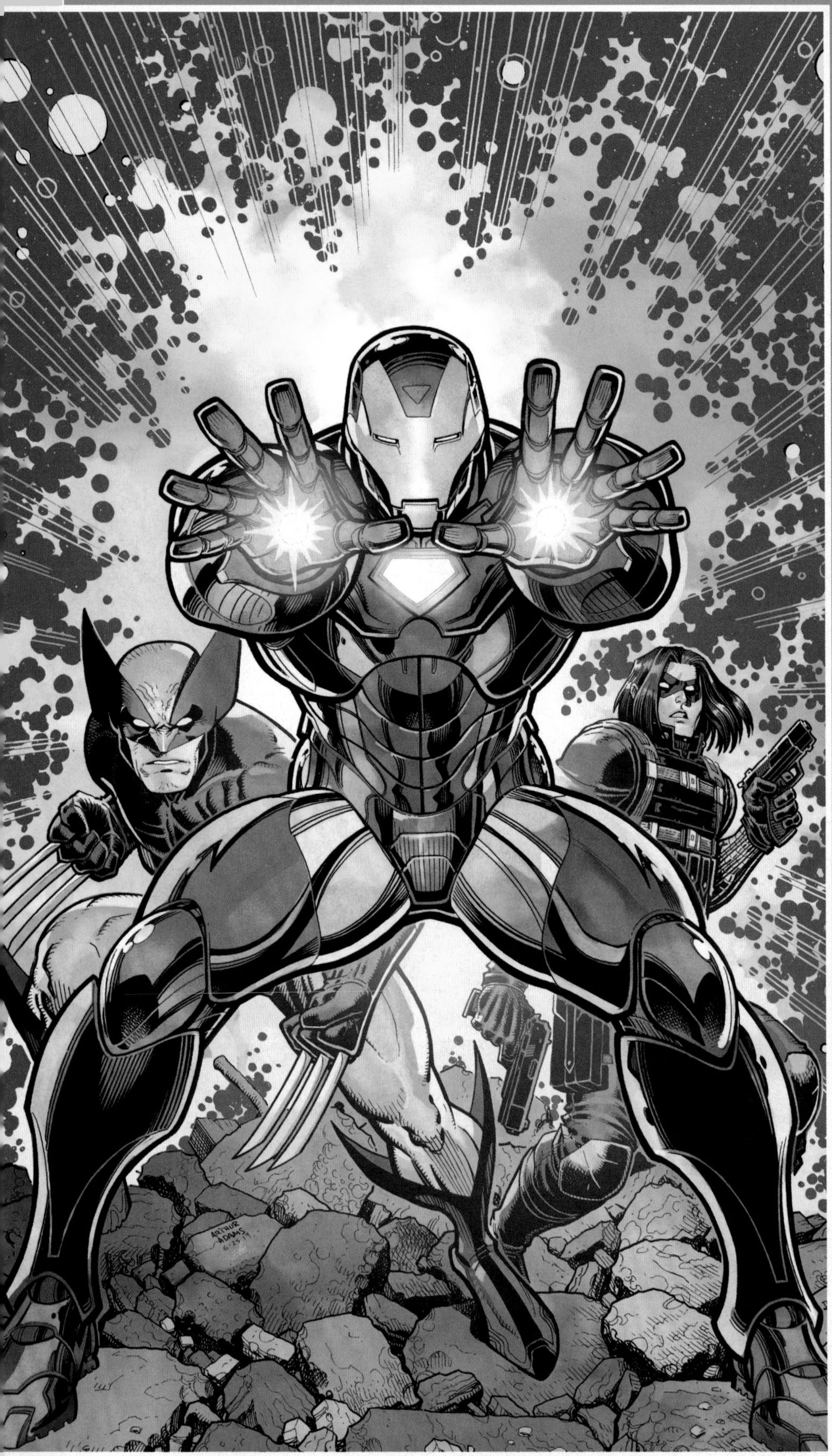
ARTHUR ADAMS 6-25-19

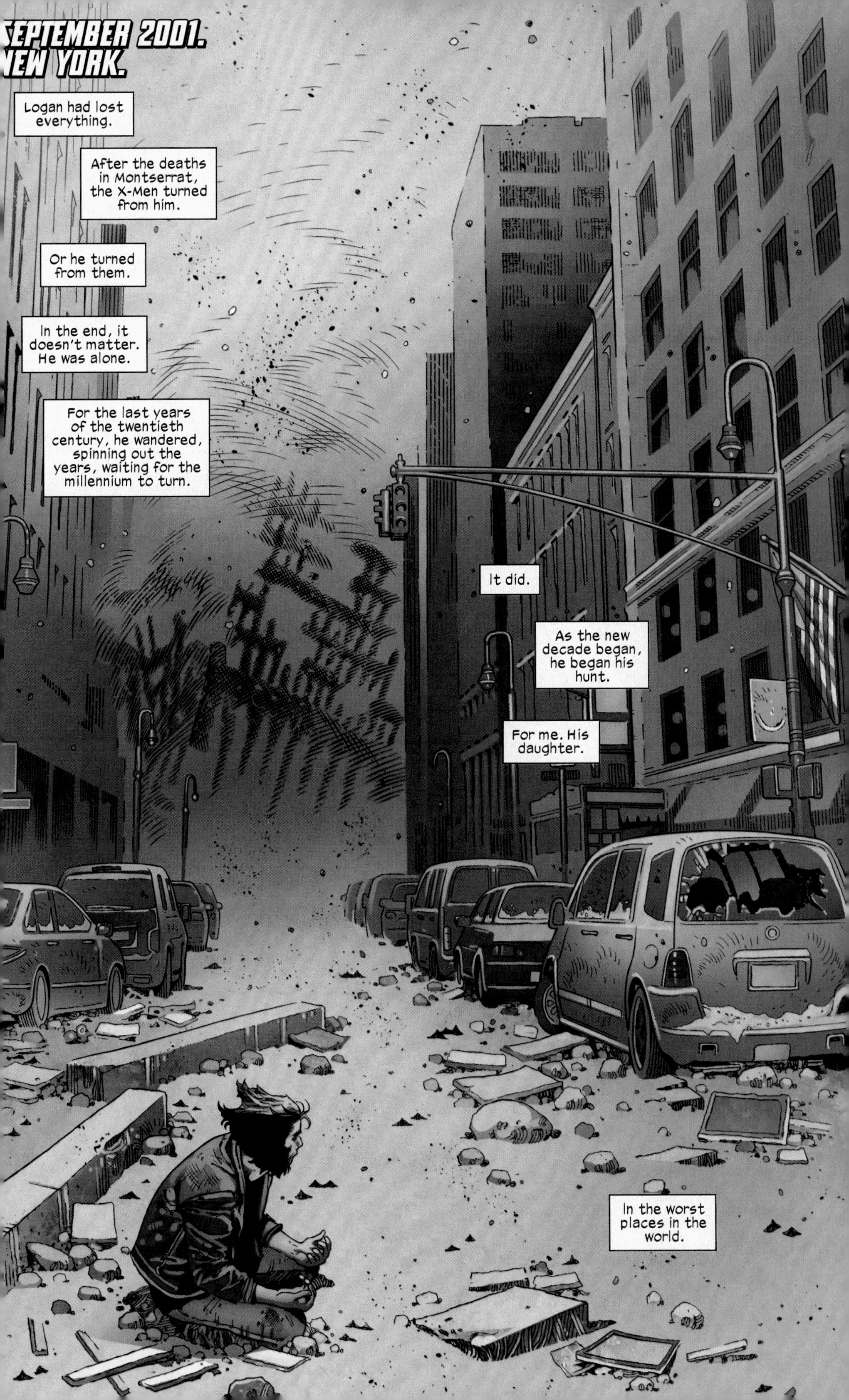
SEPTEMBER 2001.
NEW YORK.
Logan had lost everything.
After the deaths in Montserrat, the X-Men turned from him.
Or he turned from them.
In the end, it doesn't matter. He was alone.
For the last years of the twentieth century, he wandered, spinning out the years, waiting for the millennium to turn.
It did.
As the new decade began, he began his hunt.
For me. His daughter.
In the worst places in the world.

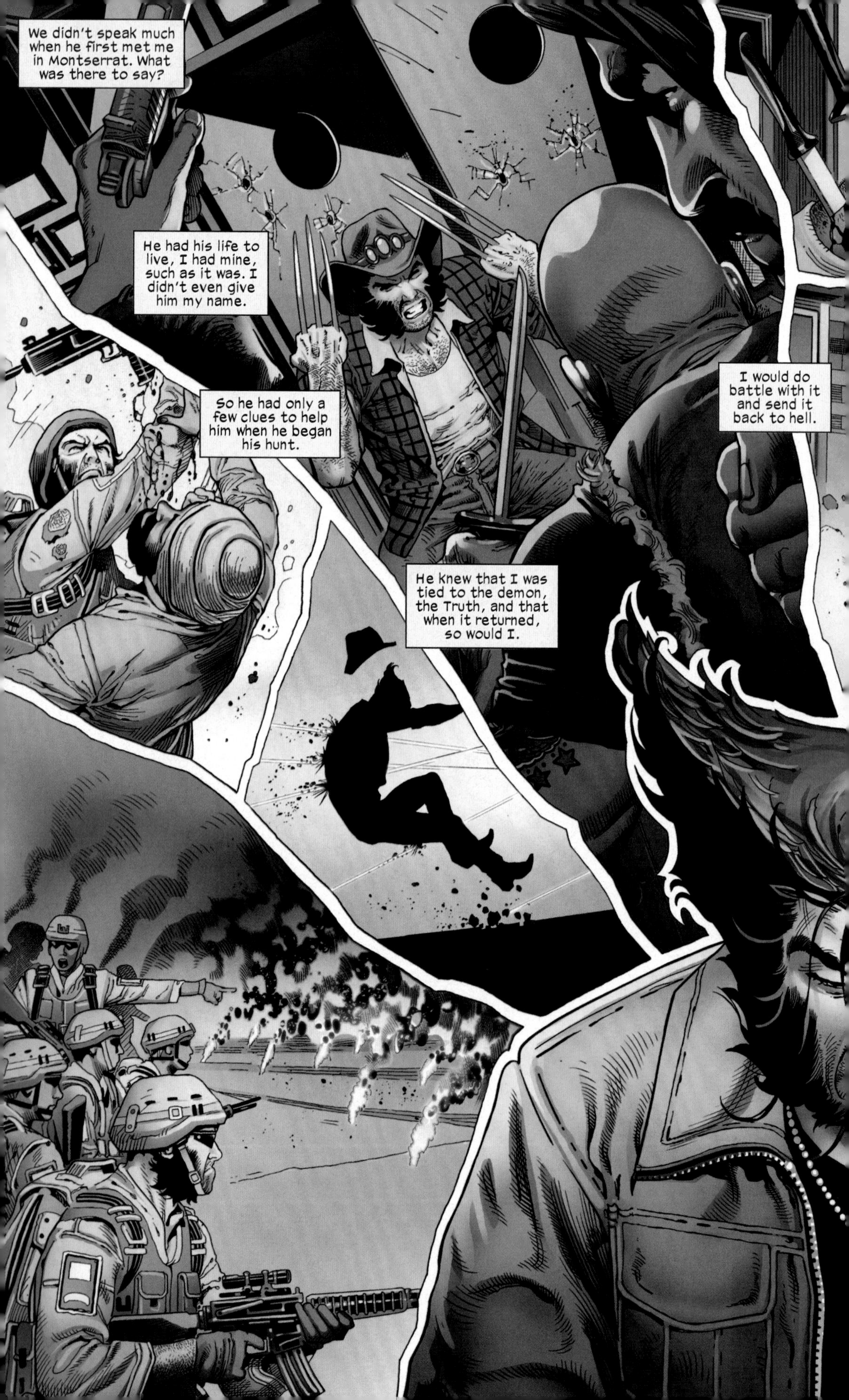
We didn't speak much when he first met me in Montserrat. What was there to say?
He had his life to live, I had mine, such as it was. I didn't even give him my name.
So he had only a few clues to help him when he began his hunt.
He knew that I was tied to the demon, the Truth, and that when it returned, so would I.
I would do battle with it and send it back to hell.

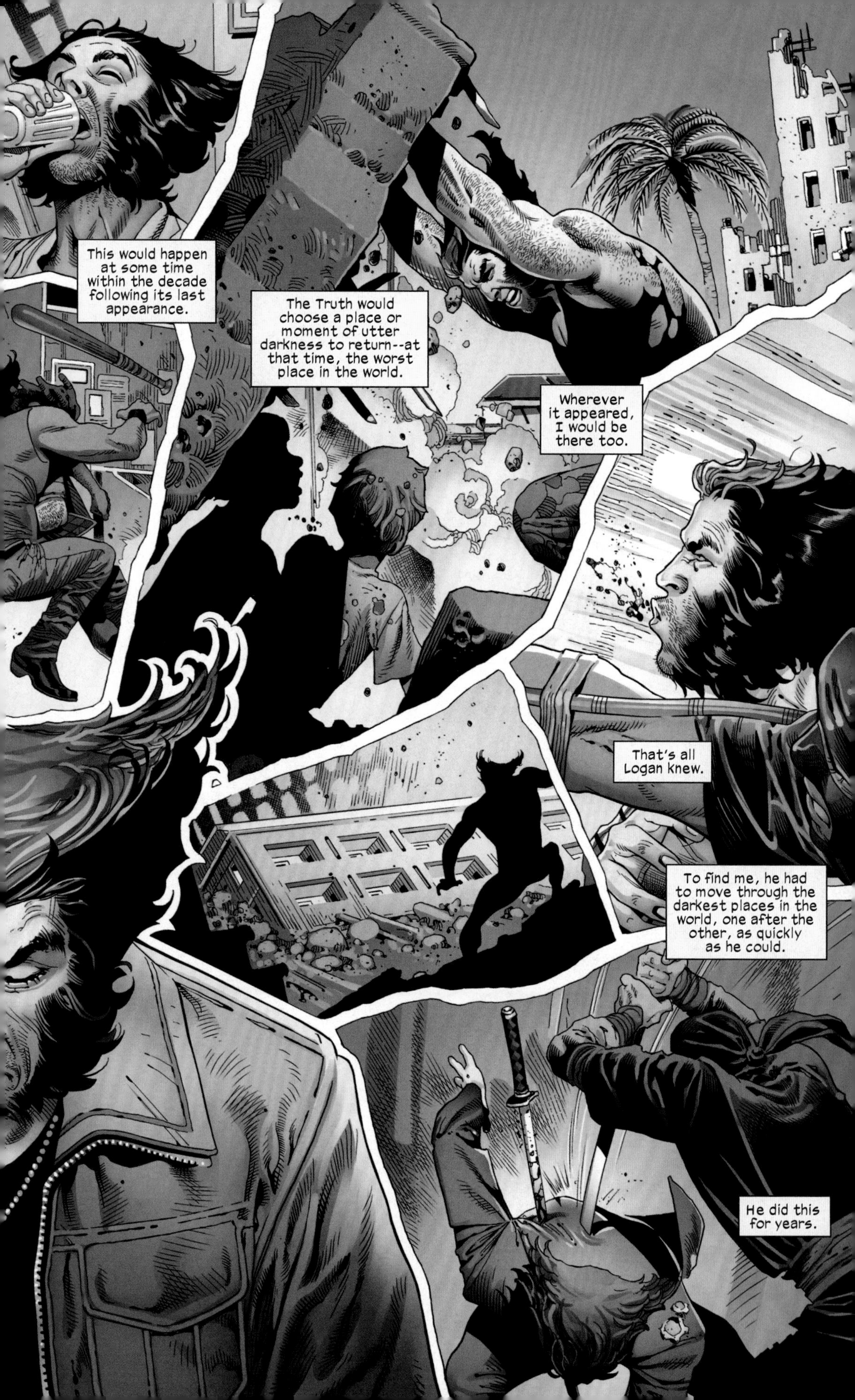
This would happen at some time within the decade following its last appearance.
The Truth would choose a place or moment of utter darkness to return--at that time, the worst place in the world.
Wherever it appeared, I would be there too.
That's all Logan knew.
To find me, he had to move through the darkest places in the world, one after the other, as quickly as he could.
He did this for years.

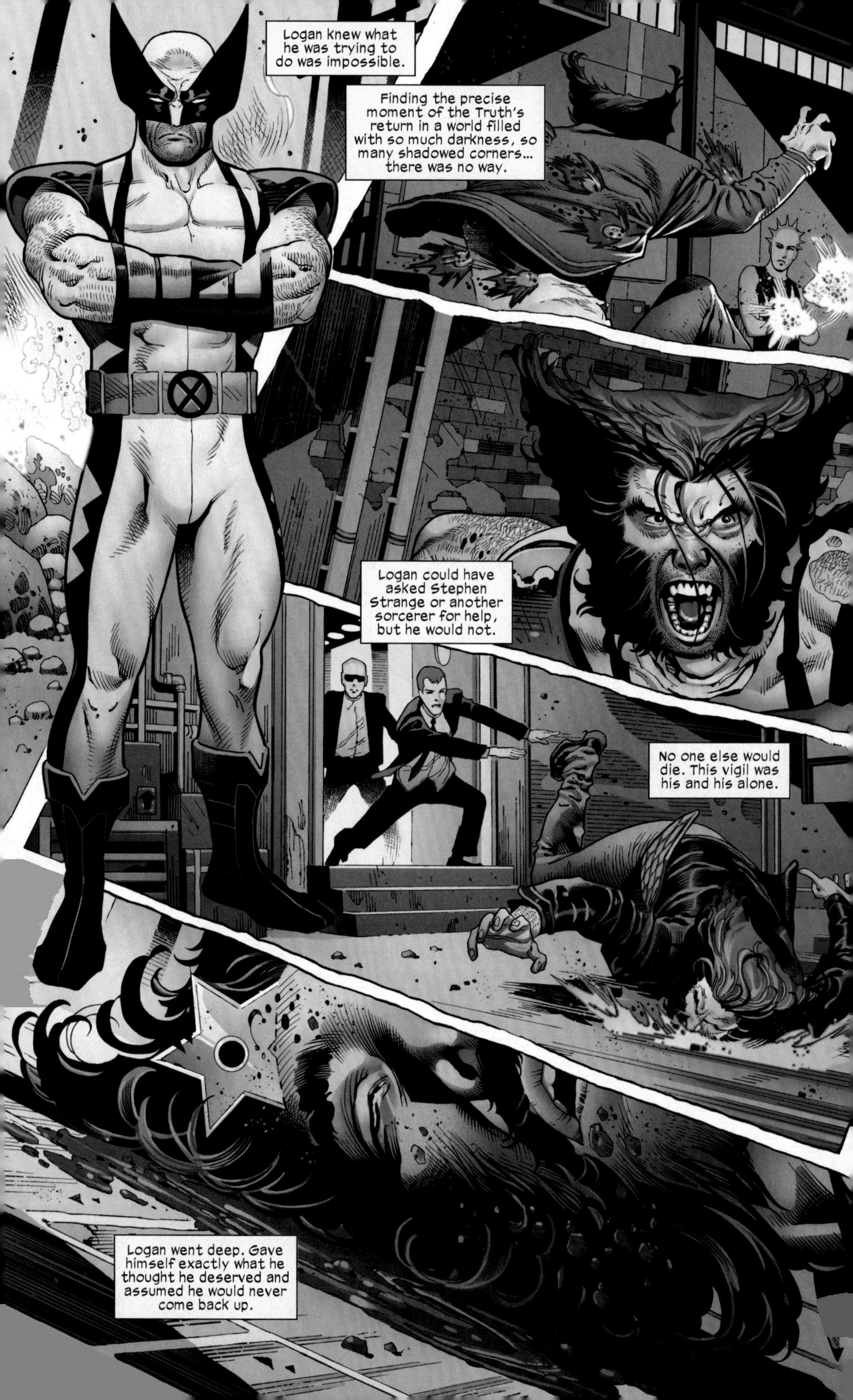
Logan knew what he was trying to do was impossible.
Finding the precise moment of the Truth's return in a world filled with so much darkness, so many shadowed corners... there was no way.
Logan could have asked Stephen Strange or another sorcerer for help, but he would not.
No one else would die. This vigil was his and his alone.
Logan went deep. Gave himself exactly what he thought he deserved and assumed he would never come back up.

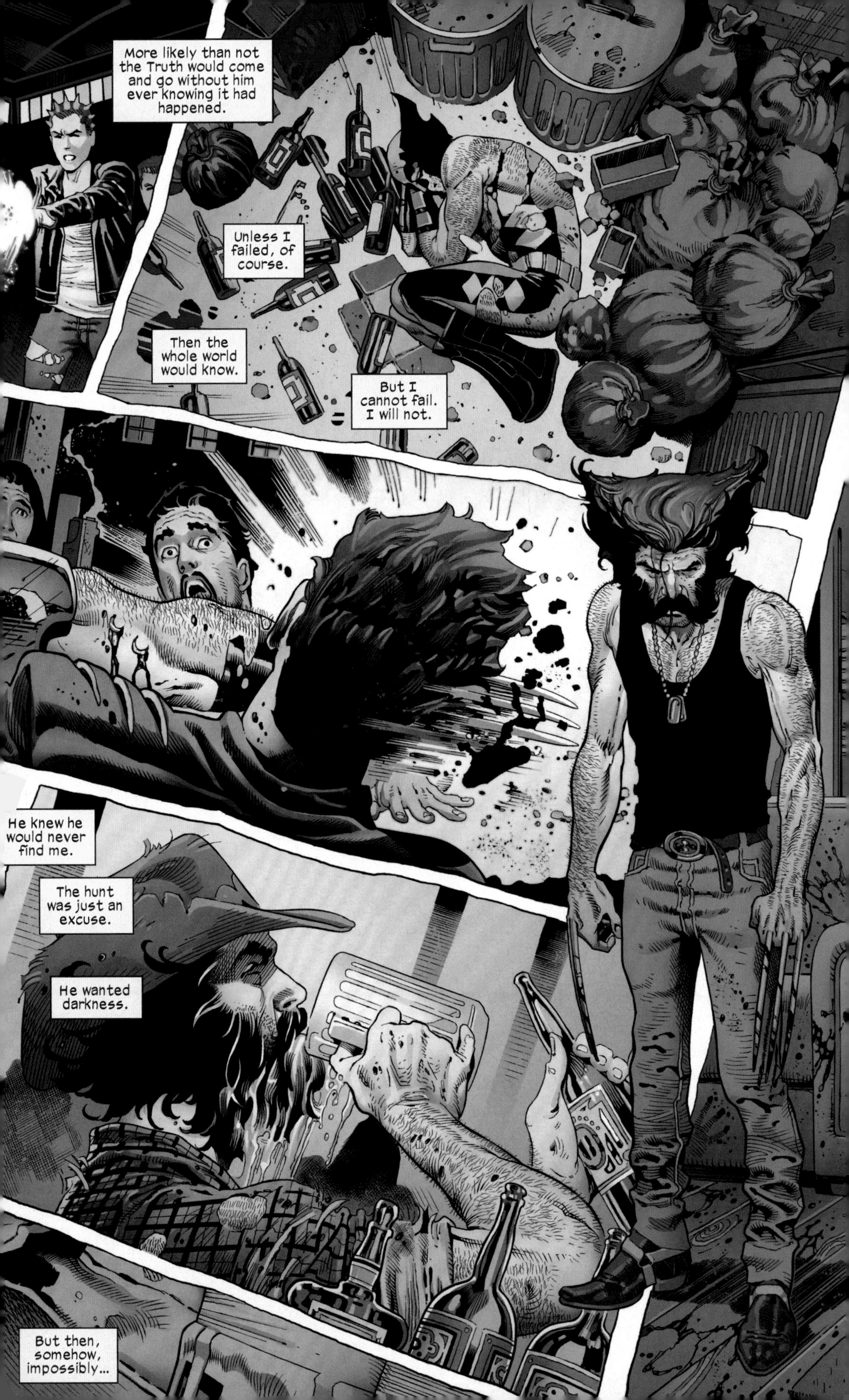
More likely than not the Truth would come and go without him ever knowing it had happened.
Unless I failed, of course.
Then the whole world would know.
But I cannot fail. I will not.
He knew he would never find me.
The hunt was just an excuse.
He wanted darkness.
But then, somehow, impossibly...

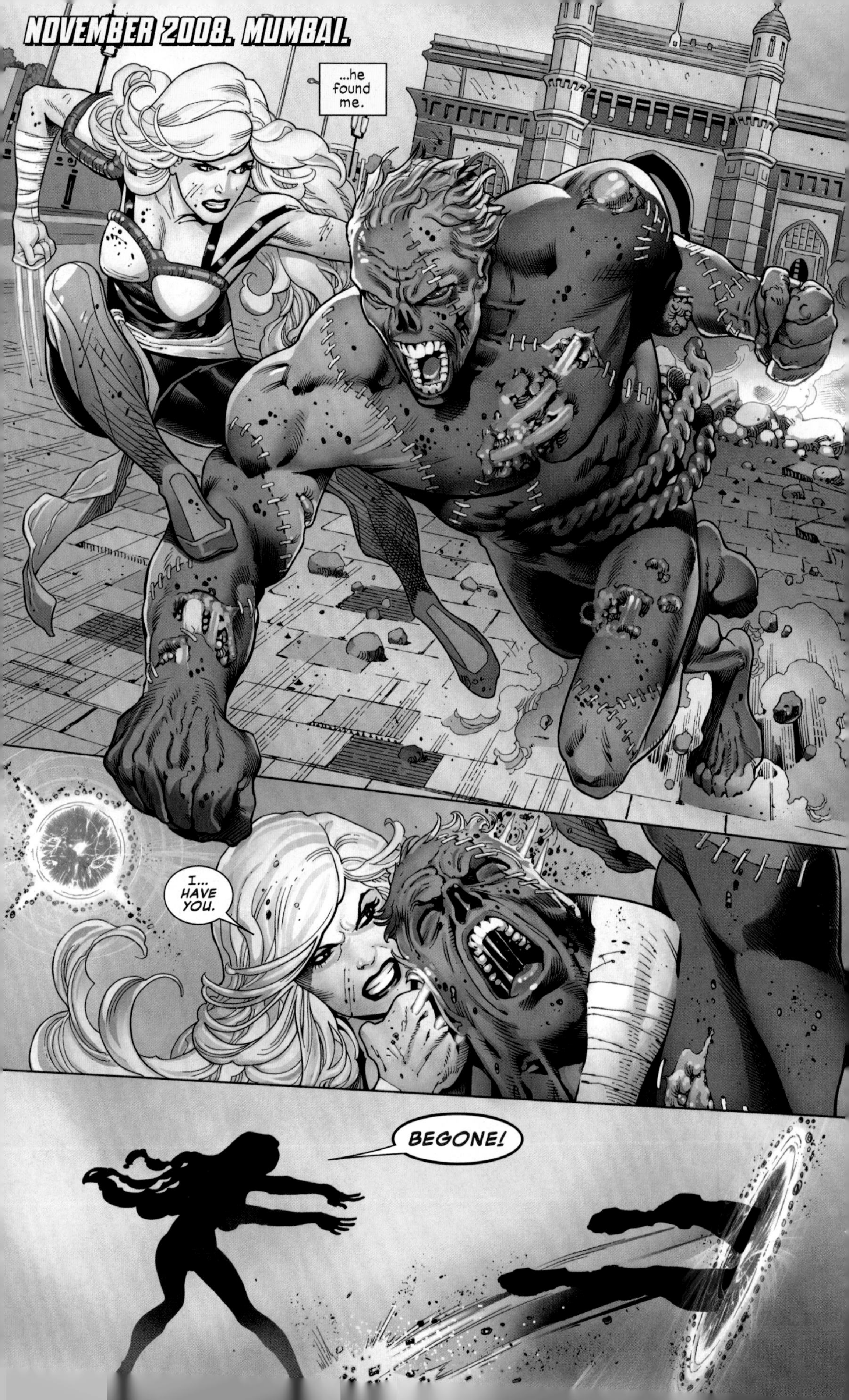
NOVEMBER 2008. MUMBAI.
...he found me.
I... HAVE YOU.
BEGONE!

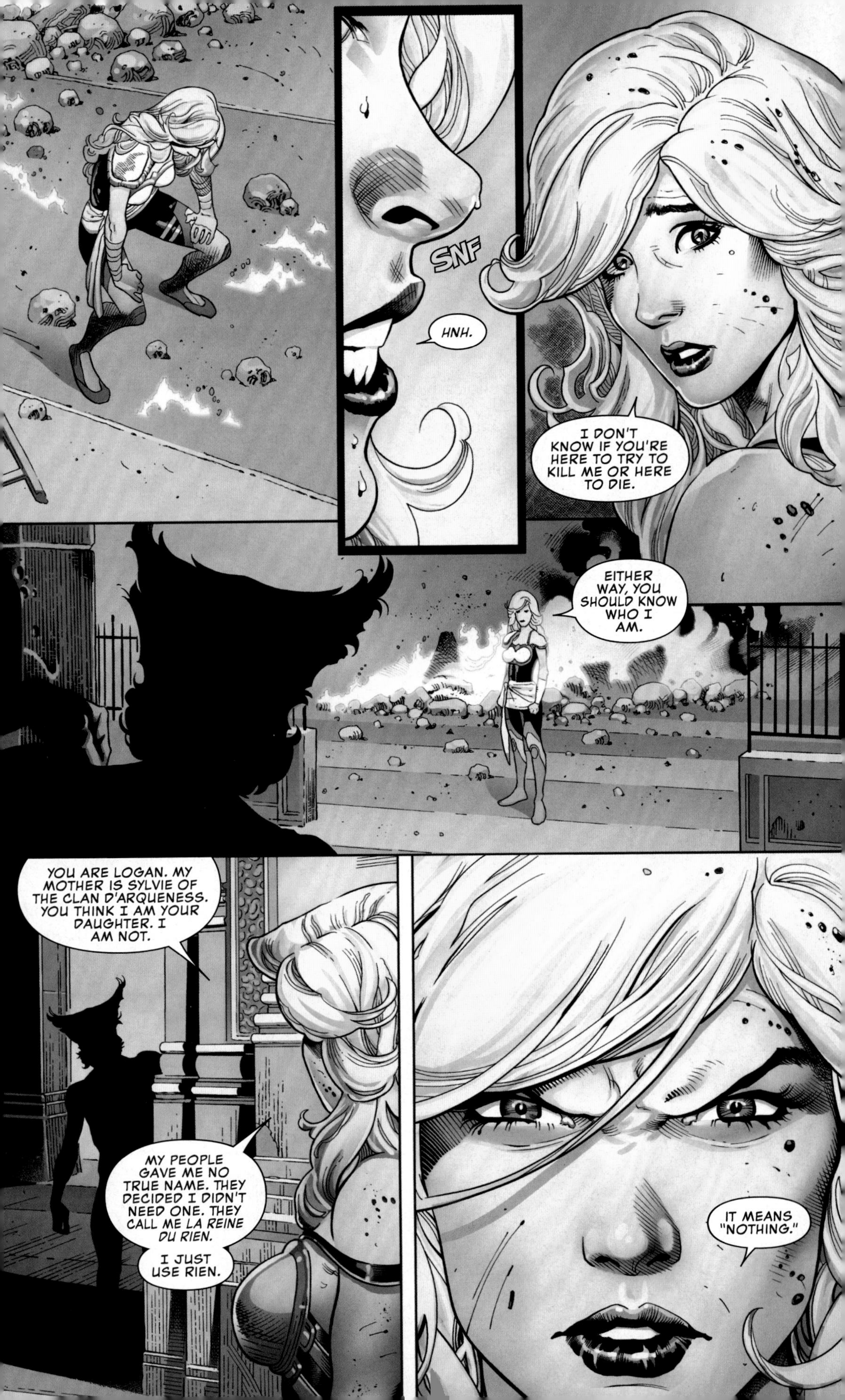
SNF
HNH.
I DON'T KNOW IF YOU'RE HERE TO TRY TO KILL ME OR HERE TO DIE.
EITHER WAY, YOU SHOULD KNOW WHO I AM.
YOU ARE LOGAN. MY MOTHER IS SYLVIE OF THE CLAN D'ARQUENESS. YOU THINK I AM YOUR DAUGHTER. I AM NOT.
MY PEOPLE GAVE ME NO TRUE NAME. THEY DECIDED I DIDN'T NEED ONE. THEY CALL ME LA REINE DU RIEN.
I JUST USE RIEN.
IT MEANS "NOTHING."

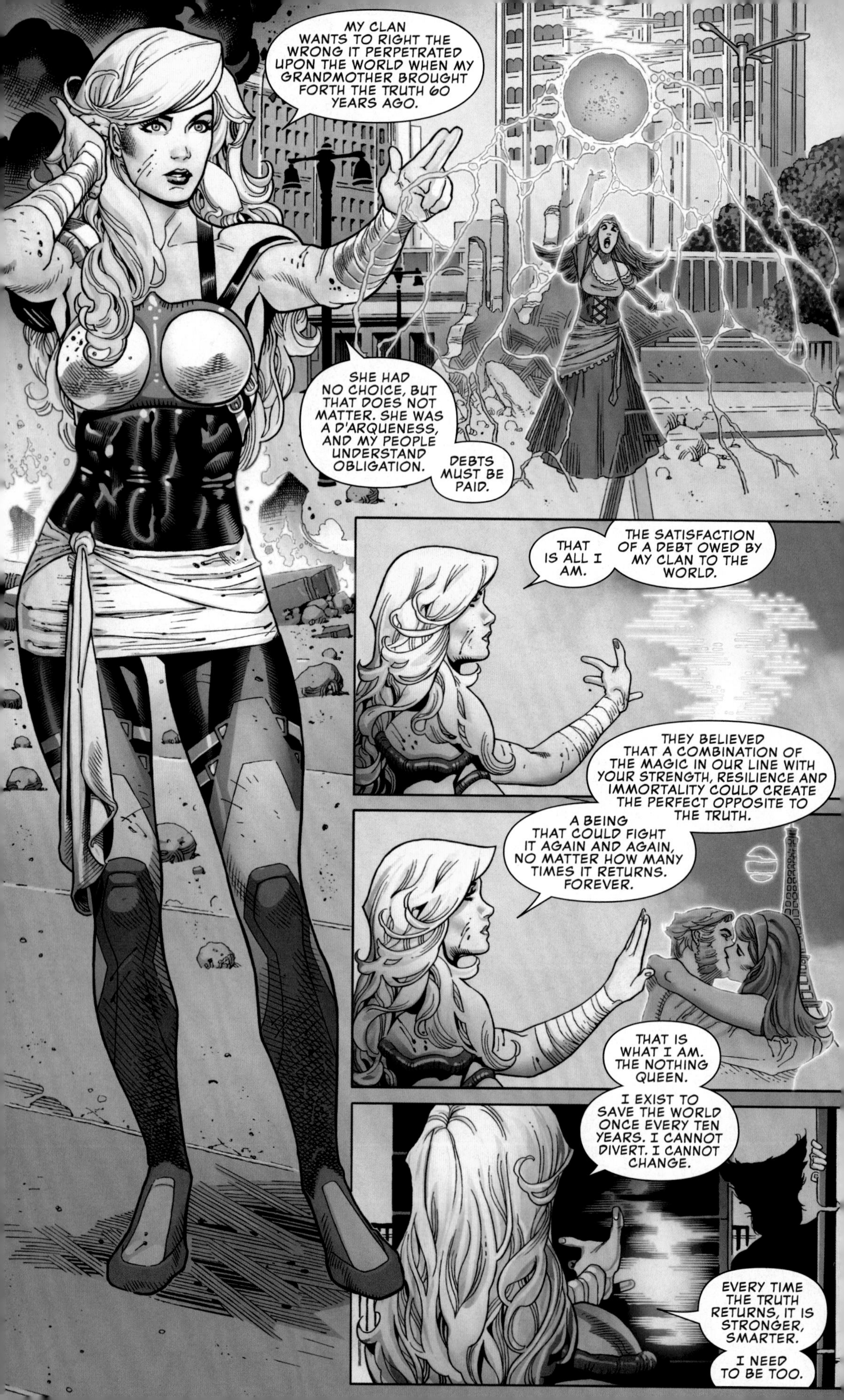
MY CLAN WANTS TO RIGHT THE WRONG IT PERPETRATED UPON THE WORLD WHEN MY GRANDMOTHER BROUGHT FORTH THE TRUTH 60 YEARS AGO.
SHE HAD NO CHOICE, BUT THAT DOES NOT MATTER. SHE WAS A D'ARQUENESS, AND MY PEOPLE UNDERSTAND OBLIGATION.
DEBTS MUST BE PAID.
THAT IS ALL I AM.
THE SATISFACTION OF A DEBT OWED BY MY CLAN TO THE WORLD.
THEY BELIEVED THAT A COMBINATION OF THE MAGIC IN OUR LINE WITH YOUR STRENGTH, RESILIENCE AND IMMORTALITY COULD CREATE THE PERFECT OPPOSITE TO THE TRUTH.
A BEING THAT COULD FIGHT IT AGAIN AND AGAIN, NO MATTER HOW MANY TIMES IT RETURNS. FOREVER.
THAT IS WHAT I AM. THE NOTHING QUEEN.
I EXIST TO SAVE THE WORLD ONCE EVERY TEN YEARS. I CANNOT DIVERT. I CANNOT CHANGE.
EVERY TIME THE TRUTH RETURNS, IT IS STRONGER, SMARTER.
I NEED TO BE TOO.

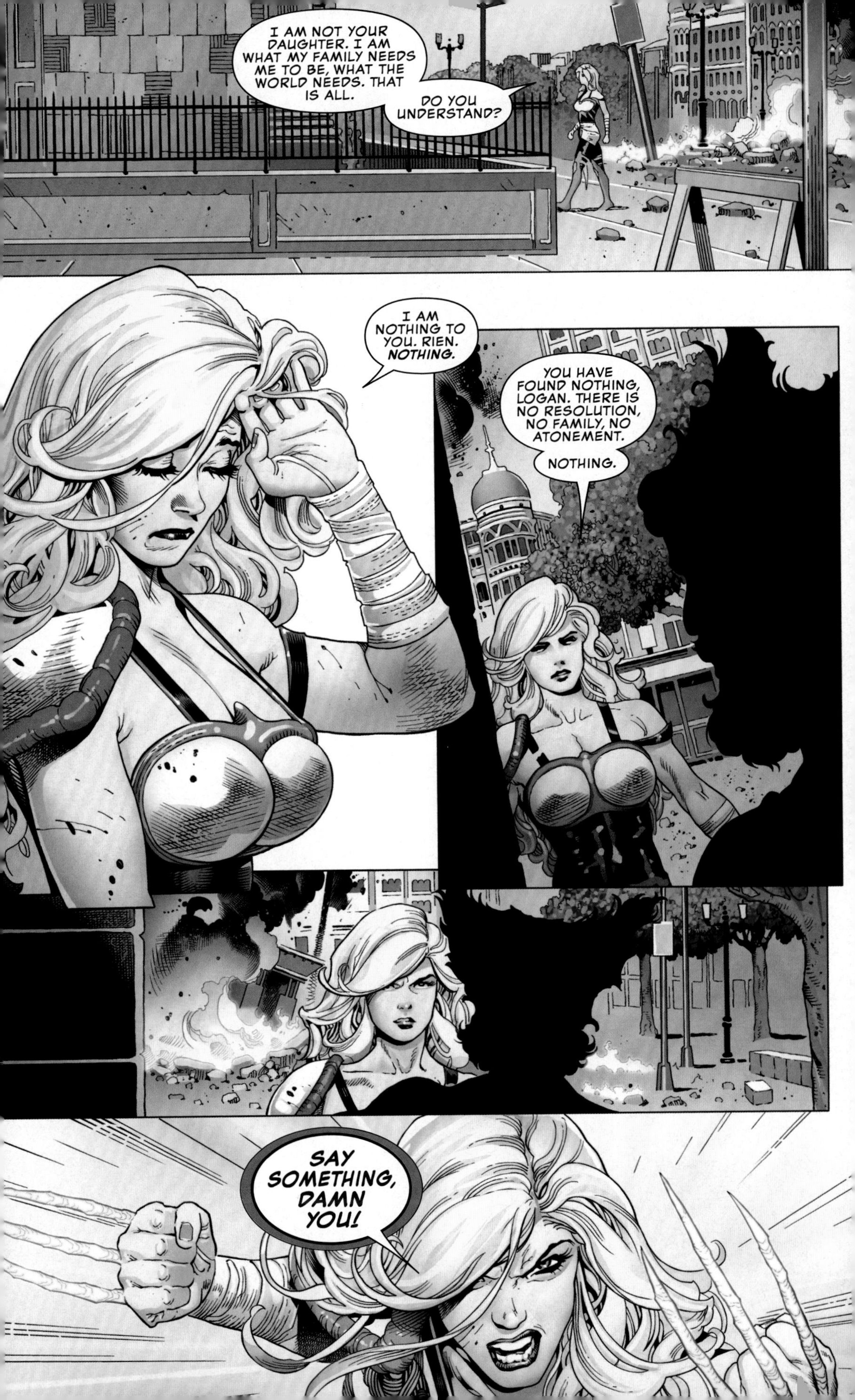
I AM NOT YOUR DAUGHTER. I AM WHAT MY FAMILY NEEDS ME TO BE, WHAT THE WORLD NEEDS. THAT IS ALL.
DO YOU UNDERSTAND?
I AM NOTHING TO YOU. RIEN. *NOTHING.*
YOU HAVE FOUND NOTHING, LOGAN. THERE IS NO RESOLUTION, NO FAMILY, NO ATONEMENT.
NOTHING.
SAY SOMETHING, DAMN YOU!

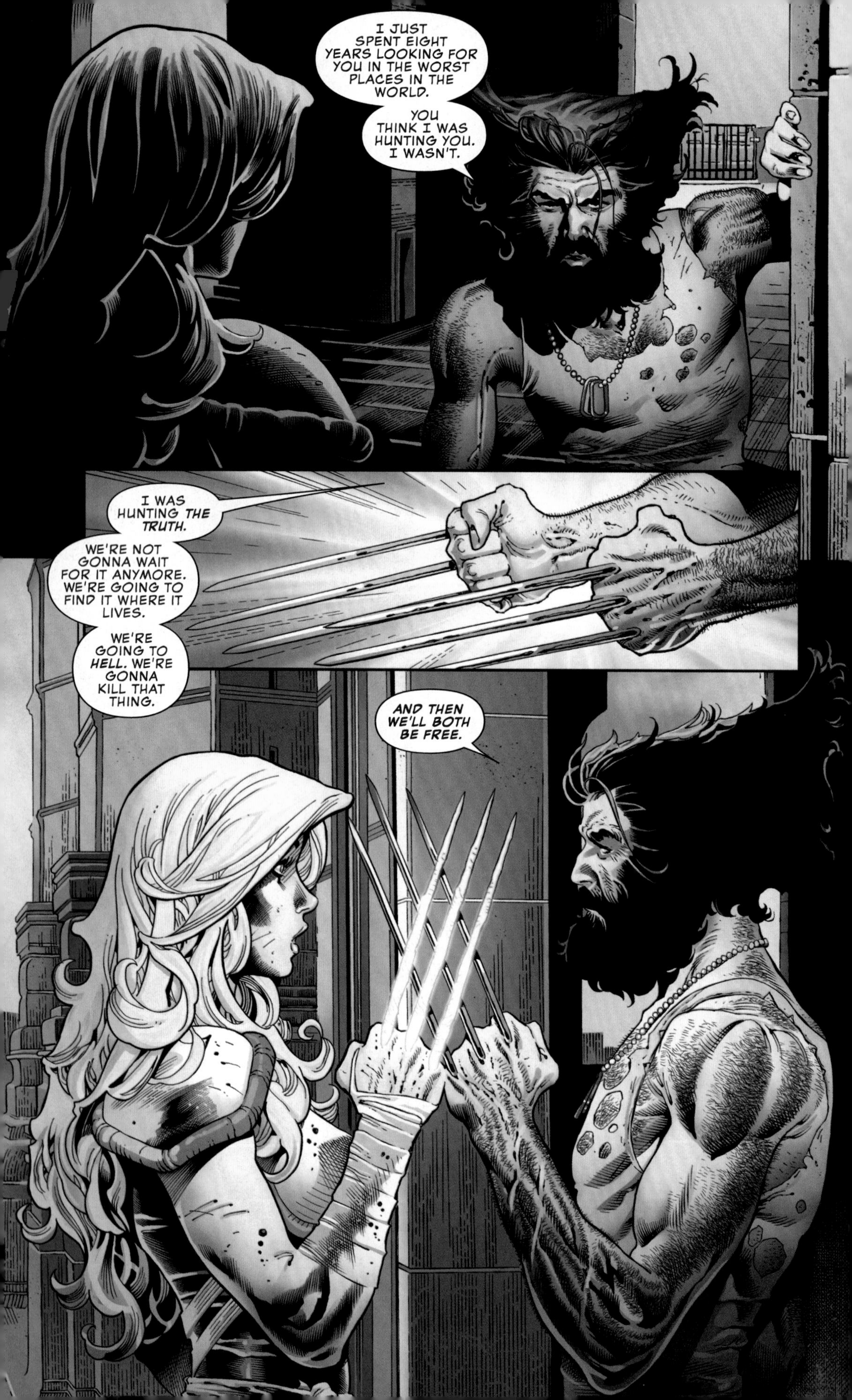
I JUST SPENT EIGHT YEARS LOOKING FOR YOU IN THE WORST PLACES IN THE WORLD.
YOU THINK I WAS HUNTING YOU. I WASN'T.
I WAS HUNTING *THE TRUTH.*
WE'RE NOT GONNA WAIT FOR IT ANYMORE. WE'RE GOING TO FIND IT WHERE IT LIVES.
WE'RE GOING TO *HELL.* WE'RE GONNA KILL THAT THING.
AND THEN WE'LL BOTH BE FREE.

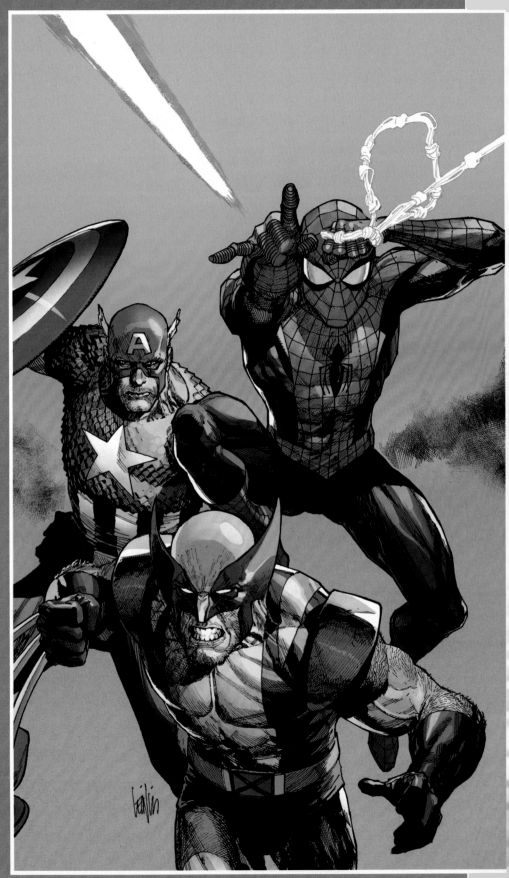

#3 variant by **LEINIL FRANCIS YU** & **SUNNY GHO**

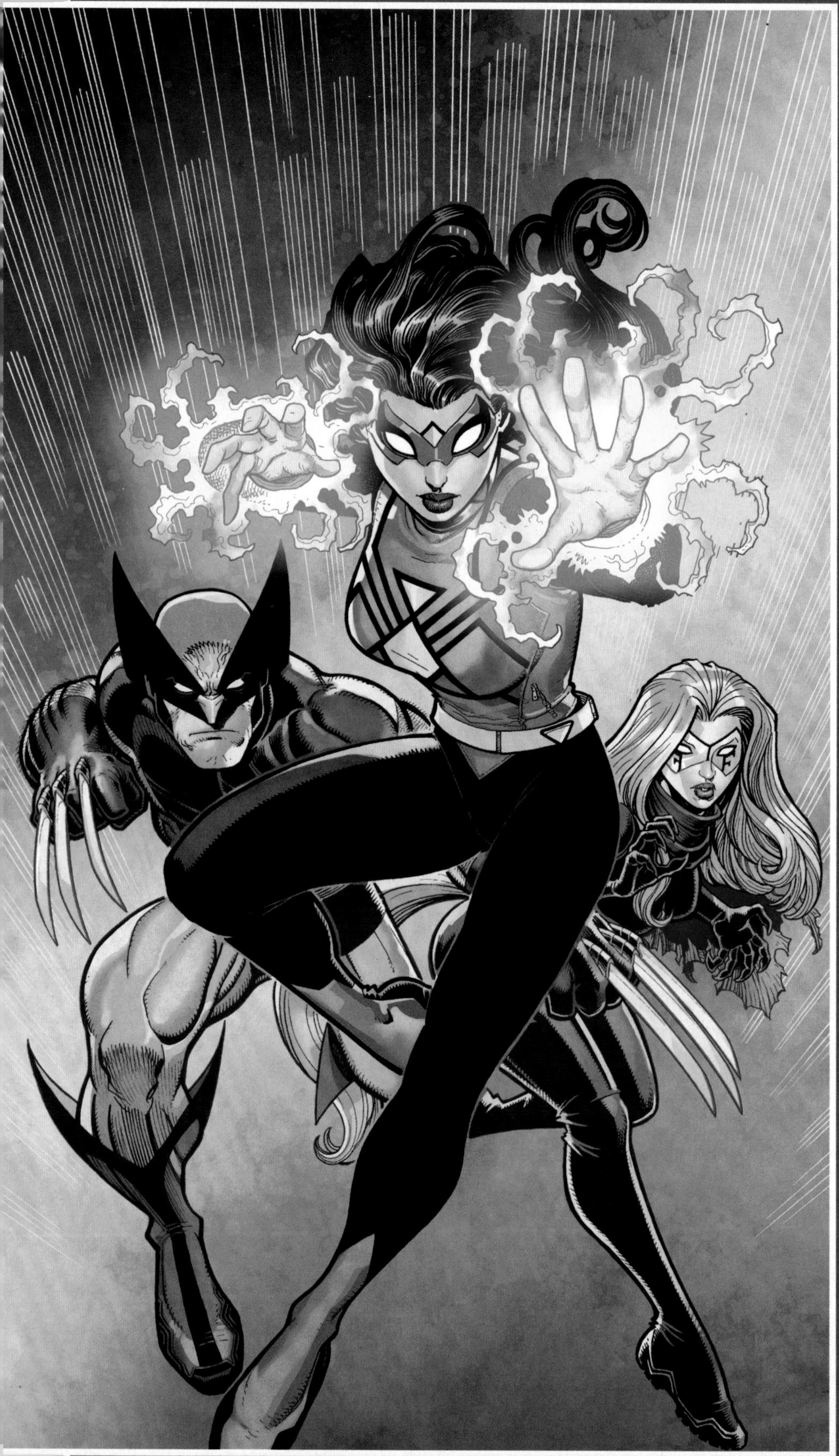

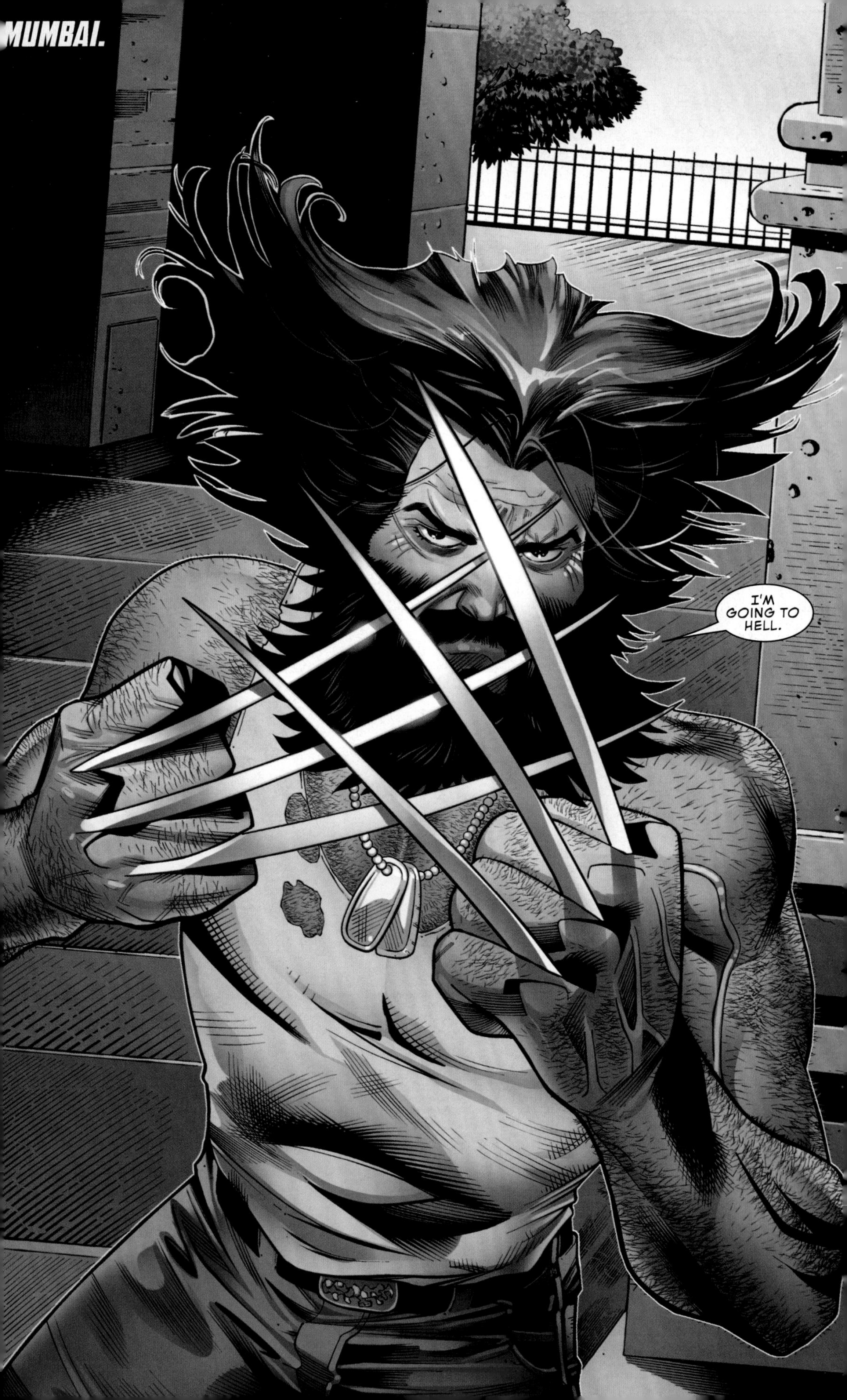
MUMBAI.
I'M GOING TO HELL.

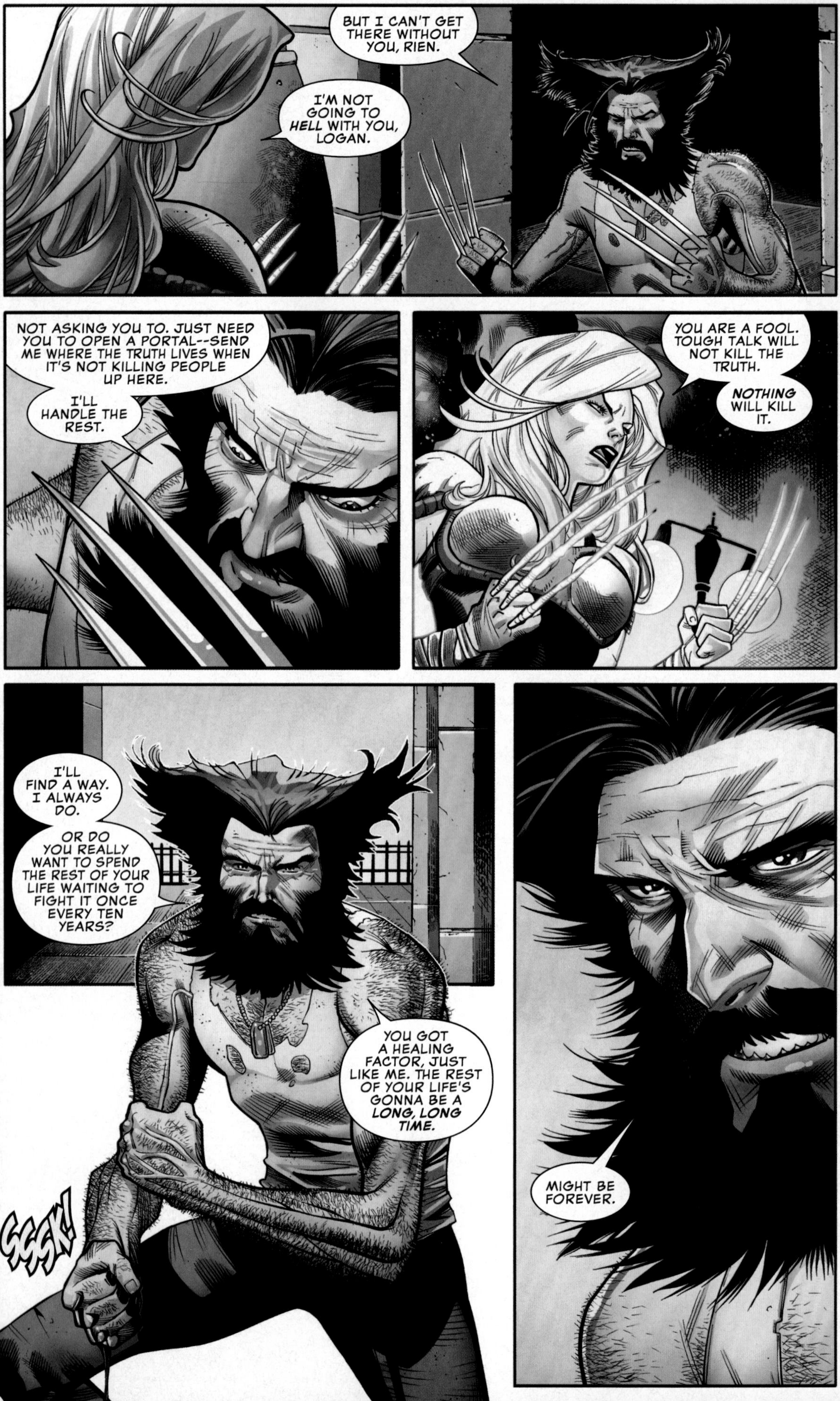
BUT I CAN'T GET THERE WITHOUT YOU, RIEN.
I'M NOT GOING TO HELL WITH YOU, LOGAN.
NOT ASKING YOU TO. JUST NEED YOU TO OPEN A PORTAL--SEND ME WHERE THE TRUTH LIVES WHEN IT'S NOT KILLING PEOPLE UP HERE.
I'LL HANDLE THE REST.
YOU ARE A FOOL. TOUGH TALK WILL NOT KILL THE TRUTH.
NOTHING WILL KILL IT.
I'LL FIND A WAY. I ALWAYS DO.
OR DO YOU REALLY WANT TO SPEND THE REST OF YOUR LIFE WAITING TO FIGHT IT ONCE EVERY TEN YEARS?
YOU GOT A HEALING FACTOR, JUST LIKE ME. THE REST OF YOUR LIFE'S GONNA BE A LONG, LONG TIME.
SSSK!
MIGHT BE FOREVER.

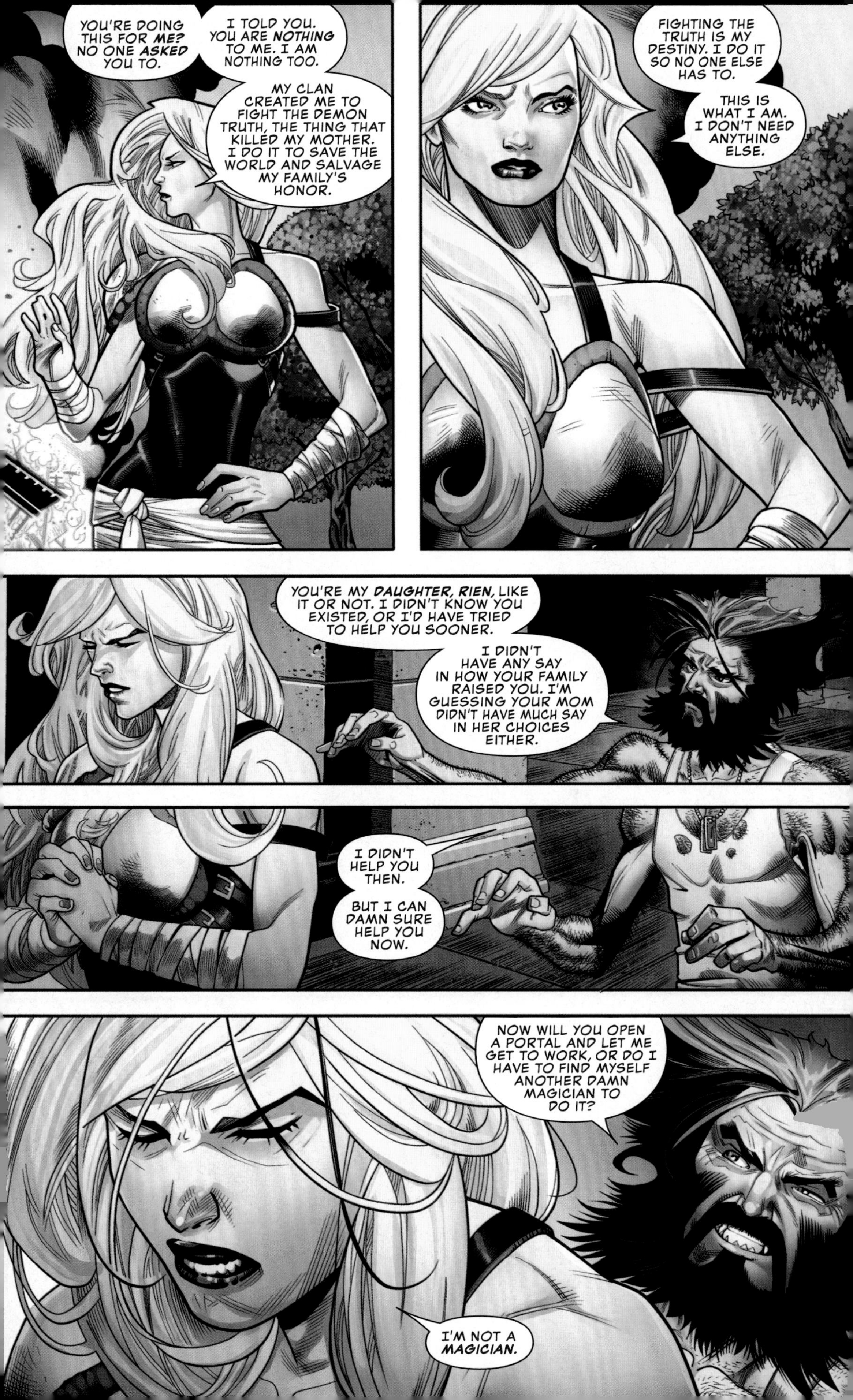

YOU'RE DOING THIS FOR ME? NO ONE ASKED YOU TO.
I TOLD YOU. YOU ARE NOTHING TO ME. I AM NOTHING TOO.
MY CLAN CREATED ME TO FIGHT THE DEMON TRUTH, THE THING THAT KILLED MY MOTHER. I DO IT TO SAVE THE WORLD AND SALVAGE MY FAMILY'S HONOR.
FIGHTING THE TRUTH IS MY DESTINY. I DO IT SO NO ONE ELSE HAS TO.
THIS IS WHAT I AM. I DON'T NEED ANYTHING ELSE.
YOU'RE MY DAUGHTER, RIEN, LIKE IT OR NOT. I DIDN'T KNOW YOU EXISTED, OR I'D HAVE TRIED TO HELP YOU SOONER.
I DIDN'T HAVE ANY SAY IN HOW YOUR FAMILY RAISED YOU. I'M GUESSING YOUR MOM DIDN'T HAVE MUCH SAY IN HER CHOICES EITHER.
I DIDN'T HELP YOU THEN.
BUT I CAN DAMN SURE HELP YOU NOW.
NOW WILL YOU OPEN A PORTAL AND LET ME GET TO WORK, OR DO I HAVE TO FIND MYSELF ANOTHER DAMN MAGICIAN TO DO IT?
I'M NOT A MAGICIAN.

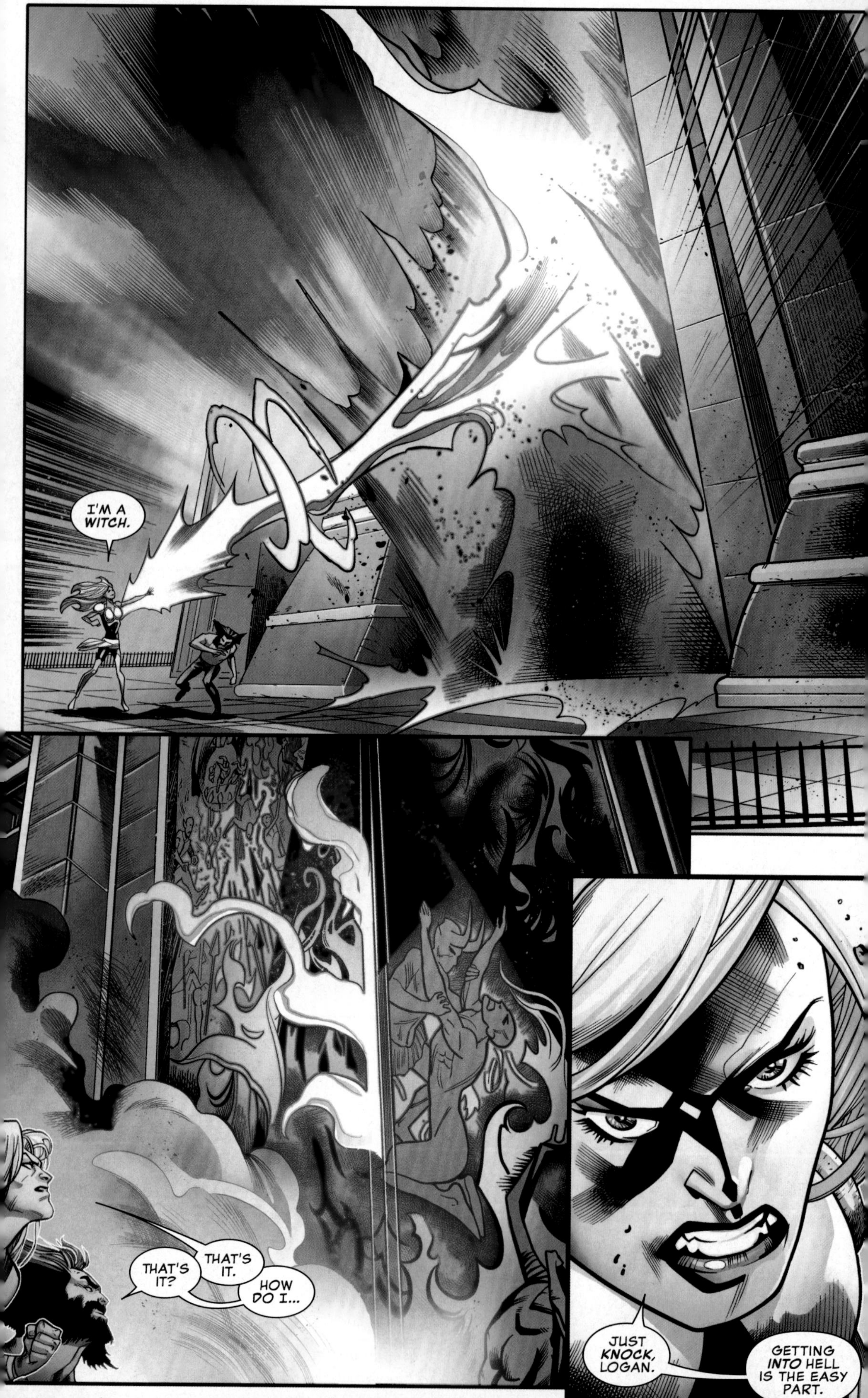
I'M A WITCH.
THAT'S IT?
THAT'S IT.
HOW DO I...
JUST KNOCK, LOGAN.
GETTING INTO HELL IS THE EASY PART.

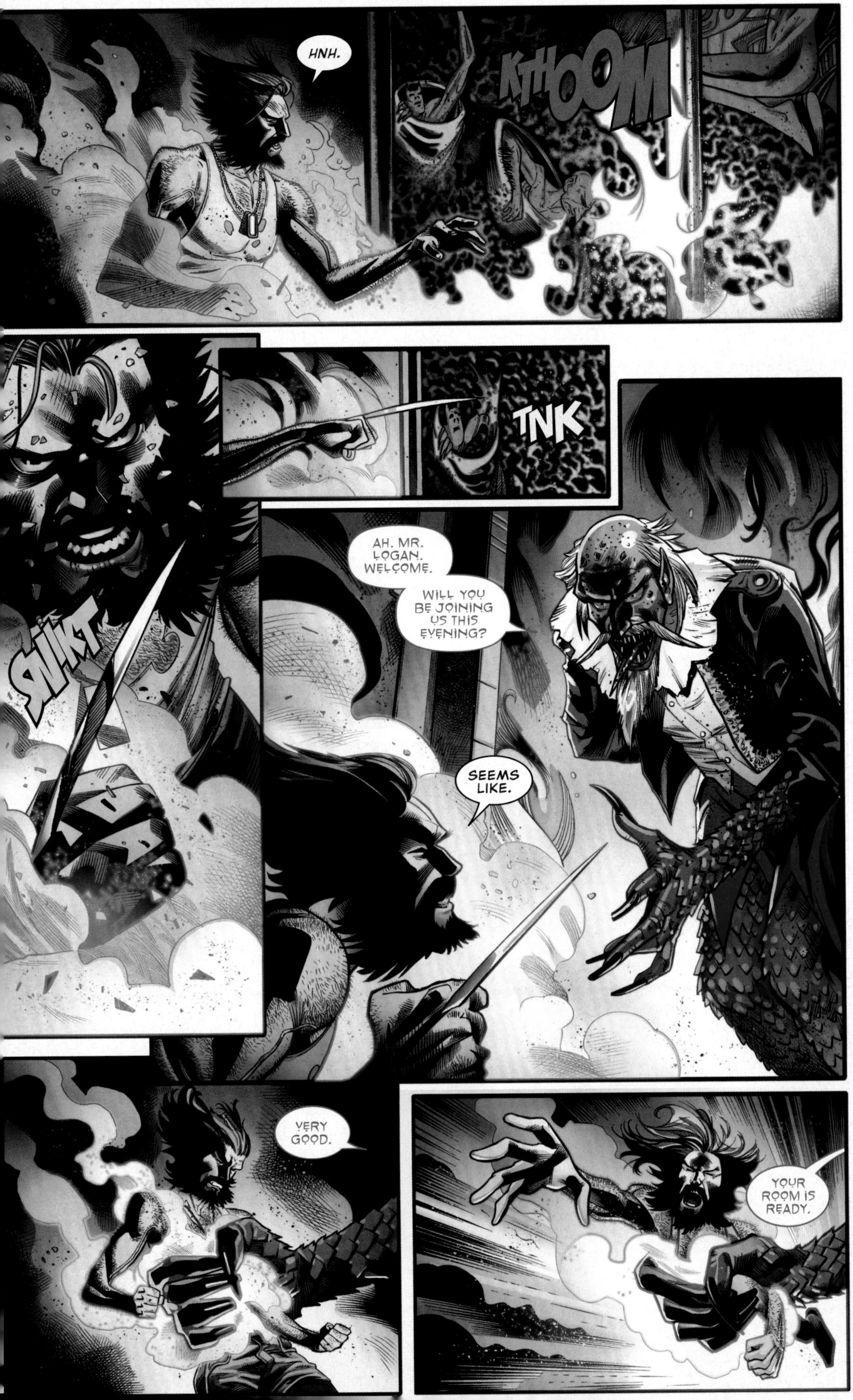
HNH.
KTHOOM
SNIKT
TNK
AH. MR. LOGAN. WELCOME.
WILL YOU BE JOINING US THIS EVENING?
SEEMS LIKE.
VERY GOOD.
YOUR ROOM IS READY.

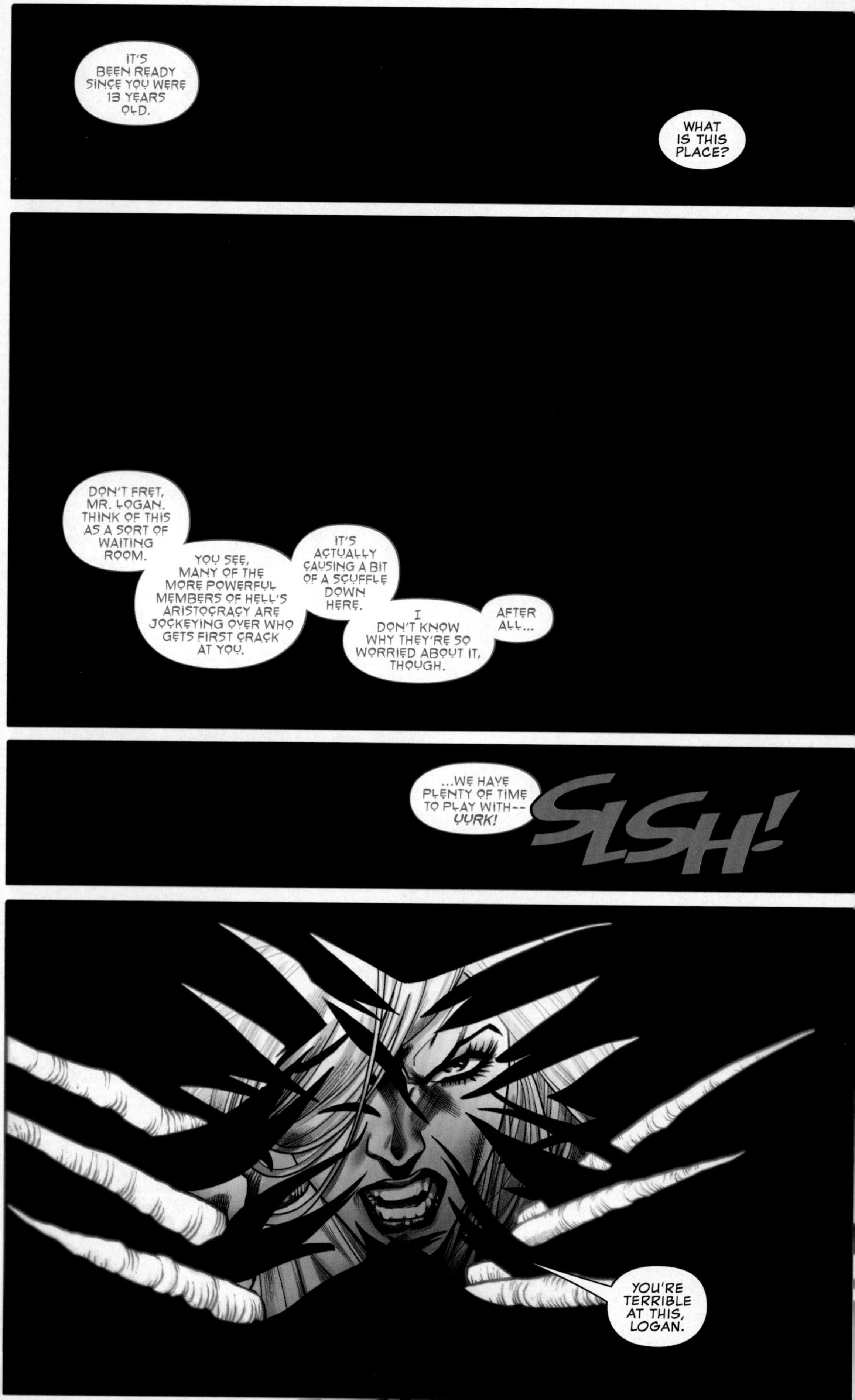
IT'S BEEN READY SINCE YOU WERE 13 YEARS OLD.
WHAT IS THIS PLACE?
DON'T FRET, MR. LOGAN. THINK OF THIS AS A SORT OF WAITING ROOM.
YOU SEE, MANY OF THE MORE POWERFUL MEMBERS OF HELL'S ARISTOCRACY ARE JOCKEYING OVER WHO GETS FIRST CRACK AT YOU.
IT'S ACTUALLY CAUSING A BIT OF A SCUFFLE DOWN HERE.
I DON'T KNOW WHY THEY'RE SO WORRIED ABOUT IT, THOUGH.
AFTER ALL...
...WE HAVE PLENTY OF TIME TO PLAY WITH-- UURK!
SLSH!
YOU'RE TERRIBLE AT THIS, LOGAN.

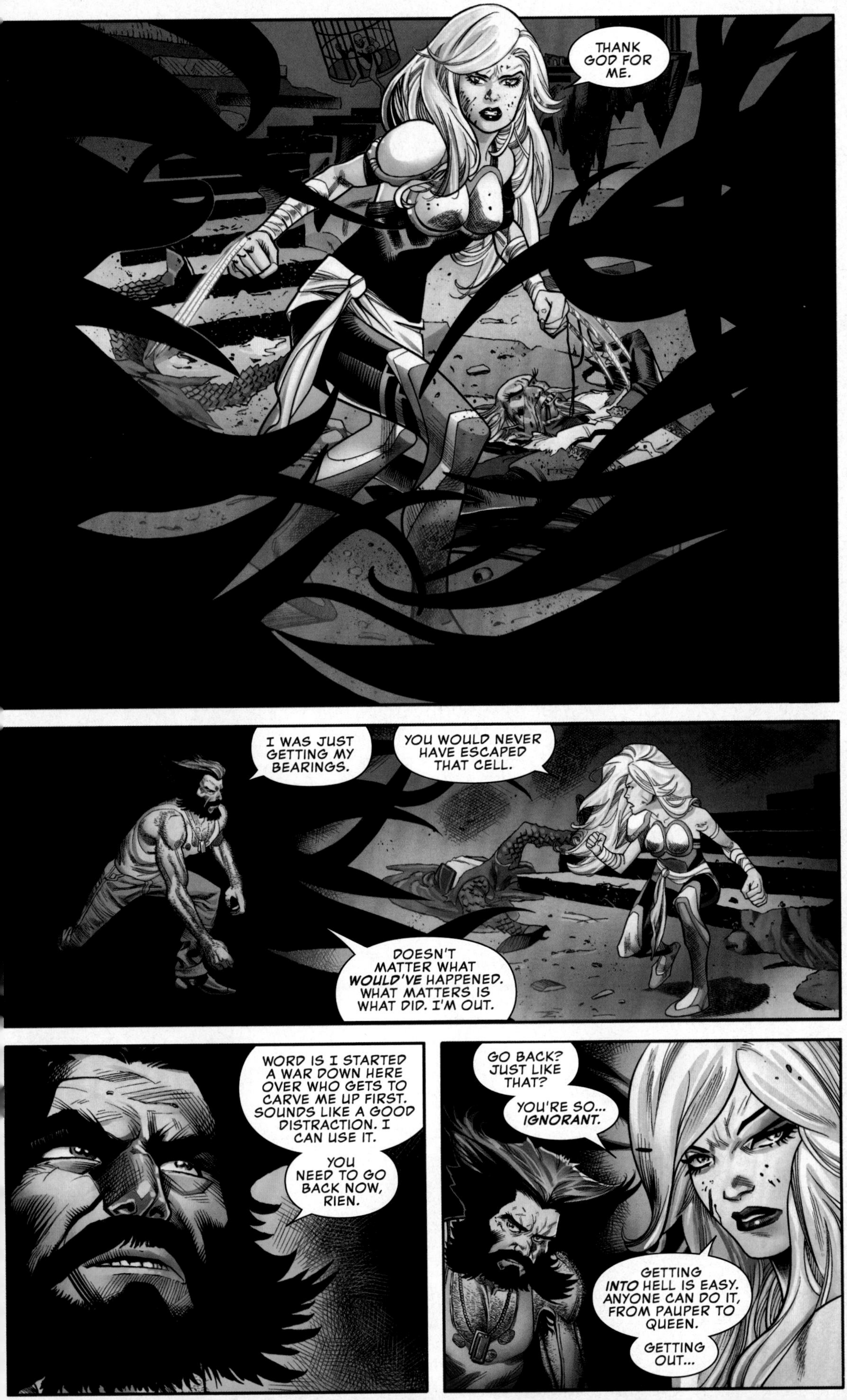
THANK GOD FOR ME.
I WAS JUST GETTING MY BEARINGS.
YOU WOULD NEVER HAVE ESCAPED THAT CELL.
DOESN'T MATTER WHAT *WOULD'VE* HAPPENED. WHAT MATTERS IS WHAT DID. I'M OUT.
WORD IS I STARTED A WAR DOWN HERE OVER WHO GETS TO CARVE ME UP FIRST. SOUNDS LIKE A GOOD DISTRACTION. I CAN USE IT.
YOU NEED TO GO BACK NOW, RIEN.
GO BACK? JUST LIKE THAT?
YOU'RE SO... *IGNORANT.*
GETTING *INTO* HELL IS EASY. ANYONE CAN DO IT, FROM PAUPER TO QUEEN.
GETTING OUT...

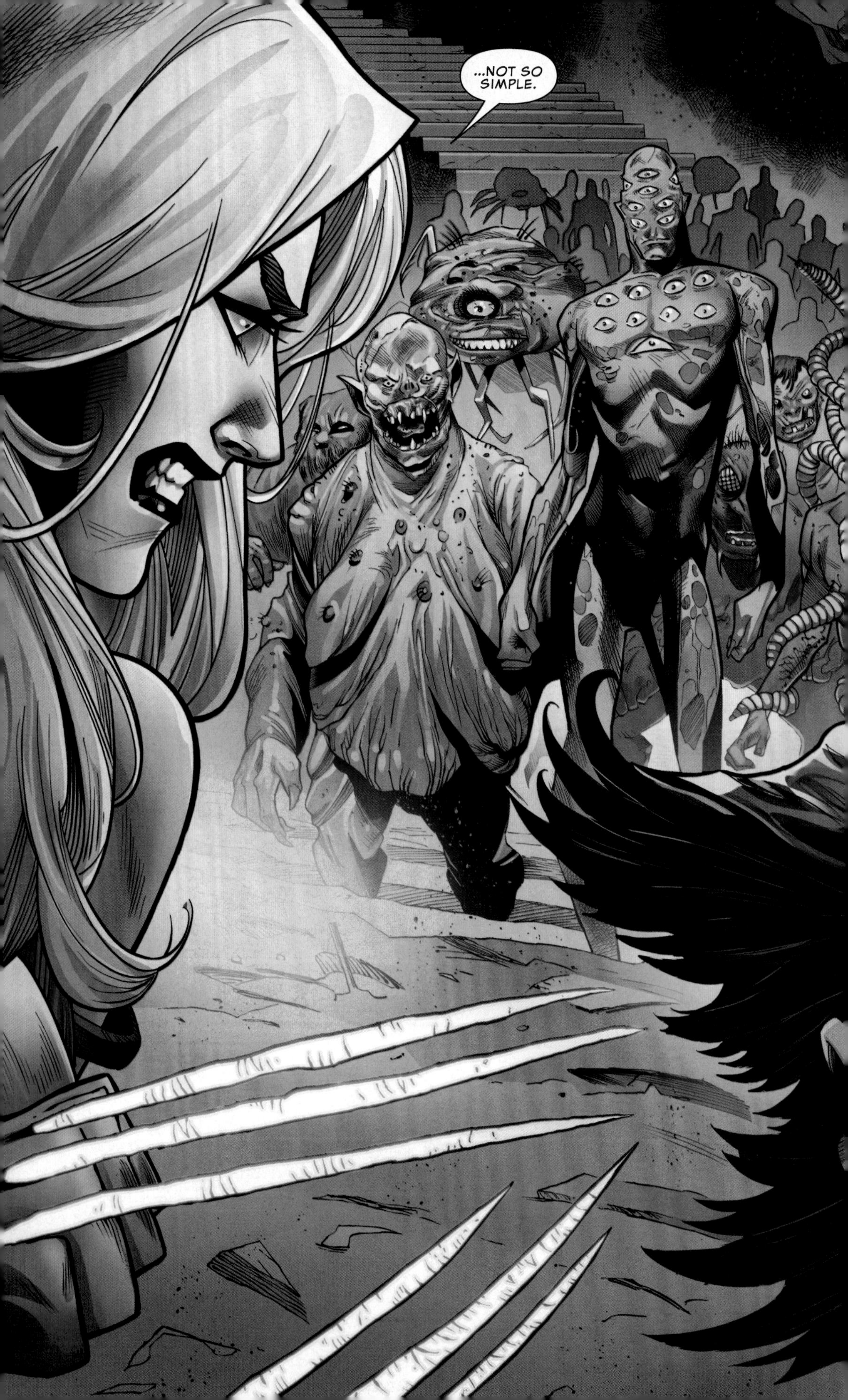
...NOT SO SIMPLE.

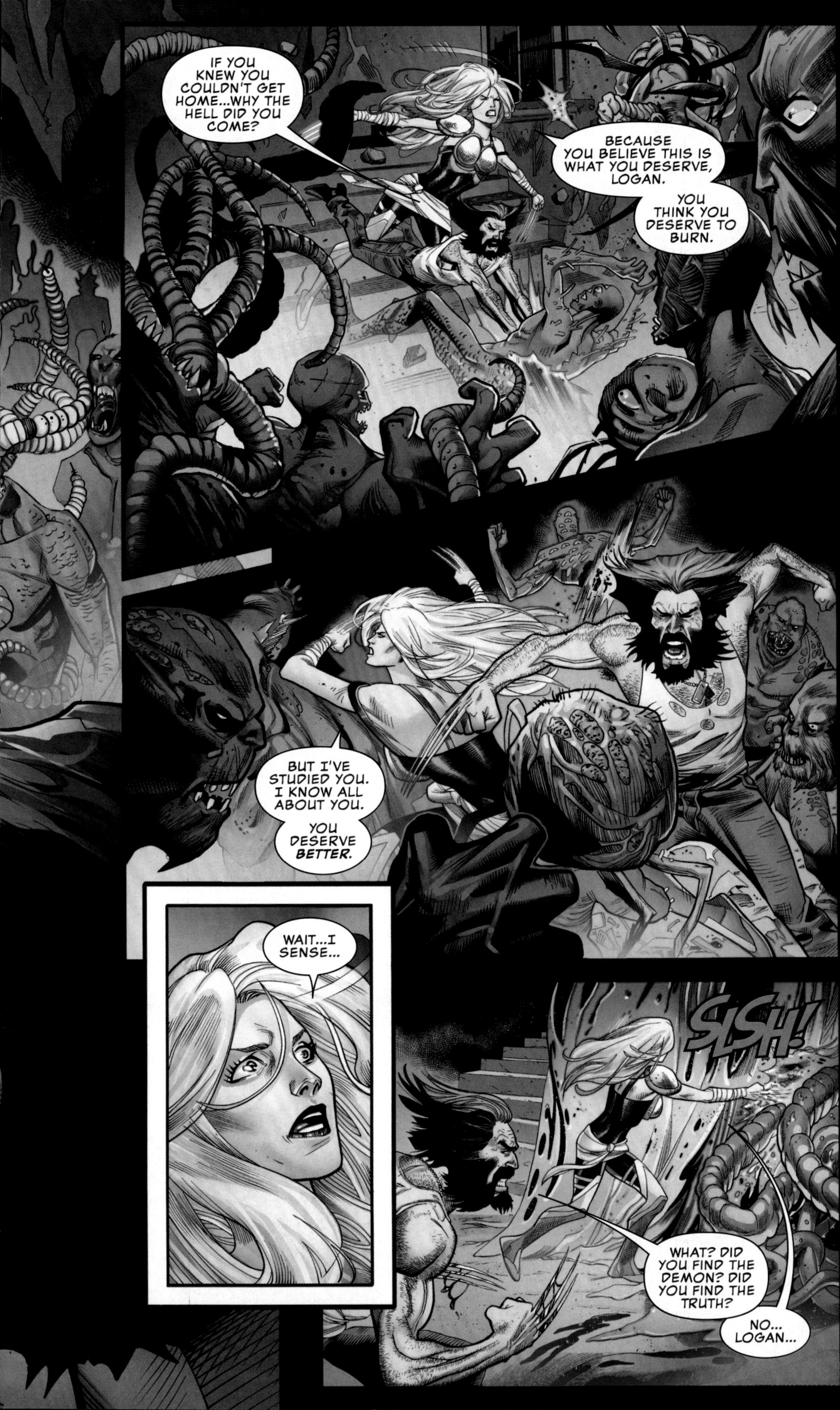

IF YOU KNEW YOU COULDN'T GET HOME...WHY THE HELL DID YOU COME?
BECAUSE YOU BELIEVE THIS IS WHAT YOU DESERVE, LOGAN.
YOU THINK YOU DESERVE TO BURN.
BUT I'VE STUDIED YOU. I KNOW ALL ABOUT YOU.
YOU DESERVE BETTER.
WAIT...I SENSE...
SLSH!
WHAT? DID YOU FIND THE DEMON? DID YOU FIND THE TRUTH?
NO... LOGAN...

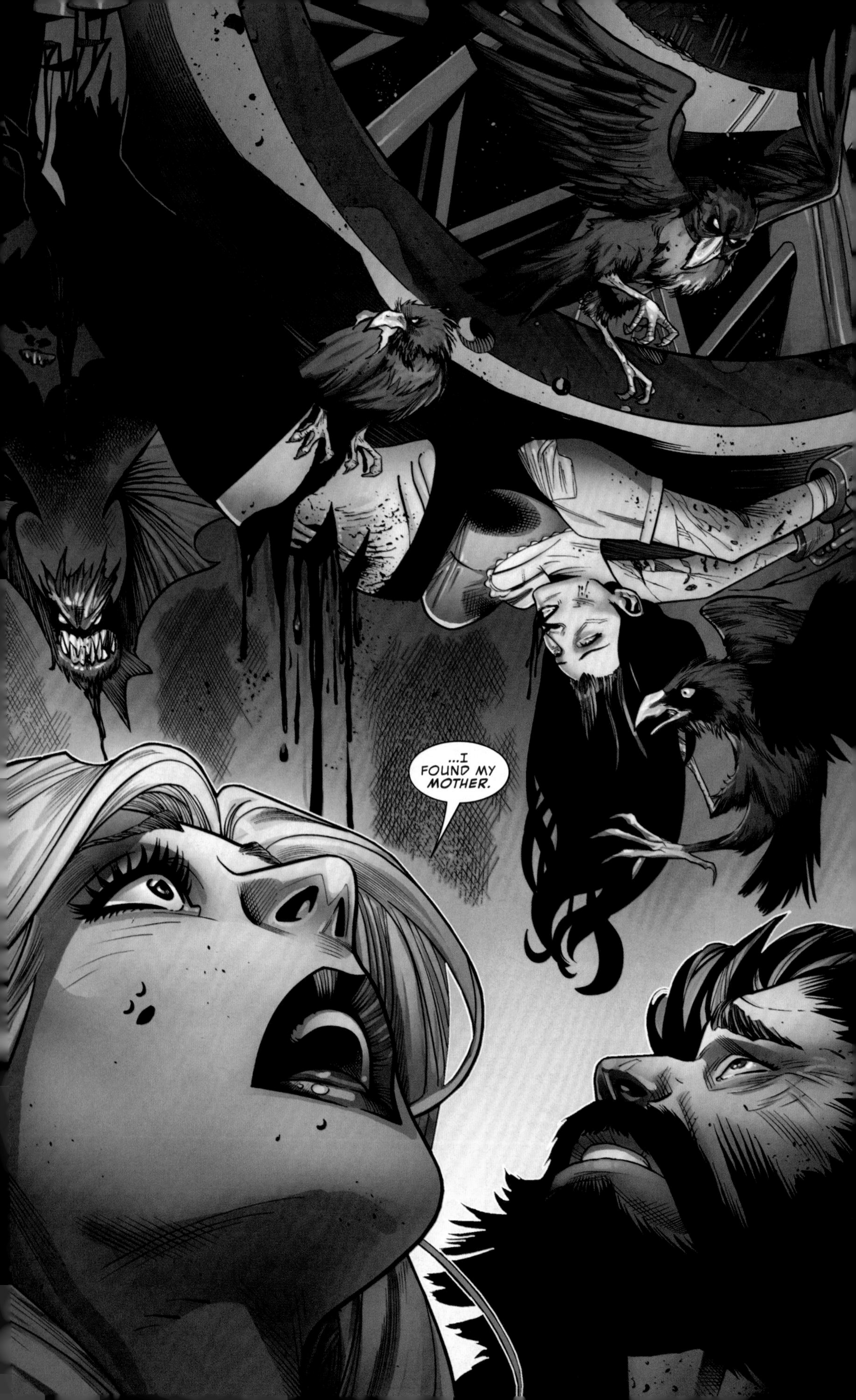
...I FOUND MY MOTHER.

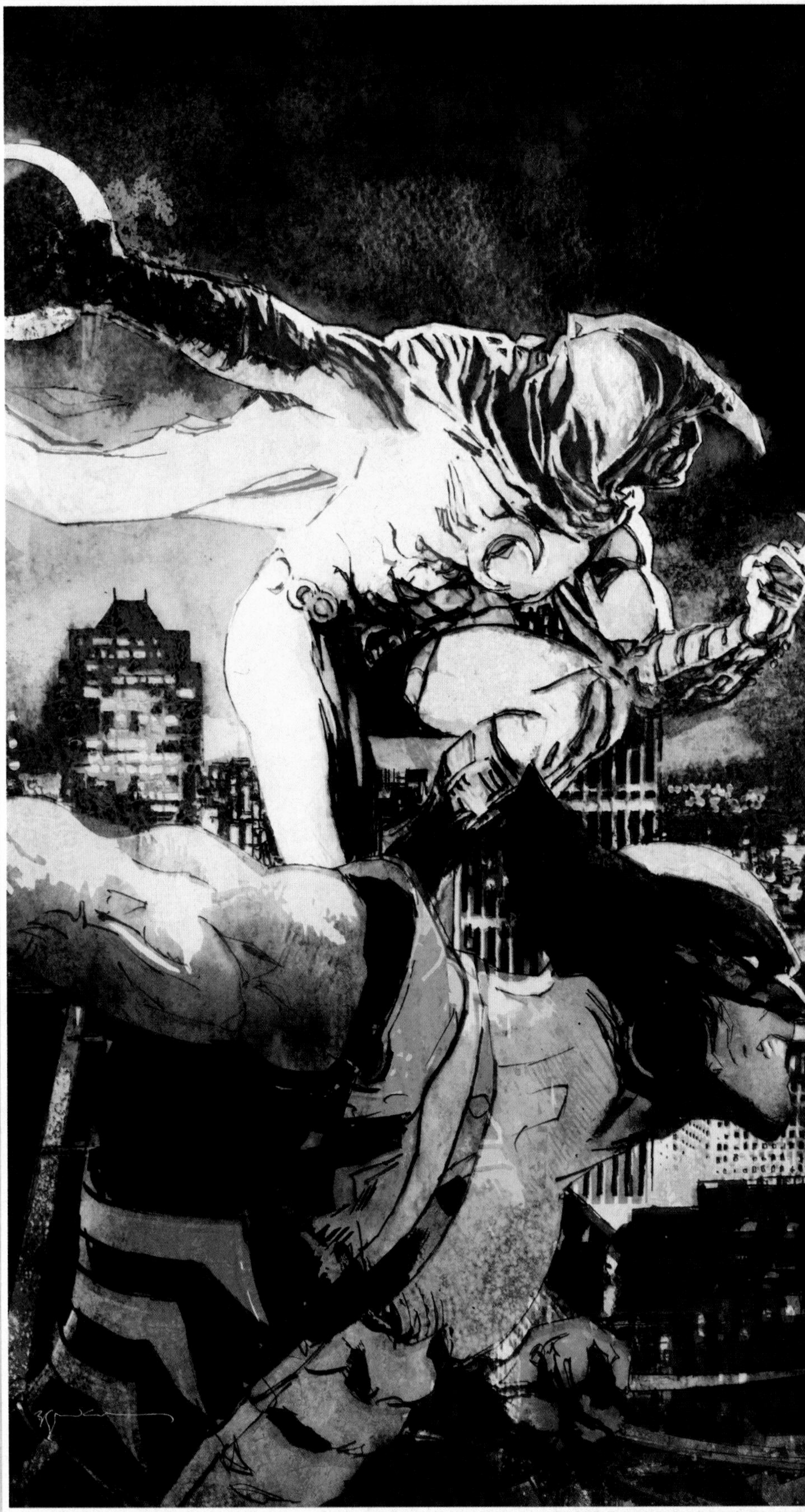

#4 variant by **BILL SIENKIEWICZ**

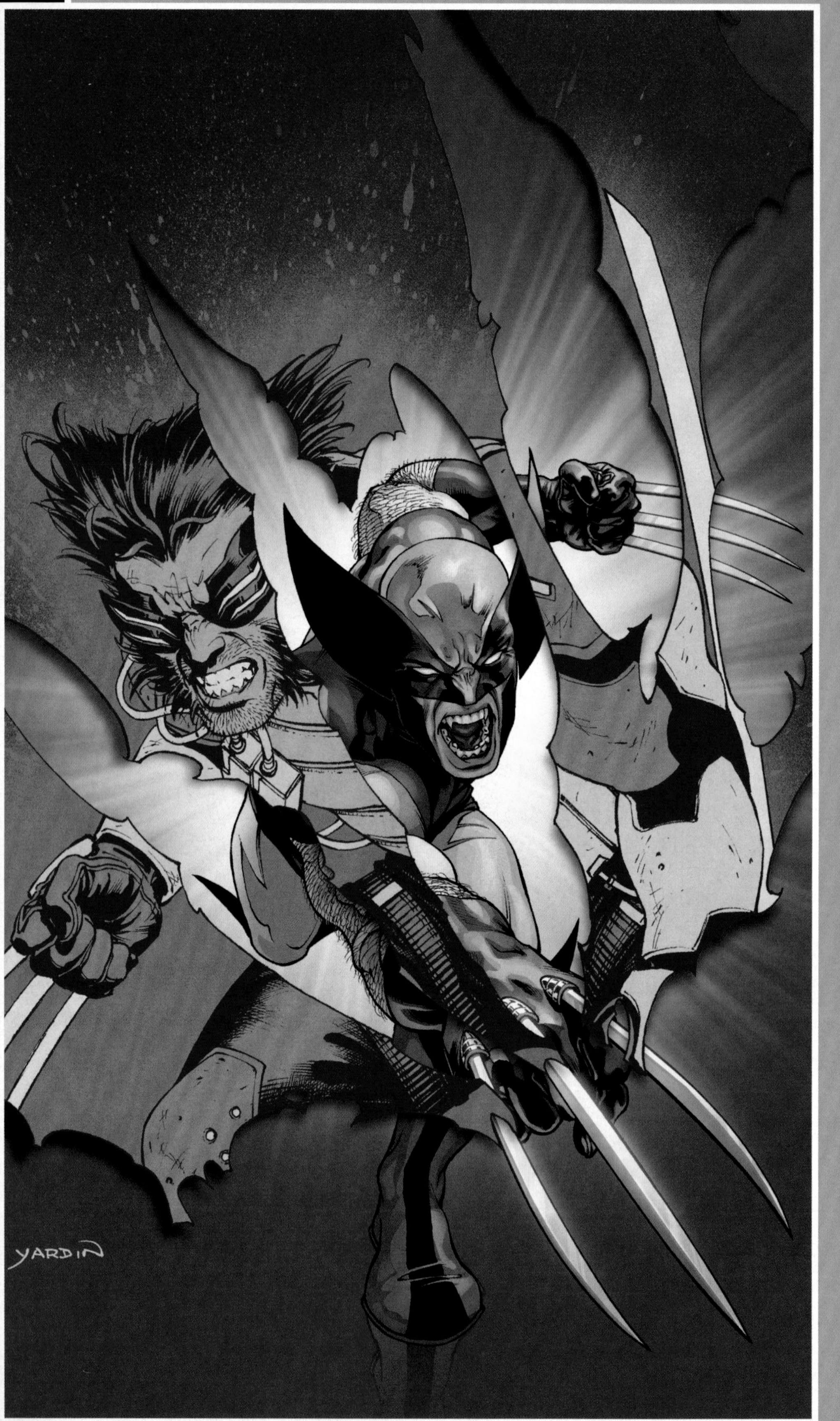
YARDIN

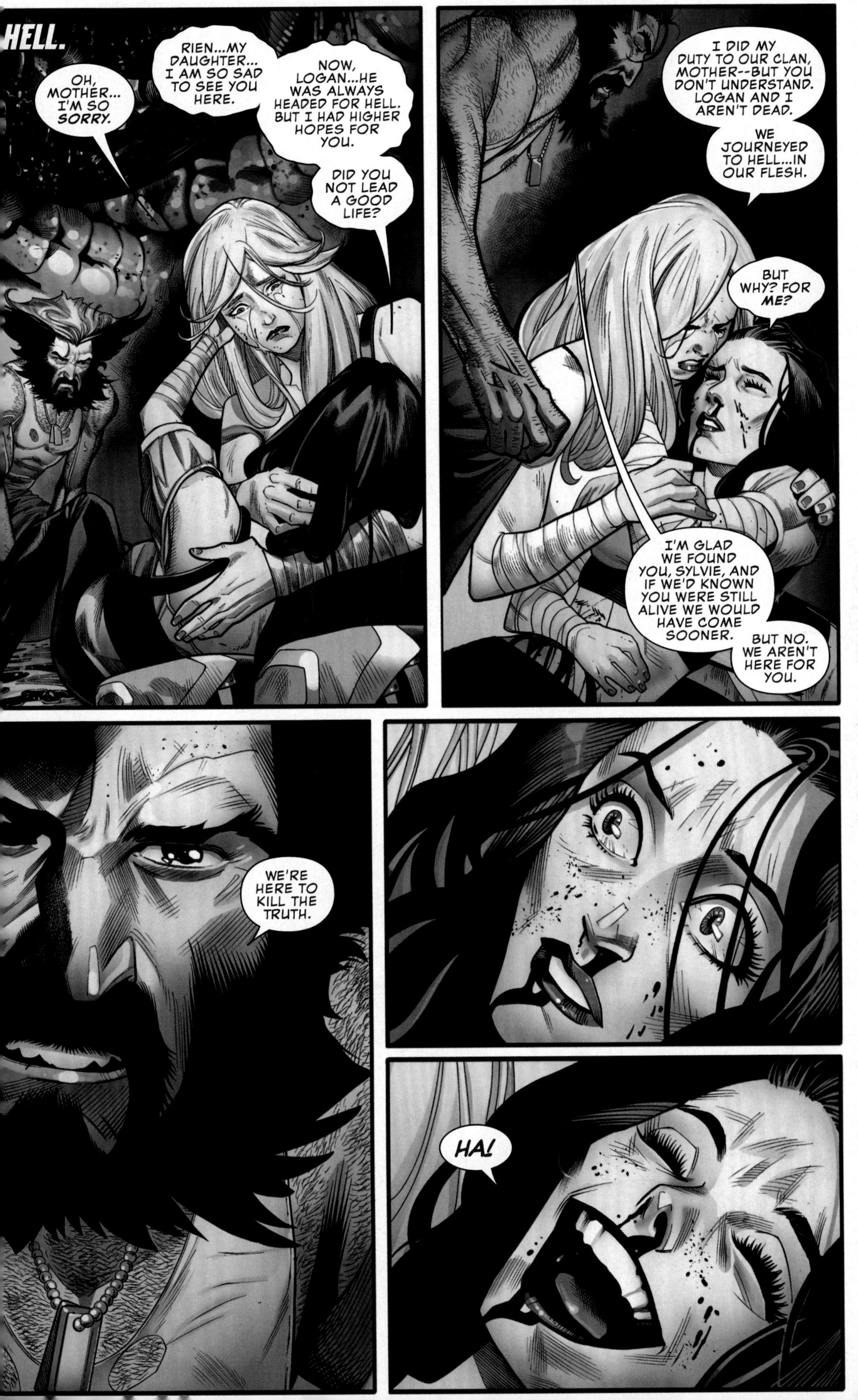
HELL.
OH, MOTHER... I'M SO SORRY.
RIEN...MY DAUGHTER... I AM SO SAD TO SEE YOU HERE.
NOW, LOGAN...HE WAS ALWAYS HEADED FOR HELL. BUT I HAD HIGHER HOPES FOR YOU.
DID YOU NOT LEAD A GOOD LIFE?
I DID MY DUTY TO OUR CLAN, MOTHER--BUT YOU DON'T UNDERSTAND. LOGAN AND I AREN'T DEAD.
WE JOURNEYED TO HELL...IN OUR FLESH.
BUT WHY? FOR ME?
I'M GLAD WE FOUND YOU, SYLVIE, AND IF WE'D KNOWN YOU WERE STILL ALIVE WE WOULD HAVE COME SOONER.
BUT NO. WE AREN'T HERE FOR YOU.
WE'RE HERE TO KILL THE TRUTH.
HA!

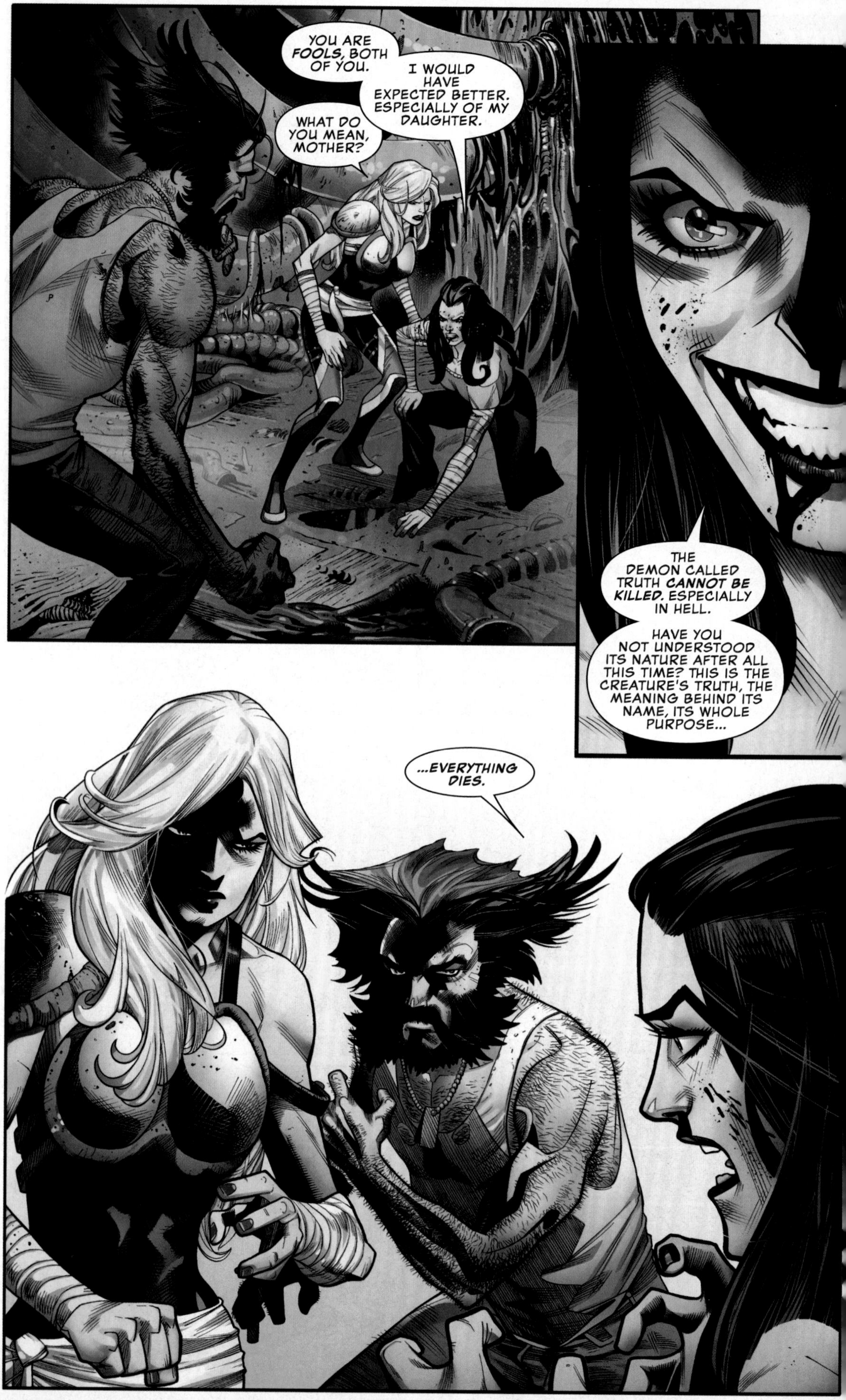

YOU ARE FOOLS, BOTH OF YOU.
I WOULD HAVE EXPECTED BETTER. ESPECIALLY OF MY DAUGHTER.
WHAT DO YOU MEAN, MOTHER?
THE DEMON CALLED TRUTH CANNOT BE KILLED. ESPECIALLY IN HELL.
HAVE YOU NOT UNDERSTOOD ITS NATURE AFTER ALL THIS TIME? THIS IS THE CREATURE'S TRUTH, THE MEANING BEHIND ITS NAME, ITS WHOLE PURPOSE...
...EVERYTHING DIES.

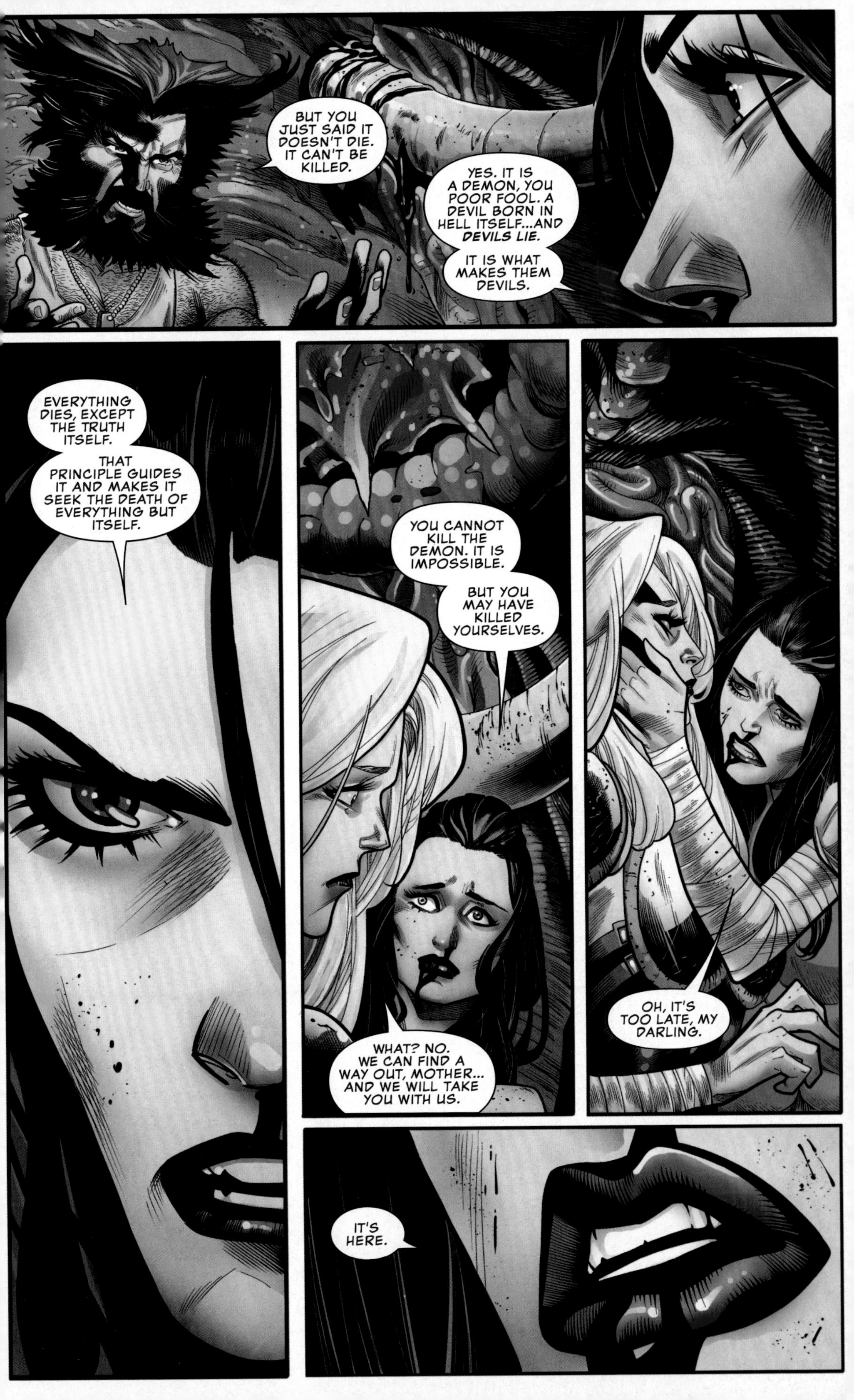
BUT YOU JUST SAID IT DOESN'T DIE. IT CAN'T BE KILLED.
YES. IT IS A DEMON, YOU POOR FOOL. A DEVIL BORN IN HELL ITSELF...AND *DEVILS LIE.*
IT IS WHAT MAKES THEM DEVILS.
EVERYTHING DIES, EXCEPT THE TRUTH ITSELF.
THAT PRINCIPLE GUIDES IT AND MAKES IT SEEK THE DEATH OF EVERYTHING BUT ITSELF.
YOU CANNOT KILL THE DEMON. IT IS IMPOSSIBLE.
BUT YOU MAY HAVE KILLED YOURSELVES.
WHAT? NO. WE CAN FIND A WAY OUT, MOTHER... AND WE WILL TAKE YOU WITH US.
OH, IT'S TOO LATE, MY DARLING.
IT'S HERE.

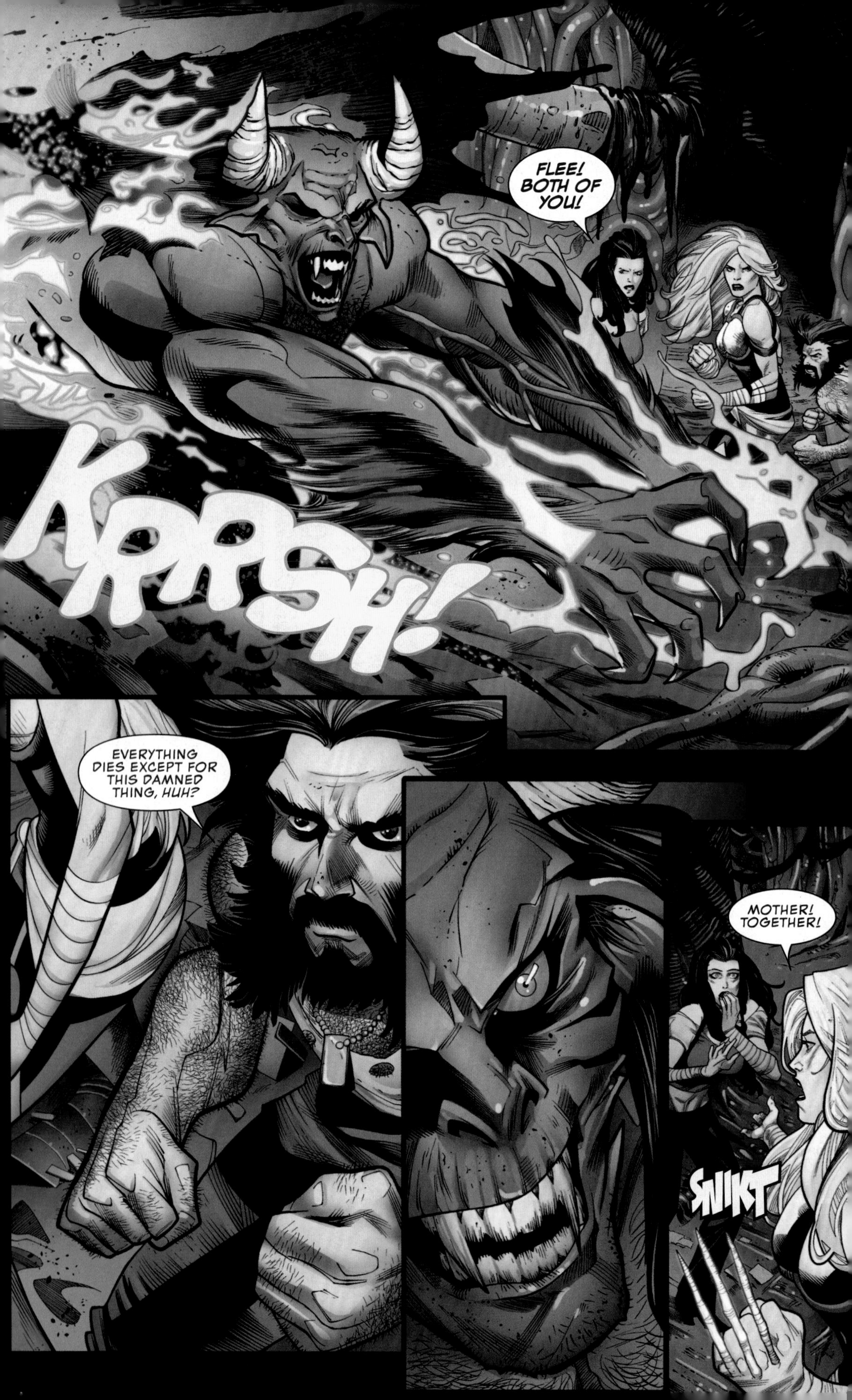
FLEE! BOTH OF YOU!
KRRSH!
EVERYTHING DIES EXCEPT FOR THIS DAMNED THING, HUH?
MOTHER! TOGETHER!
SNIKT

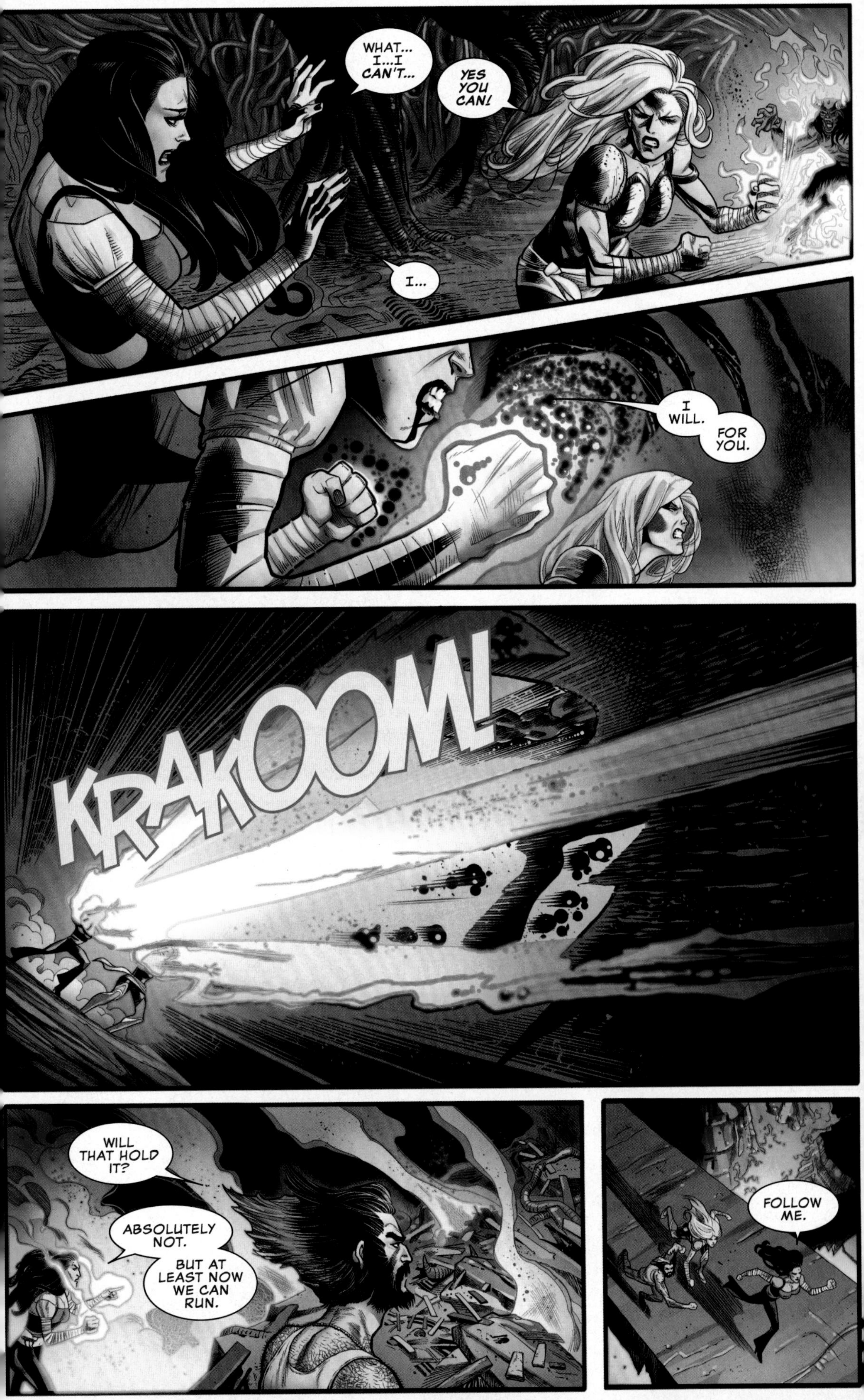
WHAT... I...I CAN'T...
YES YOU CAN!
I...
I WILL.
FOR YOU.
KRAKOOM!
WILL THAT HOLD IT?
ABSOLUTELY NOT.
BUT AT LEAST NOW WE CAN RUN.
FOLLOW ME.

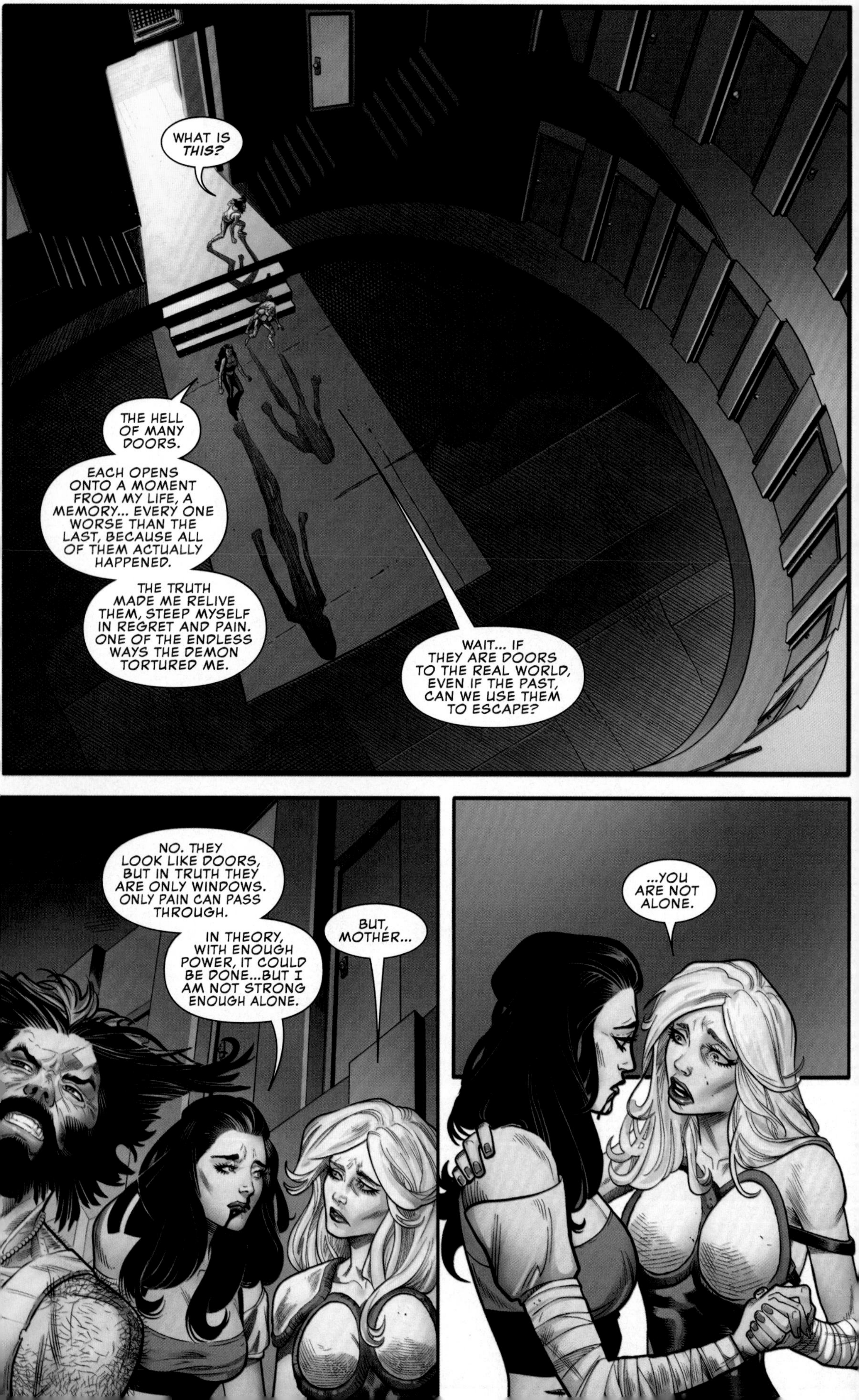
WHAT IS THIS?
THE HELL OF MANY DOORS.
EACH OPENS ONTO A MOMENT FROM MY LIFE, A MEMORY... EVERY ONE WORSE THAN THE LAST, BECAUSE ALL OF THEM ACTUALLY HAPPENED.
THE TRUTH MADE ME RELIVE THEM, STEEP MYSELF IN REGRET AND PAIN. ONE OF THE ENDLESS WAYS THE DEMON TORTURED ME.
WAIT... IF THEY ARE DOORS TO THE REAL WORLD, EVEN IF THE PAST, CAN WE USE THEM TO ESCAPE?
NO. THEY LOOK LIKE DOORS, BUT IN TRUTH THEY ARE ONLY WINDOWS. ONLY PAIN CAN PASS THROUGH.
IN THEORY, WITH ENOUGH POWER, IT COULD BE DONE...BUT I AM NOT STRONG ENOUGH ALONE.
BUT, MOTHER...
...YOU ARE NOT ALONE.

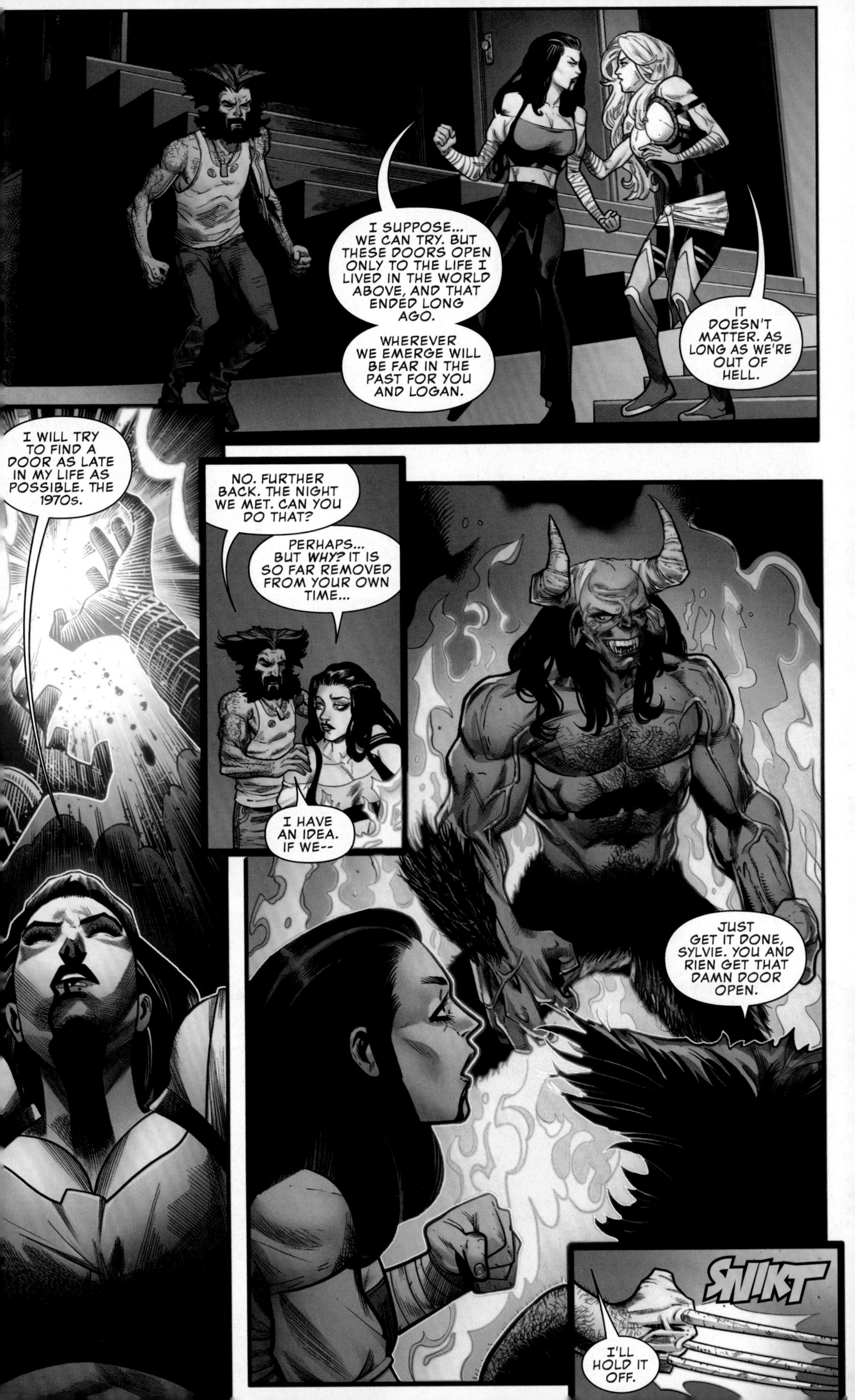
I SUPPOSE... WE CAN TRY. BUT THESE DOORS OPEN ONLY TO THE LIFE I LIVED IN THE WORLD ABOVE, AND THAT ENDED LONG AGO.
WHEREVER WE EMERGE WILL BE FAR IN THE PAST FOR YOU AND LOGAN.
IT DOESN'T MATTER. AS LONG AS WE'RE OUT OF HELL.
I WILL TRY TO FIND A DOOR AS LATE IN MY LIFE AS POSSIBLE. THE 1970s.
NO. FURTHER BACK. THE NIGHT WE MET. CAN YOU DO THAT?
PERHAPS... BUT *WHY?* IT IS SO FAR REMOVED FROM YOUR OWN TIME...
I HAVE AN IDEA. IF WE--
JUST GET IT DONE, SYLVIE. YOU AND RIEN GET THAT DAMN DOOR OPEN.
SNIKT
I'LL HOLD IT OFF.

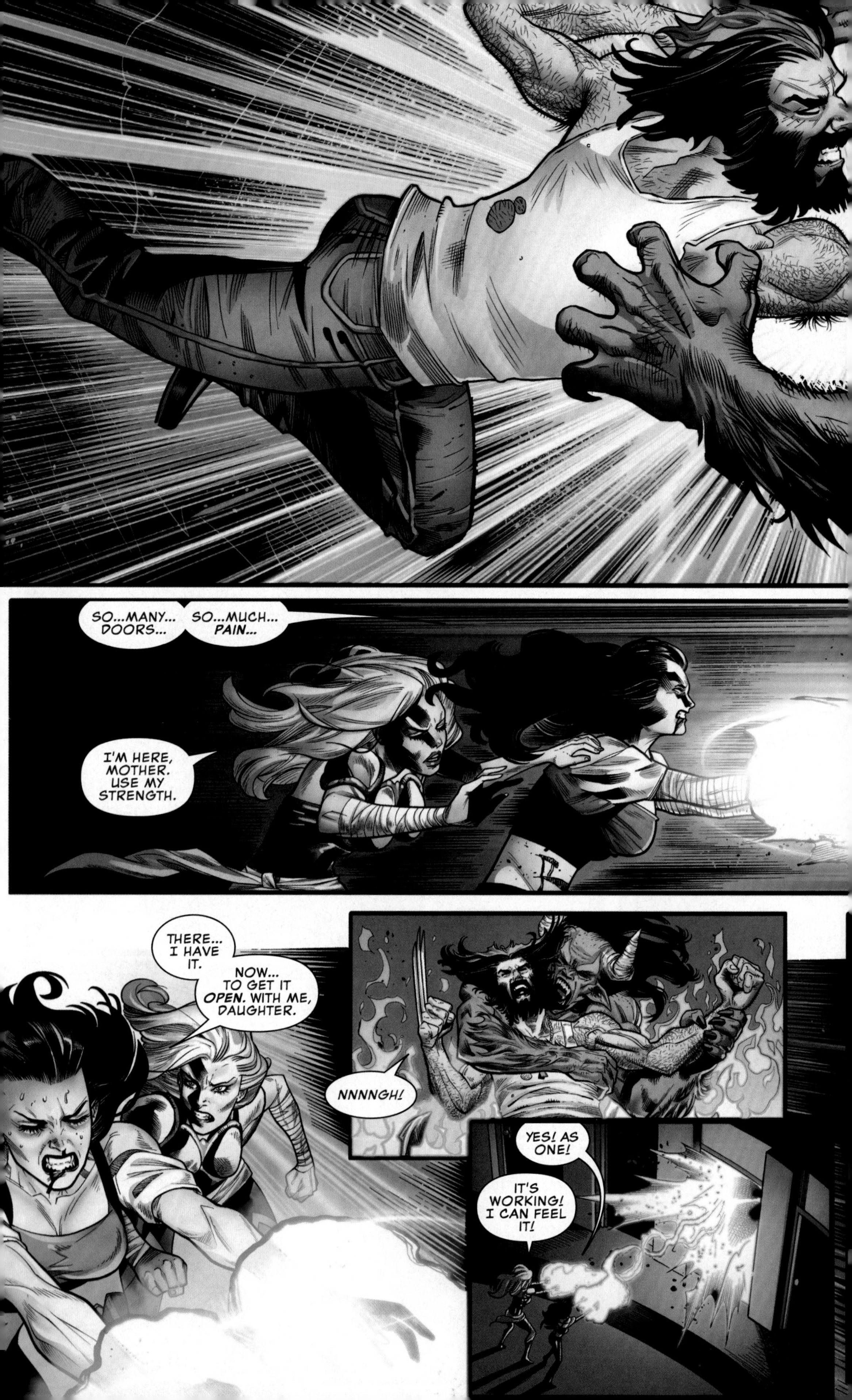
SO...MANY... DOORS...
SO...MUCH... PAIN...
I'M HERE, MOTHER. USE MY STRENGTH.
THERE... I HAVE IT.
NOW... TO GET IT OPEN. WITH ME, DAUGHTER.
NNNNGH!
YES! AS ONE!
IT'S WORKING! I CAN FEEL IT!

KRRRCH!

AAAAGH!

VRRRRR

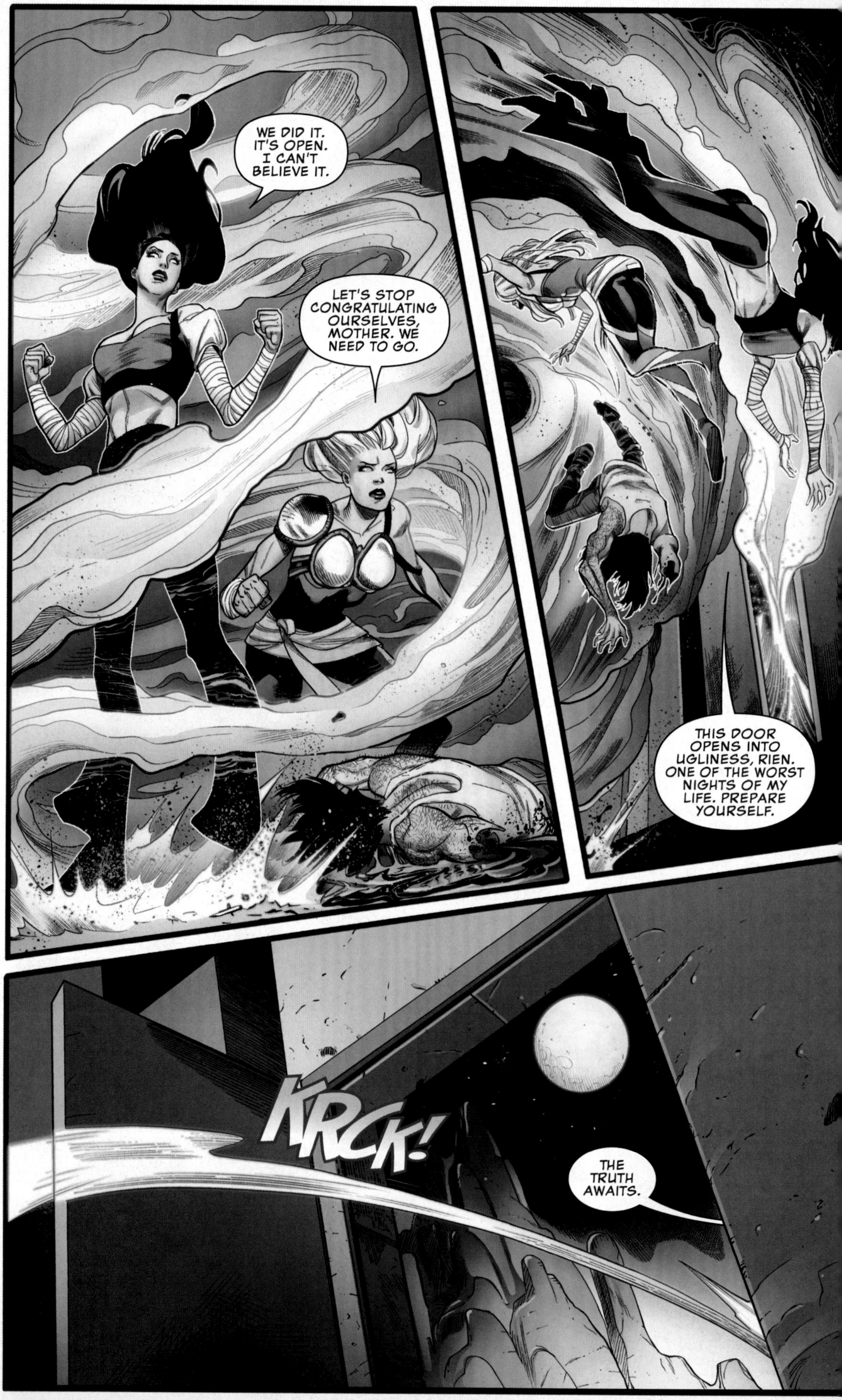
WE DID IT. IT'S OPEN. I CAN'T BELIEVE IT.
LET'S STOP CONGRATULATING OURSELVES, MOTHER. WE NEED TO GO.
THIS DOOR OPENS INTO UGLINESS, RIEN. ONE OF THE WORST NIGHTS OF MY LIFE. PREPARE YOURSELF.
KRCK!
THE TRUTH AWAITS.

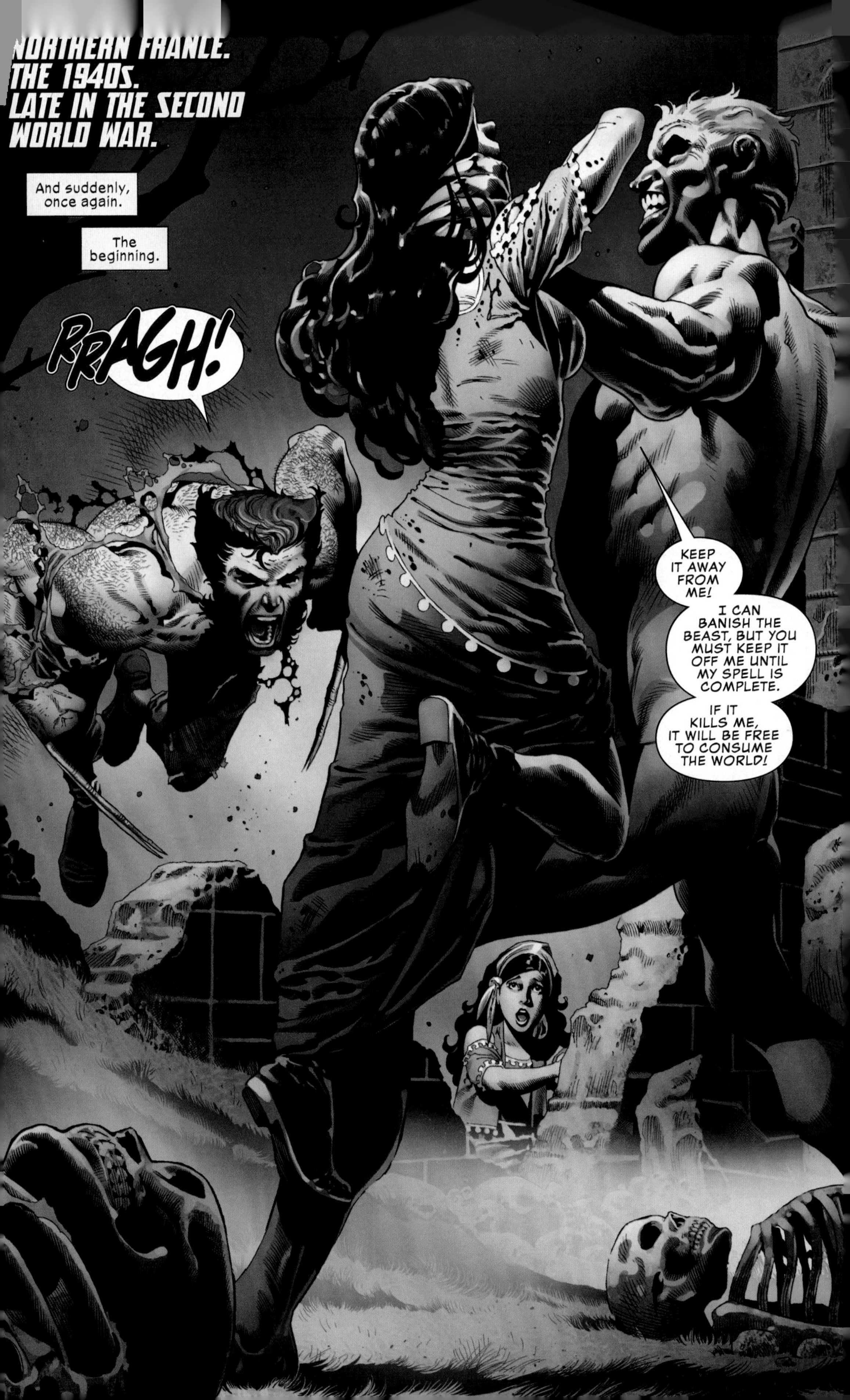
NORTHERN FRANCE. THE 1940s. LATE IN THE SECOND WORLD WAR.
And suddenly, once again.
The beginning.
RRAGH!
KEEP IT AWAY FROM ME!
I CAN BANISH THE BEAST, BUT YOU MUST KEEP IT OFF ME UNTIL MY SPELL IS COMPLETE.
IF IT KILLS ME, IT WILL BE FREE TO CONSUME THE WORLD!

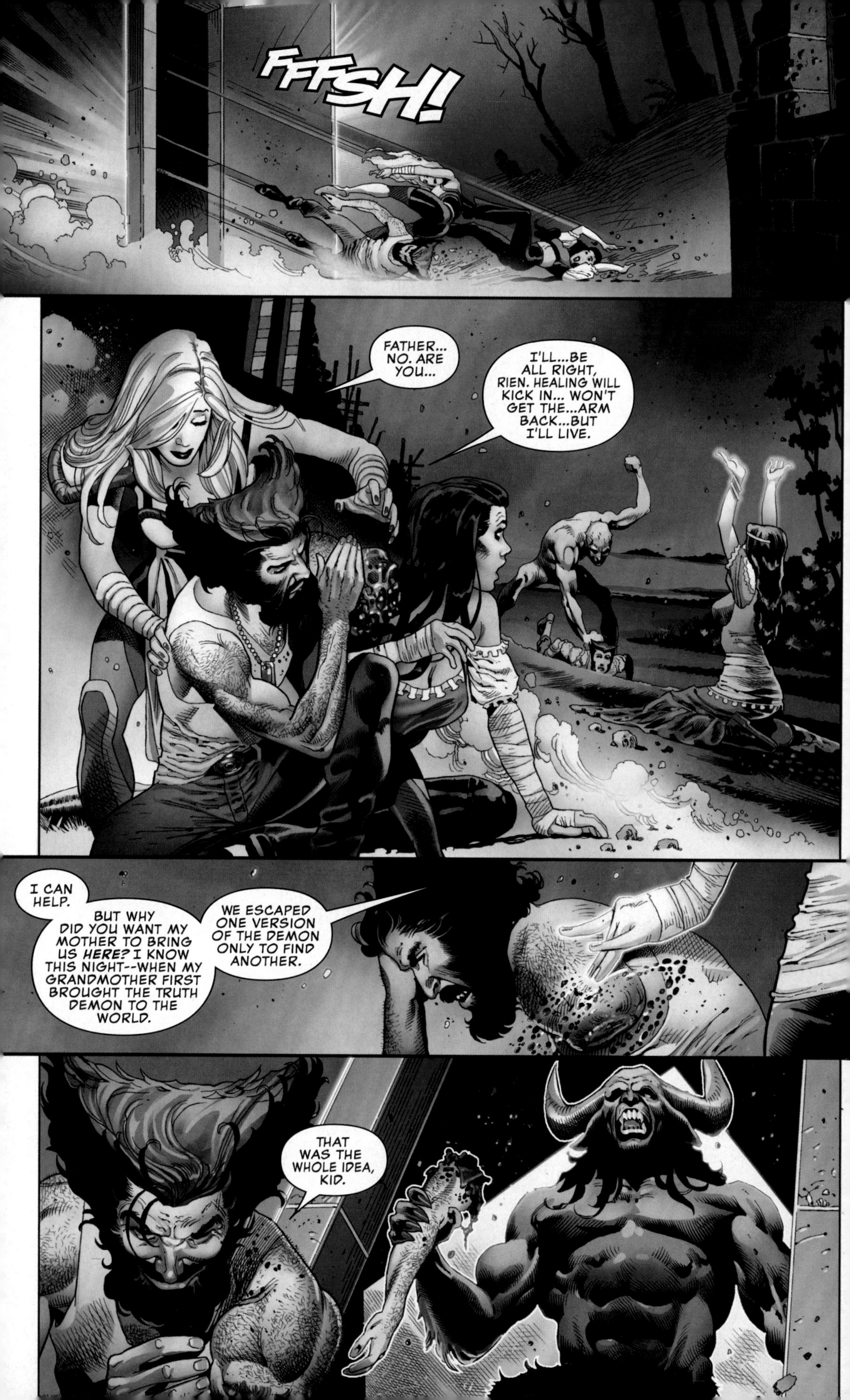
FFFSH!
FATHER... NO. ARE YOU...
I'LL...BE ALL RIGHT, RIEN. HEALING WILL KICK IN... WON'T GET THE...ARM BACK...BUT I'LL LIVE.
I CAN HELP.
BUT WHY DID YOU WANT MY MOTHER TO BRING US HERE? I KNOW THIS NIGHT--WHEN MY GRANDMOTHER FIRST BROUGHT THE TRUTH DEMON TO THE WORLD.
WE ESCAPED ONE VERSION OF THE DEMON ONLY TO FIND ANOTHER.
THAT WAS THE WHOLE IDEA, KID.

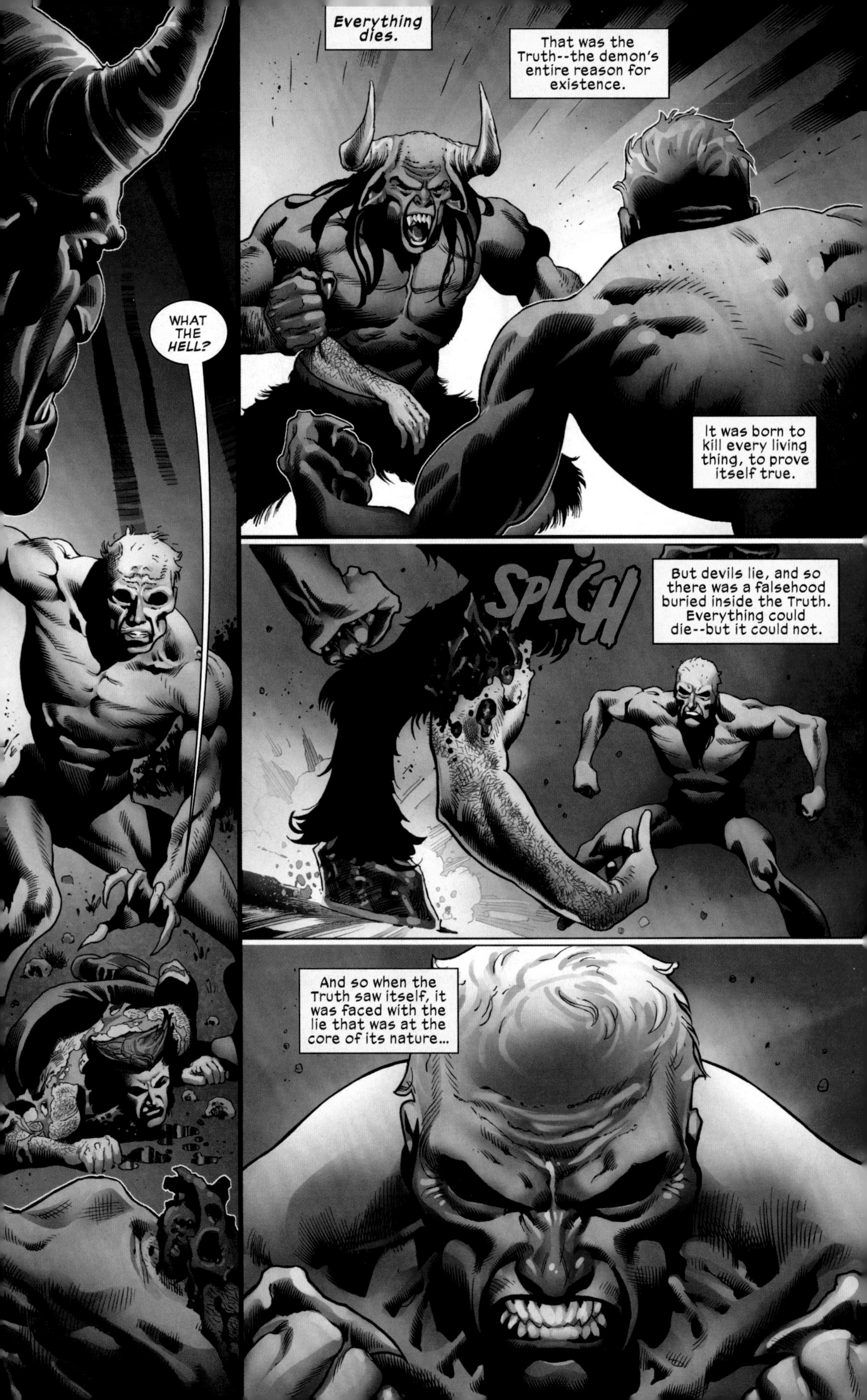
WHAT THE HELL?
Everything dies.
That was the Truth--the demon's entire reason for existence.
It was born to kill every living thing, to prove itself true.
SPLCH
But devils lie, and so there was a falsehood buried inside the Truth. Everything could die--but it could not.
And so when the Truth saw itself, it was faced with the lie that was at the core of its nature...

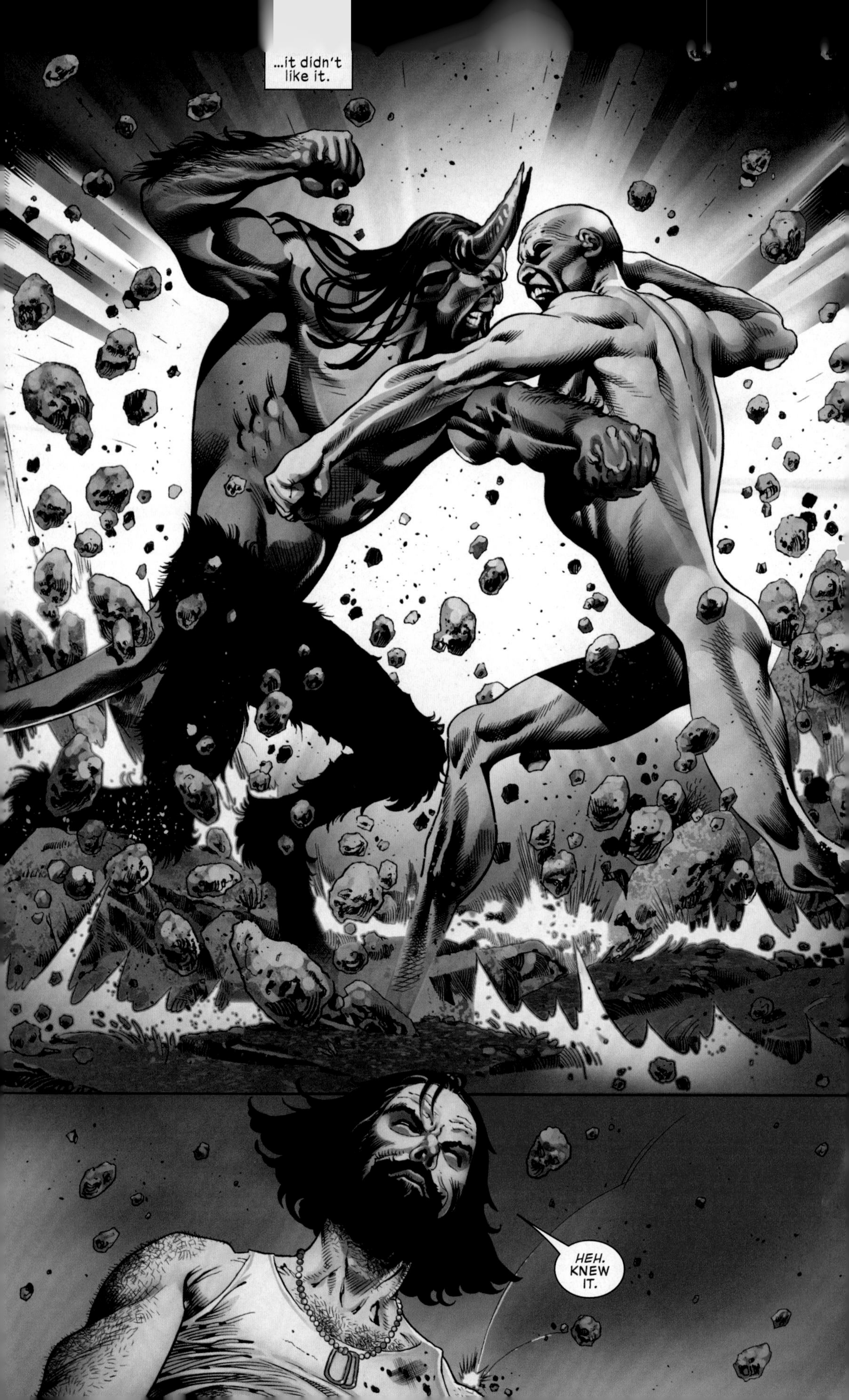
...it didn't like it.
HEH. KNEW IT.

THEY CAN'T DIE--THEY'LL FIGHT EACH OTHER UNTIL THE END OF TIME.

THAT'S WHAT I WAS THINKING. IF THEY'RE TEARING EACH OTHER UP, THEY CAN'T GO AFTER ANYONE ELSE.

BUT THEIR BATTLE... IT COULD RIP THE WORLD APART, WHETHER THEY INTEND TO OR NOT.

HEY, IT BOUGHT US SOME TIME, RIGHT? BETTER THAN NOTHING.

YES... BUT HOW MUCH?

WE MUST SEAL THEM AWAY, DAUGHTER. LET THEM BATTLE EACH OTHER FOREVER, WHERE THEY CANNOT TOUCH THE WORLD.

MOTHER... I HAVE MISSED YOU SO--

THERE IS NO TIME FOR A REUNION. WE MUST ACT NOW, BEFORE THE TRUTHS REALIZE PERHAPS THEY COULD ACT TOGETHER.

WE HAVE FOUR POWERFUL WITCHES OF THE CLAN D'ARQUENESS HERE. WE CAN CAGE THE TRUTH...

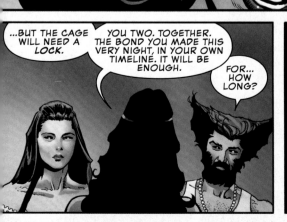

...BUT THE CAGE WILL NEED A LOCK.

YOU TWO. TOGETHER. THE BOND YOU MADE THIS VERY NIGHT, IN YOUR OWN TIMELINE. IT WILL BE ENOUGH.

FOR... HOW LONG?

YOU KNOW, LOGAN. OF COURSE YOU KNOW.

YEAH. SUPPOSE I DO.

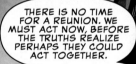

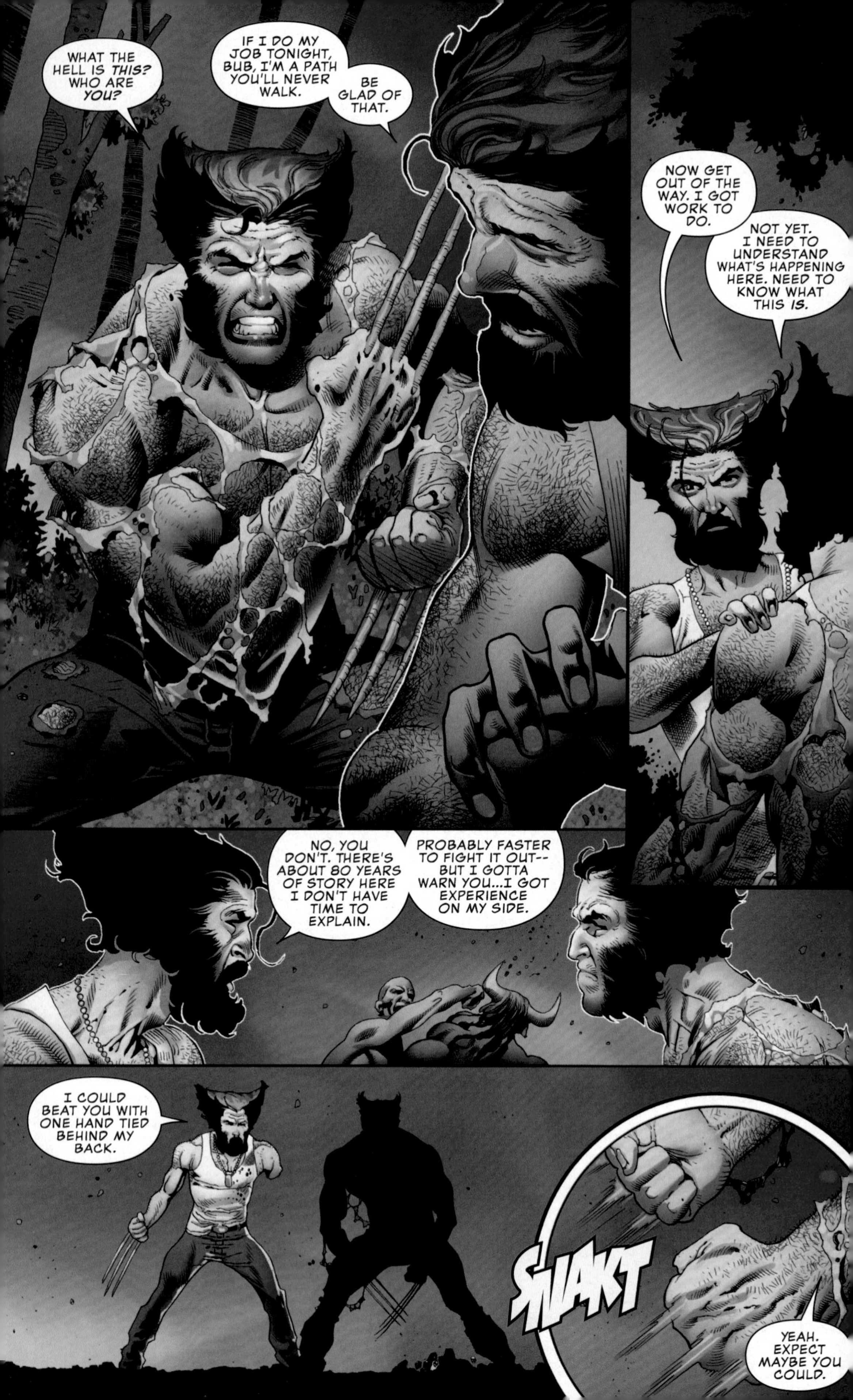
WHAT THE HELL IS THIS? WHO ARE YOU?
IF I DO MY JOB TONIGHT, BUB, I'M A PATH YOU'LL NEVER WALK.
BE GLAD OF THAT.
NOW GET OUT OF THE WAY. I GOT WORK TO DO.
NOT YET. I NEED TO UNDERSTAND WHAT'S HAPPENING HERE. NEED TO KNOW WHAT THIS IS.
NO, YOU DON'T. THERE'S ABOUT 80 YEARS OF STORY HERE I DON'T HAVE TIME TO EXPLAIN.
PROBABLY FASTER TO FIGHT IT OUT-- BUT I GOTTA WARN YOU...I GOT EXPERIENCE ON MY SIDE.
I COULD BEAT YOU WITH ONE HAND TIED BEHIND MY BACK.
SNAKT
YEAH. EXPECT MAYBE YOU COULD.

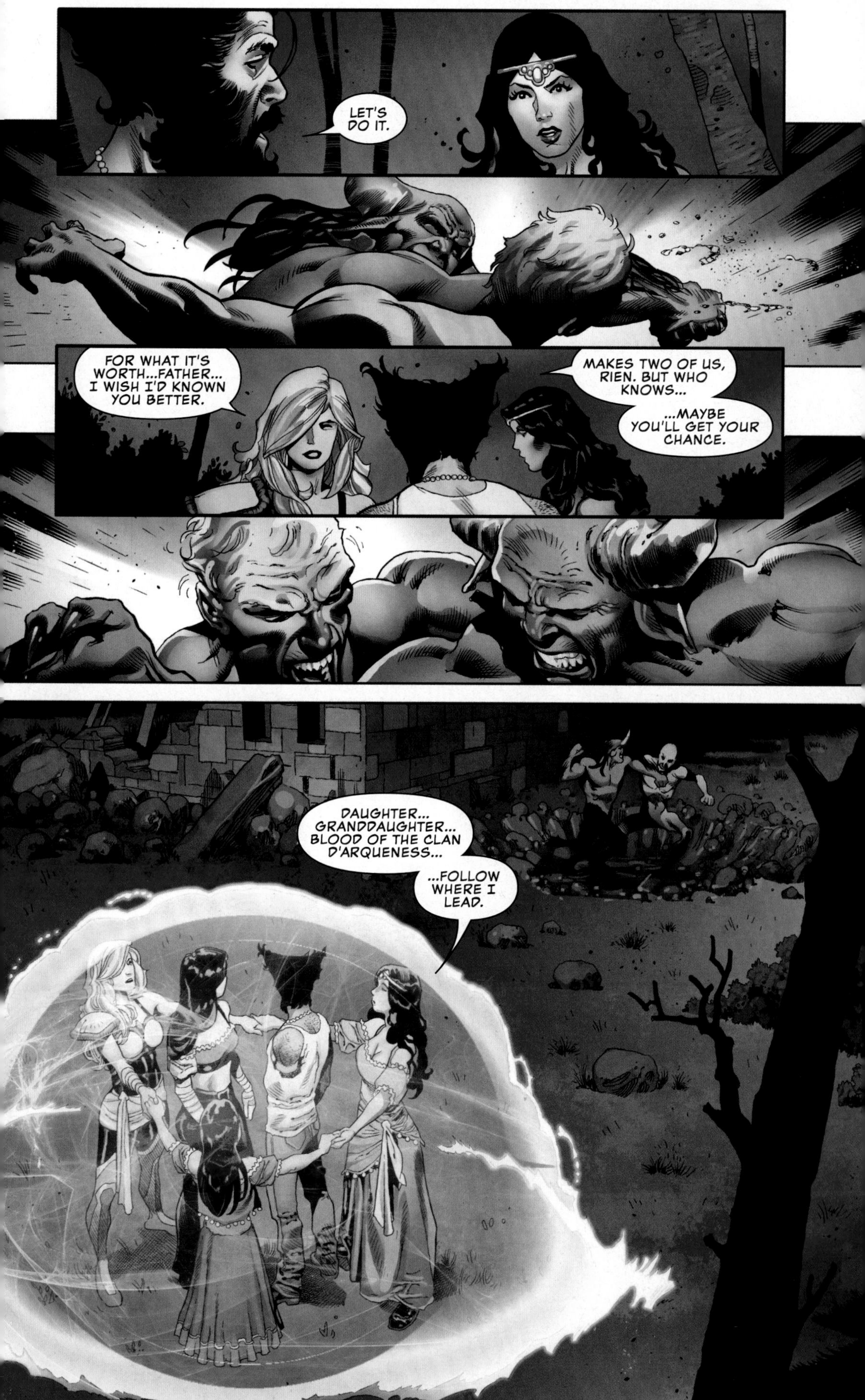

LET'S DO IT.
FOR WHAT IT'S WORTH...FATHER... I WISH I'D KNOWN YOU BETTER.
MAKES TWO OF US, RIEN. BUT WHO KNOWS...
...MAYBE YOU'LL GET YOUR CHANCE.
DAUGHTER... GRANDDAUGHTER... BLOOD OF THE CLAN D'ARQUENESS...
...FOLLOW WHERE I LEAD.

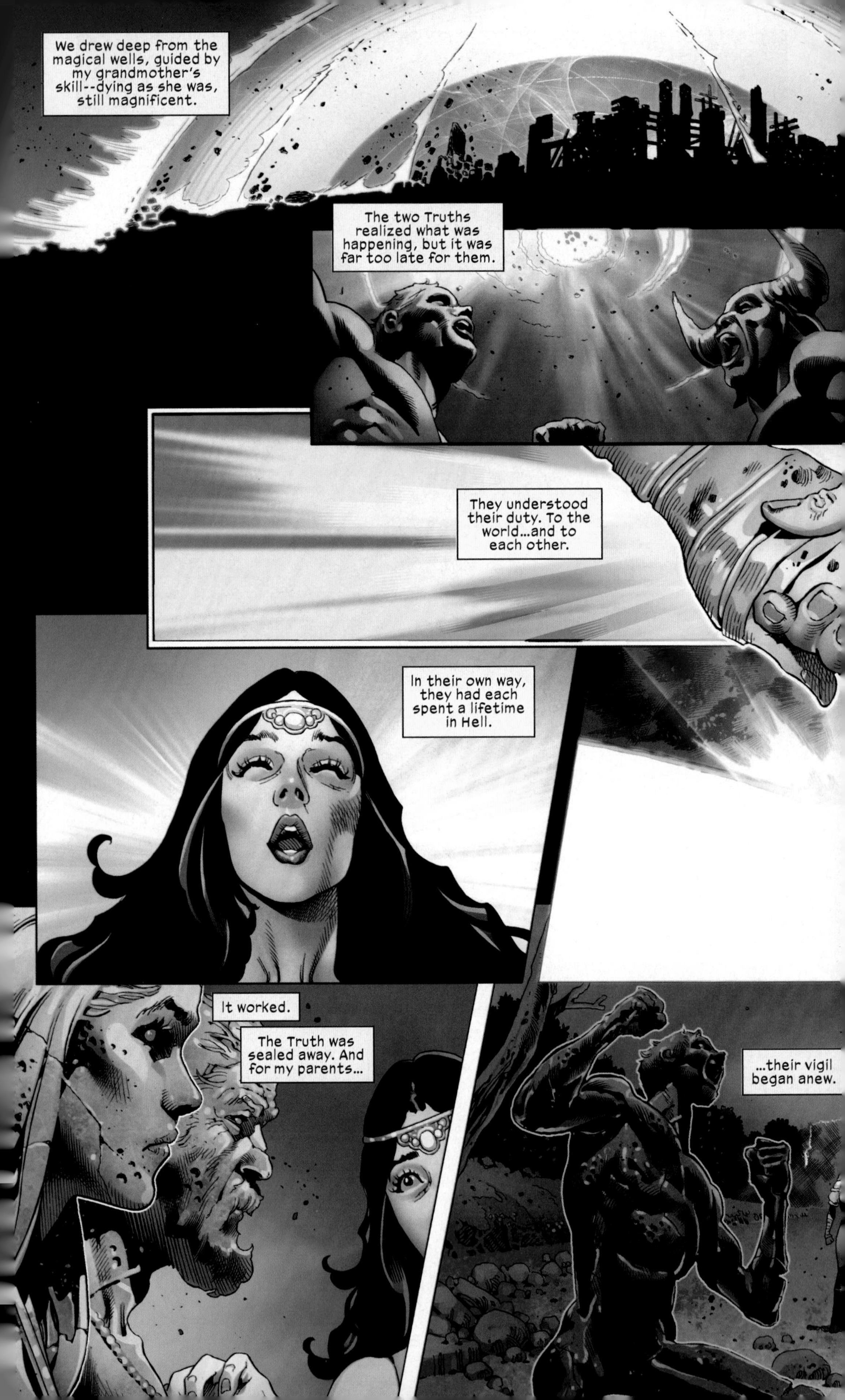

We drew deep from the magical wells, guided by my grandmother's skill--dying as she was, still magnificent.
The two Truths realized what was happening, but it was far too late for them.
They understood their duty. To the world...and to each other.
In their own way, they had each spent a lifetime in Hell.
It worked.
The Truth was sealed away. And for my parents...
...their vigil began anew.

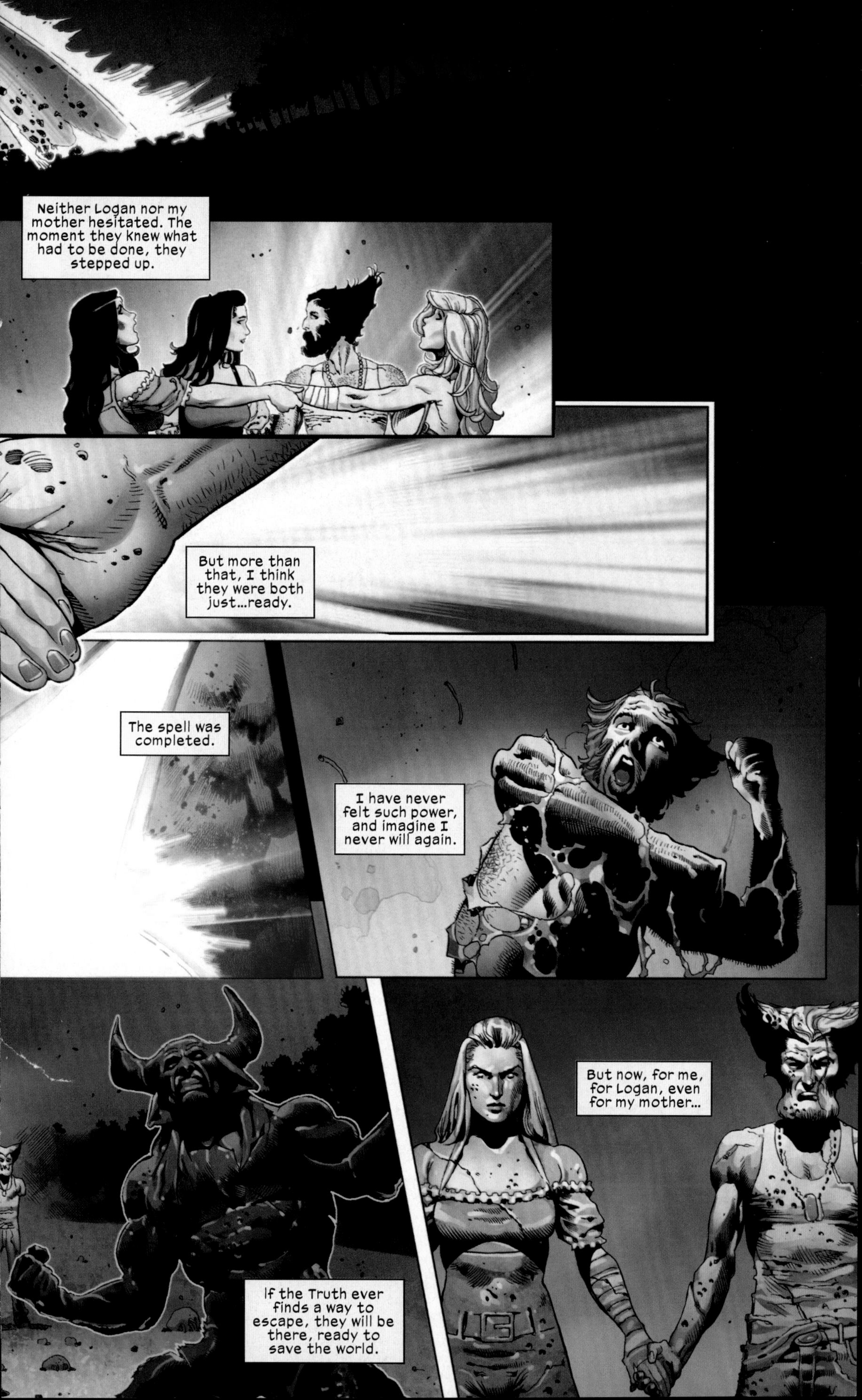
Neither Logan nor my mother hesitated. The moment they knew what had to be done, they stepped up.
But more than that, I think they were both just...ready.
The spell was completed.
I have never felt such power, and imagine I never will again.
But now, for me, for Logan, even for my mother...
If the Truth ever finds a way to escape, they will be there, ready to save the world.

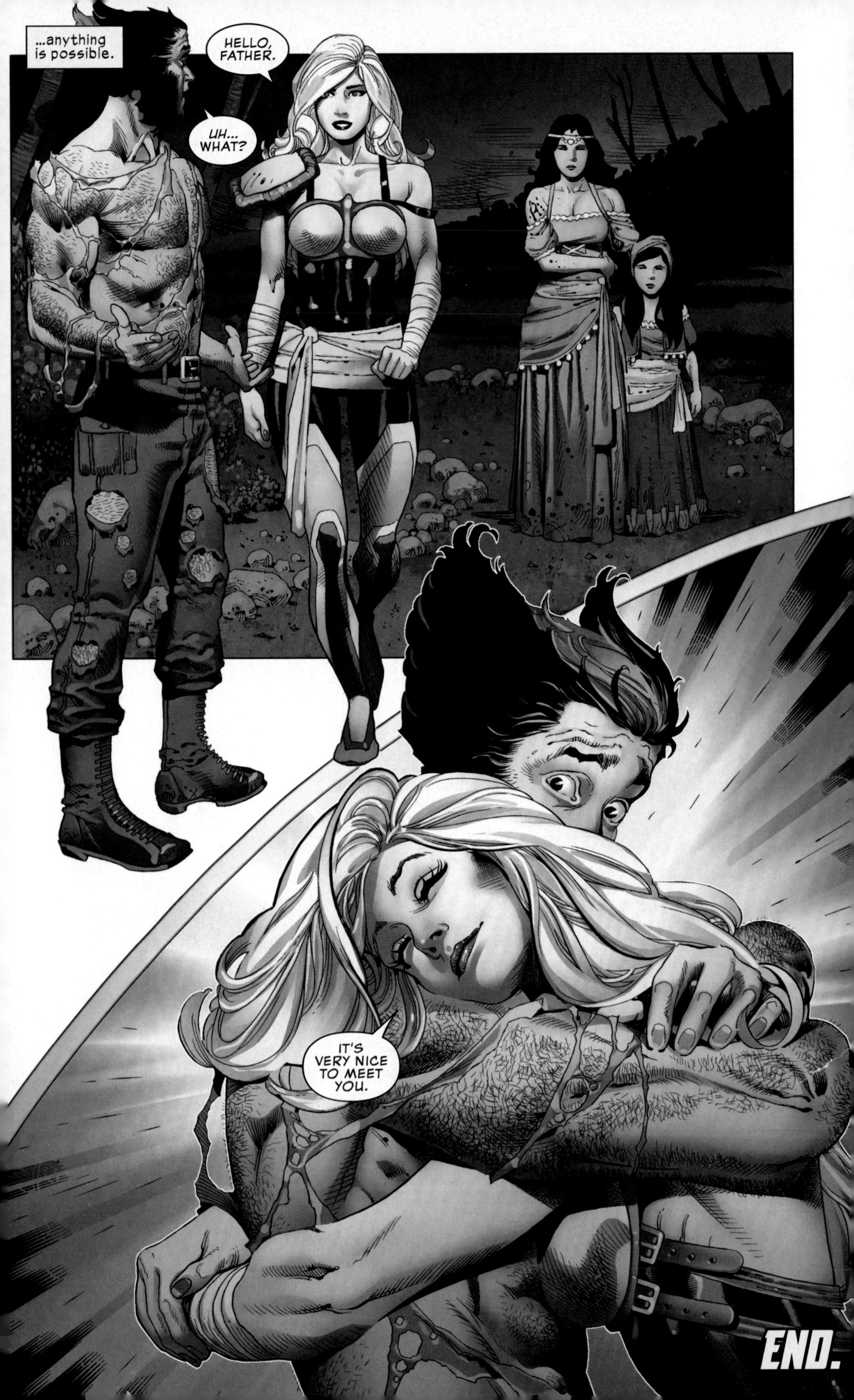
...anything is possible.
HELLO, FATHER.
UH... WHAT?
IT'S VERY NICE TO MEET YOU.
END.